DANCING WITH PRINCIPLE

DANCING WITH PRINCIPLE

Hanya Holm in Colorado, 1941-1983

CLAUDIA GITELMAN

University Press of Colorado

© 2001 by the University Press of Colorado

Published by the University Press of Colorado
5589 Arapahoe Avenue, Suite 206C
Boulder, Colorado 80303

The University Press of Colorado is a cooperative publishing enterprise supported, in part, by Adams State College, Colorado State University, Fort Lewis College, Mesa State College, Metropolitan State College of Denver, University of Colorado, University of Northern Colorado, University of Southern Colorado, and Western State College of Colorado.

The paper used in this publication meets the minimum requirements of the American National Standard for Information Sciences—Permanence of Paper for Printed Library Materials. ANSI Z39.48-1992

Library of Congress Cataloging-in-Publication Data

Gitelman, Claudia.
  Dancing with principle : Hanya Holm in Colorado, 1941–1983 / Claudia Gitelman.
    p. cm.
Includes bibliographical references (p.) and index.
    ISBN 0-87081-644-6 (Hardcover : alk. paper) — ISBN 0-87081-651-9 (Paperback : alk. paper)
    1. Holm, Hanya, 1893–1992. 2. Choreographers—United States—Biography. 3. Dance—Study and teaching—Colorado—Colorado Springs—History. I. Title.
  GV1785.H6 G58 2001
  792.8'2'092—dc21

                                                                    2001003076

Design by Daniel Pratt

10   09   08   07   06   05   04   03   02   01   10 9 8 7 6 5 4 3 2 1

for Howard

CONTENTS

*I*LLUSTRATIONS

ACKNOWLEDGMENTS

I am honored that the Holm family trusted me with documents pertinent to Hanya Holm's summers in Colorado and that Madeleine Nichols, curator of the Dance Division, New York Public Library for the Performing Arts, allowed me to use the materials before turning them over to the library. The staff at the Dance Division aided my research, and I received help at Colorado College from Virginia Kiefer, librarian of Special Collections, Tutt Library, registrar Margaret Van Horn, and the Summer Session office. Staff at the *Colorado Springs Gazette* and the Penrose Library also helped me, as did the staff at J. Henry Meyer Library, Stanford University. Daniel Nagrin, Gerald Myers, and Randy Martin gave wise counsel at the beginning of this project. Joanna Harris, Janet Soares, Judith Finley, Elizabeth Zimmer, Esther Geoffrey, and consulting editor Elaine Long read and discussed various drafts with me. Rutgers University's Office of Research and Sponsored Programs provided a summer grant in support of my research. Barbara Palfy's friendship and watchful eye sustained me during all stages of the book's development.

I am deeply grateful to all of the above and to the many generous individuals who gave me their memories: Geulah Abrahams, Mary Anthony, Laurie Archer, Peggy Berg, Harry Bernstein, Bernice Bronson, Alfred Brooks, Chris Burnside, Jerry Cochran, John Colman, Norman Cornick, Marianne Crowder, Edna Jane

Dexter, K. Dunkley, John Fetler, Melvin Fillin, Judith Finley, Lindsay Fisher, Kenneth French, Tim Fuller, Esther Geoffrey, Ursula Gray, Elizabeth Hayes, Doris Hering, Martha Hill, William Hockmann, Klaus Holm, Heidi Jasmine, Gilbert Johns, Tom Kanthak, James Kelly, Mimi Kim, Louise Kloepper, Stephan Koplowitz, Oliver Kostock, Henry Kurth, Phyllis Lamhut, Hortense Loeb, Murray Louis, Molly Lynn, Dorothy Madden, Bernadine Madole, James Malcolm, Edward Martinez, Allan Miles, Ellen Moore, John Munger, Elmer Peterson, Luc Peton, Donald Redlich, Stephanie Reinhart, Gresham Riley, Jessica Sayre, Bessie Schönberg, Louise Spizizen, Julia Sutton, Nancy Topf, Karen Trautlein, Sharry Traver, Margery Turner, Frances Wessells, Joan Woodbury.

DANCING WITH PRINCIPLE

Chapter One
ꝶ ORTY-THREE ꟿ UMMERS
AN INTRODUCTION

Hanya Holm was a blue-eyed cricket, a bird, a serene Buddhist monk, a German powerhouse—or so said the New York press in the 1930s. This tiny, complicated woman fascinated the public from the day she stepped off the ocean liner *Aquitania* onto a Manhattan pier in September 1931. An emissary from a sophisticated European dance culture, she became a leader among modern dance artists in the United States and contributed to the apotheosis of the book musical on Broadway with choreography for *Kiss Me, Kate; My Fair Lady; Camelot;* and other shows. Holm made another contribution to her adopted country when in 1941 she formed an alliance with a small college at the foot of the Rocky Mountains and produced one of America's great dance institutions.

This book is about the Hanya Holm/Colorado College Summer School of the Dance. It addresses a gap in our knowledge about institutions that shaped a dance culture in the United States.[1] To their mutual advantage, artist and college preserved their relationship for forty-three years, and in 1983 neither Holm, her Colorado audiences, nor the dance community was ready for its abrupt end.

At a time when arts achievement away from the East and West Coasts was seldom recognized, Holm accepted the invitation of visionary Colorado College president Thurston Jenkins Davies to teach and choreograph in the middle of the country. Colorado College is 70 miles south of Denver in Colorado Springs, a community of 37,000 inhabitants in 1941. It perches on the lip of Monument Creek where the vast American high plain gives way to the Front Range of the Rocky Mountains. To the west, snow-capped Pikes Peak shoulders its way to 14,110 feet, rising in majestic symmetry behind mesas, foothills, and attendant smaller peaks. To the southwest, Cheyenne Mountain surges up directly from the plains. Other mountains and ridges swell and fold north and south along the Front Range and back from the big peaks, teasing mind and eye. Thin air lifts the spirit as lungs expand to bring in oxygen at an elevation of 6,000 feet. Dancing in this place, for people who must dance, can be celestial.

The college campus of the 1940s was a pleasant conglomerate of three-story structures united by flat lawns, its walkways shaded by carefully cultivated trees. Most college halls had been built between 1885 and 1917 with the largesse of speculators who amassed fortunes in the Colorado gold rush of 1858–1859 and the Cripple Creek gold strike of 1890. Frontier capitalists settled in Colorado Springs, and an educated, well-traveled social elite took root. A health and tourist trade attracted wealthy visitors from Europe and the Americas. Colorado Springs took on the image of a Newport of the Rockies.[2]

Holm's teaching brought many hundreds of dance professionals, teachers, and novices from all parts of the country to Colorado College. Bessie Schönberg, like Holm a legendary teacher, once said, "There was a time when, if you wanted good training, you better get yourself out to Colorado."[3] During peak enrollment years in the 1960s and 1970s, tuition dollars Holm generated carried the college summer program. Her reputation supported the college's ambition for national stature as a cultural center, and her European background helped the Colorado Springs social elite maintain an international identity. When her own career glided between concert art and popular theater, Holm used deeply rooted modern dance values and a pedagogic strategy grounded in principles of movement to enlighten her Colorado students and audiences.

Among centers for summer dance training, Holm's in Colorado was unique. Study was guided by one master teacher, rather than several, and radiated from a single dance theory. The spine of

Holm's curriculum was a daily class in dance technique where the body was drilled and coaxed into mastery of itself. The flesh of her program was creative work. Holm's European dance heritage equipped her with a teaching method that stimulated invention and released imagination. Her students committed themselves to daily movement explorations.

In the early years a few advanced students performed with Holm's own company in her annual productions. Later, guest artists and some advanced students were allowed to see their choreography to the stage. Still later, Holm found ways to include all willing dancers in the performance experience, even if that meant only a few stage crossings. Submitting to the discipline of the theater before a sophisticated audience that Holm had cultivated was a peak experience—a life-changing experience—for many.

Some professionals, their epiphanies behind them, practiced their craft and moved on, the inspiration of Holm's training now a part of their heritage. Glen Tetley—Broadway star, ballet principal, choreographer in demand the world over—is one. So is Alwin Nikolais, a choreographer who changed the way we look at theater. Ray Harrison, Katherine Litz, David Wood, Joyce Trisler, Jessica Sayre, Jeff Duncan, Steve Koester, and Susan Hadley are just a few great performers who passed through Holm's program. Elizabeth Hayes, Joan Woodbury, Chris Burnside, Paul Chambers, Annalise Mertz, and Jerry Cochran are some of the prominent educators. In the category of students awakened to dance is Don Redlich. His special relationship with Holm began when he was a young student in 1949 and continued into the 1980s when she choreographed for his dance company.

Holm had come to the United States in 1931 to direct a school for the great German modern dance pioneer Mary Wigman, with whom she had worked since 1920. The cachet of Wigman's name put Holm in the first rank of modern dance artists in this country, but by the mid-1930s Holm found herself walking a fine, stressful line between loyalty to her mentor and America's outrage at the fascist menace in Europe. Wigman was the most famous dancer in Germany when Adolf Hitler came to power in 1933. By choosing to remain in her homeland, she seemed to lend support to the Third Reich, even though she was not a member of the Nazi Party.

In New York Holm lost students as the Wigman School came under suspicion of fascist connections. Finally, suffering what Schönberg called "the torture of the damned," Holm explained her troubles to Wigman, and the two women agreed to sever their business ties. Although the school continued to founder, Holm sustained a dance company, and in 1937 she choreographed a masterpiece. *Trend* was a nonliteral work of epic scale concerned with social disintegration and ultimate reaffirmation of humanity's vital forces. It won the *New York Times* award for best group choreography in 1937.

Holm's invitation to Colorado College was brokered by Martha Hill, director of the important Bennington Summer School of the Dance. Hill had previously chosen Holm as one of the four major artists around whom the curriculum was organized at that influential institution. From its founding in 1934, Bennington supported the work of "the Big Four"—Martha Graham, Doris Humphrey, and Charles Weidman, along with Holm—and established many emerging figures who danced and choreographed there. Bennington trained educators who spread across the country to teach modern dance; it created links with composers, designers, and writers and educated the public to a new art of human movement. Holm took on all these tasks when she established her own summer program at Colorado College.

By 1941 Holm welcomed the opportunity to pull away from Bennington and direct a dance program that was entirely her own. She was familiar with Colorado, having taught at the Perry-Mansfield School, a women's summer outpost of outdoor recreation and the arts at Steamboat Springs, not far from the Continental Divide. Colorado had given her company its first opportunity to perform for a general audience, and she had helpful friends in the state. Those were the pull mechanisms. The push mechanisms were wounding professional rivalries at Bennington and also the anti-German feelings that haunted her even after she made the prudent move of breaking her business ties to Wigman.

In Colorado Holm was able to sanitize her German background; dances she made in the West, then toured and produced in New York, finalized her American identity for the New York journal *Dance Observer*, which in 1943 proclaimed all doubt about her understanding of the American idiom dispelled.[4] Her work in Colorado was also crucial for Holm's success as a Broadway choreographer. Her Colorado experiments with Americana and dance-drama prepared her to triumph with the dance opera *Ballet Ballads* in 1948. That success led her into the high-stakes arena of commercial theater. Meanwhile, with her teaching in Colorado Holm fully realized the purpose for which she had come to the New World: she adapted a theory-based modern dance practice with roots in Germany to American bodies and American needs. From Colorado her reformation spread to colleges, universities, and professional settings throughout the country as her students passed on their learning to their own students and other audiences.

This chronicle of forty-three summers of dancing and dance learning is written for students, teachers, and all readers who are interested in artistic expression and want to know how a dance heritage is passed from generation to generation. To assemble a record of this overlooked institution I used Holm's own papers, which her heirs entrusted to me. Among them are concert programs, photographs, correspondence, notes on students, and plans for Holm's productions. Colorado College provided other material, including class rosters, brochures, and pertinent college publications. I read press clippings in Holm's microfilmed scrapbooks in the Dance Division of the New York Public Library for the Performing Arts. College administrators, Holm's colleagues, and observers of her program spoke with me, and I found at least one student from each of the forty-three summers to interview. From evidence in the record I suggest dynamics of the founding of the institution in 1941 and propose what I think is a logical scenario for its bitter and contested ending in 1983.

The story is told in chronological fashion, divided into chapters of uneven length. I give 1941 a full chapter as a love affair between Colorado Springs and a star visitor begins and Holm confronts contradictions in her situation. The war years are given another chapter. In the next chapter, covering 1946 through 1949, Holm develops the craftsmanship with which she triumphs in commercial theater. From 1950 to 1956, her modern dance company five years in the past, Holm attracts Broadway dancers and other professionals to form a company of irregulars to perform in Colorado as she choreographs prolifically.

The next chapter, 1957 through 1965, takes the college and Holm through a reassessment of their codependency and ends with a reaffirmation of their partnership. Holm's contribution to the dance boom takes up another chapter. I limit Chapter 8 to the three-year period 1975 through 1977, when I was in Colorado as an assistant to Holm, and I can reflect on the complex ingredients of her success. From 1978 through 1981, summer arts projects at Colorado College build to a frenzied pitch with Holm at their center. The bubble bursts in the penultimate chapter, "Curtain," which is followed by a brief "Aftermath." A first appendix lists Holm's students by year, and a second gives programs in abbreviated form for each of her concerts.

By paralleling Holm's summers in Colorado with accounts of her full career, I show how Holm's work in the East affected her behavior in Colorado and the ways in which Colorado influenced her life. This is not a biography of Hanya Holm, but it provides evidence that must be considered when a new biography is undertaken.[5] It reveals a complex artist whose foibles frustrated some people while endearing her to countless others. Holm exercised iron self-discipline and expected the same of others, yet she was an improviser who cherished the moment and trusted spontaneity. She could articulate original, profound ideas, yet she loved nonsense and hilarity. She knew how to be a team player and defer to the authority of others, but at times she was stubborn and unyielding.

Hanya Holm is the stage name Johanna Kuntze adopted when her professional career began. Everyone who knew her, from Broadway luminaries to beginning students, addressed her as "Hanya." Her biographer and other writers also refer to her by her first name. I suggest that by stepping back from the intimacy the first-name choice implies, we legitimatize the artist and her work. It is time to begin an assessment of the institution Holm led in Colorado and to analyze its place in American dance.

Chapter Two

FRONTIER CROSSINGS 1941

If a frontier is a boundary between the known and the unknown, then modern dance in 1941 was on the frontier of America's performing arts. Modern dance artists had achieved their goal of a contemporary and national identity, but they had not developed a sustainable audience. Major choreographers had partisans in New York; their work appealed to intellectuals in other urban centers and to acolytes in college dance classes. But laypeople were bewildered, even when they could be enticed into theaters to see modern dance. As early as 1938 a critic who championed the new form worried about pretension and a failure to communicate. In 1940 another feared that cultism and fanaticism were holding the field back. Even a major choreographer admitted that modern dance was excessively grim.[1]

Hanya Holm helped dance to cross frontiers between modernism and accessibility and between regionalism and East Coast hegemony. After her first summer in Colorado, Holm's successes inspired the influential journal _Dance Observer_ to state that the response of Holm's regional audience "shows that modern dance has reached the place wherein it can command the admiration and attention heretofore accorded only the larger ballet companies." The journal further concluded that its readers could look forward to Colorado College becoming a new Mecca of the dance.[2] The story of Holm's forty-three-year partnership with

Colorado College reveals strategies and opportunities she used to promote an inclusive vision of American dance culture.

In 1941 Holm was forty-eight and still young-looking. She was small—just five feet one inch tall—and blond. Roundness softened her features and delicate frame. Her hair—which she had worn in the short, smooth bob de rigueur in the heady days of Weimar Germany where she began her career—had grown long, and she wore braids wound up in various styles. For the cameras recording her first summer in Colorado, Holm projected a robust let's-get-going enthusiasm for life, often sporting a grin that seemed to say she was ready to accept any dare.

She had an accent, used German word order, and had a seemingly endless repertory of aphorisms that heightened the fun of her conversation and intensified the profundity of her message. She was fast gaining a complete command of English vocabulary, as Scrabble opponents through the decades would discover. She was a single parent, having agreed to a divorce shortly after the birth of her son. Klaus was cared for in Germany while his mother established herself in the New World, but Holm brought him to the United States in 1936, just before he turned sixteen and would have been enrolled in the Hitler Youth. Friends marveled at Holm's success in this maneuver. One said, "We knew if anybody could do it, Hanya could."[3]

Everyone she encountered recognized Holm's magnetism and the inner resources that supported her authority. Coloradans also saw her playful side. She motored through the canyons and climbed Pikes Peak. She made enduring friendships with interesting people and brought a lot to their parties. She tied flowers in her hair, watched owls in the trees and sunsets over the mountains. She and her company posed in cowgirl hats.

One could wonder if the exuberance Holm displayed was the acting out of a European myth of the American West she had brought from Germany. But Colorado Springs was proud of frontier characters in its past, proud of nearby ghost towns and abandoned railroad beds, and proud of its mountain skyline. That a famous eastern artist with credentials from Europe would play "Wild West" charmed them and disarmed their resistance to an unfamiliar theater experience. By reminding Coloradans of their historical frontier, Holm helped them cross a frontier in the arts.

The Colorado Springs community had been introduced to professional modern dance in 1936, when Martha Graham performed on a series of programs inaugurating the Colorado Springs Fine Arts Center, a gift to the town from heiress Alice Bemis Taylor. A young athletics coach who, along with the rest of the college faculty and staff, had been given a ticket remembered that although the guests enjoyed the music concerts, "Martha Graham's leaping and gesturing left most of them in an uncomprehending stupor. Only a few of those in attendance had seen a modern dance performance before."[4] Later that year they could see another modern dance concert when Holm and a company of dancers performed at the Fine Arts Center after concerts in Denver and Boulder.

Those were the first public performances Holm gave with a company under her own name. She had tested her program before dance audiences twice that summer, July 25 at Mills College in California and August 7 and 8 at Bennington College in Vermont, and the company had performed earlier in the summer at a Dance Congress in New York City. For all those concerts Holm's group was still named for the New York Mary Wigman School of the Dance.

Publicity that heralded the debut of her own company afforded Holm the opportunity to declare her new nationality and her regional connections. In a radio interview from Denver she asserted, "The spirit of America has become the vital inspiration of my work." She explained that in the five years since coming to the United States, "I have found myself becoming more and more a part of the country." Asked why she had happened to choose Colorado for the debut of her company, she replied, "Colorado is the place, since my dearest friends live here."[5]

One of those friends, Martha Wilcox, who was interviewed with Holm on another radio station, talked about meeting Holm in 1933 at the Perry-Mansfield School. Wilcox, who ran a studio for dance on Sherman Street in Denver, said, "Her work and her teaching that summer inspired me to abandon all the old principles of the dance, the ballet, and the interpretive type of performance. I have been an enthusiast for the new ever since."[6]

Colorado College president Thurston Jenkins Davies sympathized with Wilcox's enthusiasm, and he was familiar with modern dance and its milieu in the East, for he was a close friend of

Martha Hill. Soon after taking up the leadership of Colorado College in 1934, Davies had begun to promote the arts. He forged a partnership with the Fine Arts Center, and the two institutions announced a combined effort to advance the arts. In spring 1938 they joined in sponsoring an annual Conference on the Fine Arts. Grants from the El Pomar Foundation, endowed by millionaire Spencer Penrose, expanded musical offerings of the college. A professional string quartet, the Belgian, became resident, and composer Roy Harris and his wife, pianist Johana Harris, joined the faculty.

One of Davies's first actions as president had been to reinstate the summer session that had been a casualty of the Depression. Davies wished to add dance to the summer offerings. "But," he complained to Hill, "you have all the stars," referring to his friend's leadership of Bennington. "I told him to have Hanya out," said Hill, and she explained how impressed she was with the lecture-demonstrations in which Holm demystified modern dance and made it enjoyable for the uninitiated. Hill saw Holm as the best proselytizer of a new art form to help Davies build a regional audience for the arts. Holm was verbal and charming. Good teaching would be important, and Hill knew Holm was an excellent teacher. "And," Hill remembered telling Davies, "Hanya is having a hard time because of the anti-German feeling in the East."[7] Hill, who had invited Holm to the Bennington Summer School of the Dance, was responsible for offering her a new path.

Holm's responsibilities were to direct an eight-week summer dance program, extending two weeks beyond the regular college summer session, and to create a new dance on a regional theme to a score by composer-in-residence Roy Harris, who was best known for Americanist music. Accepting a regional theme and nationalistic music presented Holm with a dilemma. Her colorful friend, the musician John Colman, said later, "Hanya felt the same way I do about nationalistic art. It's terrible! Nationalism has nothing to do with music or with dance."[8]

Holm faced another dilemma as support for the arts became linked to regional chauvinism and national patriotism. Throughout 1941, Colorado watched devastation on the Continent and the bombing of Britain with increasing anxiety. By early summer the college was honoring its alumni who were in the National Defense Program and noting the number of current students in uniform.

Bonds between patriotism and the arts were forged during the 1941 Colorado Springs Fine Arts Conference "The Arts, the Public, and the Crisis." Chicago music critic Olin Downes, the keynote speaker, declared, "Artistically as well as socially, America must take up the torch of the spirit that Europe has let fall." A second speaker, like Holm a German expatriate, also invoked patriotic spirit when he distinguished between totalitarian art, which is directed by a government, and democratic art, which involves all the people.[9]

Holm readily accepted her new country's righteous response to Germany's militarism and eugenic fervor. A fine reading of her situation, however, shows contradictions in her position. When she had put her name to the school she directed for Mary Wigman, she made a statement that read in part: "In my opinion there is no room for politics in art."[10] Shortly after the United States entered the war in December 1941, Davies would proclaim, "The arts can and should be aids to national morale. In promoting activities that help to stabilize people emotionally, we are directly aiding the maintenance of morale and thereby helping the war effort."[11]

Holm had three reasons to accommodate Davies's enthusiasms and Harris's musical interests. One was financial and professional survival. In 1941 Holm's financial situation was precarious, and her company would disband in two-and-a-half years. "She was a soldier in her poverty," said Bessie Schönberg of exactly this period.[12] A second reason was Holm's need to reconfirm her new nationality. Hill had acknowledged that some in the dance world still connected Holm to the enemy culture of Germany when she recommended her to Davies. That this was a major issue for Holm is evidenced by a 1941 press release, which begins: "It is interesting to note that the nine young dancers who comprise the Hanya Holm Company . . . are all Americans, gathered from the widely separated states of the Union, and as such bring to the dance theatre that healthy attitude which is the mainstay of any healthy institution."[13] The need to emphasize American connections exposes insecurity in the director's self-image.

Holm may also have had a genuine interest in exploring American folk idioms. In an essay she had written for the book *The Modern Dance,* published in 1935, Holm suggested that America's phenomenal material growth had left the country's folk arts in an incongruous crude state. In "The German Dance in the American Scene," Holm negotiated a position above the parochialisms of both the German and American camps of modern dance, but she hinted that American arts suffered from an immaturity that could be corrected by the development of their own folk tradition.[14] A recent immigrant, she may have projected her own rootlessness onto her new homeland. For her, folk idiom was not implicated in political or social agendas but was a necessary exercise for grounding herself and American dance.

Holm and her dancers gave a lecture-demonstration on Saturday, July 27, the first day of the Colorado Springs Fine Arts Conference. The next morning an ecstatic review, signed by Elizabeth Hylbom, in the *Colorado Springs Gazette* reported that "an ovation of shouting proportions" had greeted the demonstration. The reviewer was well versed in the vocabulary and arguments that had engaged the German art community twenty years previously—the question of whether dance could be absolute, that is, whether it could speak through movement alone. She had seen in Holm's demonstration a dance freeing itself of "slavery to the picture, the story, the poem, [and] of its artificial techniques." She told her readers that dance of the kind she had seen the previous night "now approaches the realm of the absolute," and she celebrated dance that "can now touch and play upon the depths of universal experience and emotion . . . without literal tale-telling or glamorous ballet music."[15]

Hylbom was a music critic and the daughter of a banker who had helped to shape the gold-glutted city at the turn of the twentieth century. She had studied in Europe and at Vassar College. Hylbom represented the community's cosmopolitan social elite that embraced Holm because of her German heritage rather than in spite of it. To the advantage of her readers and the artists she reviewed, Hylbom researched thoroughly and wrote intelligently about music and dance.

Her review continued with promotion of Holm's August concerts:

> If such an effect could be produced last night through the highly matured technique of the art, the leaps, the falls, the swings and rhythms, how much more can be expected in the near future when all this is brought to the focus of creative artistic expression. The rapidly growing public with a taste for

such things will see on August 7, 8, and 9, and it is hoped that many who have passed by with "oh, the modern dance," will be on hand for conversion.

As Hylbom helped her readers to step from the unknown to what would become a beloved theater experience, she herself stepped onto an aesthetic frontier. Although she returned to ideals of absolute dance in subsequent reviews of Holm's work, she ultimately followed Holm into a dance partnership with music, text, and design and toward a modernism that modified absolute principles of modernism in northern Europe and became American.

Thus while teaching daily, rehearsing her company, and choreographing a new work, Holm was touched by two debates— one about the dependence of dance on music, character, and situation and the other about the role of the artist vis-à-vis political agendas. Her concert at the end of the summer session would reveal a principled response to her delicate situation. She found a way to address these political and artistic questions while leading the community to accept her work on her terms.

For forty-three summers the college gave Cossitt Gymnasium over to Holm's dancers. Most classes and rehearsals were held on the big floor. It had a mellow patina just right for the bare feet of modern dancers. High windows let in all the light needed in daytime. One entered Cossitt on a level above the big floor, descended a staircase through a railed, circular opening, and went down a hallway to a door in the long south side of the studio. A piano stood close to where teachers positioned themselves. A balcony over the east end gave visitors a foreshortened perspective of the activity below. An archaic Greek theater spilled out from the south side of Cossitt on a lower level, its cement platforms hard for sunbathing but its columns irresistible background for camera buffs.

Small classes were held in rooms tucked into corners above the big floor. A wood-paneled reception room just to the left of the main entrance was an especially cozy place for small classes and rehearsals; after their classes students vied for any studio space in which to rehearse composition assignments.

Holm offered four courses. *Course* was used in the European sense of the word to mean what Americans now mean by *program of study*. Students chose to be in a course for beginners, in an advanced course for teachers of dance and advanced dancers, or in a course for laypeople. Each course was composed of several classes. Workshop was the fourth course. Open by audition, it gave some experienced students the opportunity to perform in Holm's choreography in the concert that closed the eight-week session. All students studied Technique and Theory together. In Theory Class Holm lectured, engaged her students in discussion, and directed improvisations precisely structured around one element of dance. Afternoon classes were in Dance Composition and Rhythmic Training. Advanced dancers had an additional class, called Review, for more detailed study of principles on which the morning classes were based.

Technique classes began with floor exercises Holm had designed with physical therapist Joseph Pilates to develop strength and flexibility. Then came standing exercises: first were knee bends in six positions of the feet and arms that prepared the dancer for working in cardinal directions of space, side-side, diagonal forward–diagonal backward, and forward-backward; then came leg swings in various patterns, foot exercises, and jumps. Sometimes there were arm and torso swings, and occasionally dancers practiced falling and rebounding from the floor.

Holm's evaluations often combined German and English vocabulary and word order. After class, students would laugh about such remarks as "a knee bend can do any idiot" and "don't *schleppen,* children!" Holm taught confidently and with enthusiasm, yet she was stern and uncompromising. Anger, which often accompanied her demands for perfection, increased her authority in the eyes of her students and created camaraderie among them.

Holm began the across-the-floor section of class with simple traveling steps, usually the walk. She built slowly, adding variations such as a turn into backward walking or a change in rhythm. If the group did not perform as Holm wished, more explanations and exhortations were given, and simple locomotion was repeated at length. When the class was working well, Holm amplified the basic pattern. Students remember with delight the fluency and beauty of Holm's elaborations and the mounting excitement in class as everyone tried to imitate her.

Each class was precisely focused, and each was fresh, because Holm did not train her students with patterns of dance material carried over from one class to another. Rather, she invented

movement on the spot to highlight a particular understanding—
it could be the correct lift and placement of the foot to accom-
plish a smooth forward walk, the technique of turning, or stability in the shoulders while arms are gesturing. She ended every
class with exuberant runs, leaps, turns, and springs into the air,
leaving dancers joyous and dewy with perspiration.

Louise Kloepper was Holm's principal assistant. Kloepper had
been Holm's assistant teacher at her New York school since 1932.
She was the first American dancer to have earned a certificate at
the Wigman School in Germany, and at the suggestion of Wigman
she joined the New York staff, instantly becoming a loved and
respected teacher. When Holm formed a company, Kloepper
was her leading dancer and, some say, rivaled the powerful
Martha Graham as a performer.

Martha Wilcox, who taught part-time at Colorado College as
well as in her Denver studio, was Holm's second assistant. Wilcox
had made possible the debut of Holm's company in Denver in
1936 and was also partly responsible for Holm's coming to Colorado College; Davies had consulted Wilcox to assess Holm's local
reputation after Martha Hill's recommendation. Wilcox's students
swelled the roster of Holm's students in the first years of the session.

Both assistants taught Technique Class, but Holm taught all
theory classes herself. Sometimes Kloepper was trusted with
Rhythm Class. Both assistants sat with Holm during Composition
Class. In the advanced Composition Class one student would
choreograph a dance using a small group of her classmates. The
product was discussed at length and then abandoned as other
dancers took their turn to choreograph.

In 1941 Holm taught a group of thirty-one dancers, twenty-
four registered students, Wilcox, and Holm's company of three
women and three men: Robin Gregory, Kloepper, Barbara Hatch,
Kipp Kiernan, Gregory McDougall, and Paul Sweeney (Kloepper
and Wilcox took Technique Class when Holm taught). Students
were aspiring dancers, teachers, and seasoned performers; three
were advanced students at Holm's New York studio. A prominent ballet teacher from Georgia and two of her assistants were
among the students. Dorothy Alexander would soon found the
Atlanta Ballet and become a leader of the country's regional ballet movement. Alexander spoke of the many altitude-induced
nosebleeds she had seen during the summer. She was surprised

that Holm did not slow down her classes to accommodate sufferers or even seem to notice the bloody cotton wads hanging from noses as dancers did their best to control their affliction.[16]

Another experienced educator who studied with Holm in 1941 was Elizabeth Hayes, who taught physical education and dance at colleges in West Virginia and Illinois. Hayes had taken three courses with Holm in New York and had been to Germany for a course with Wigman. During her long and illustrious teaching career at the University of Utah, Hayes sent many students to Holm's summer courses. Her descriptions of the 1941 summer and the memories of another student, Frances [Davies] Wessells, color in the outlines of the first Hanya Holm summer session. Both women saw a threatening side to Holm, yet both have positive memories of their dance learning in Colorado—learning, they say, that influenced their long careers.

Hayes summarized Holm's teaching manner as affable and demanding but sometimes cruel. As an example of Holm's cruelty, Hayes recalled an occasion when an advanced student was asked to teach a class, enabling Holm to rehearse with her company. "Hanya returned before the end of the class, watched, and after the class finished said, 'That was the most superficial lesson I have ever seen.'" Hayes remembered only one time Holm chastised her: "She just about destroyed me, the worst thing she could have done right before a performance." Despite her one unhappy experience, Hayes remains loyal to Holm. Her strongest memory is of a dynamic person who was an expert and meticulous teacher. "Hanya," she said, "impressed on us the importance of teaching thoroughly; in those days she was the only one teaching how to teach."[17]

Wessells was a professional chorus-line dancer in Denver. She was "overwhelmed," she said, when she saw a modern dancer rehearsing in a studio, and she knew instantly that she wanted to do more than chorus-line dancing. She sought out Wilcox, who convinced her to take Holm's summer course. Wessells elaborated on Hayes's descriptions of Holm's teaching persona: "She was a Dr. Jekyll and Mr. Hyde. Usually she was wonderful, like a mother, but she could be wicked; she could pick on one person for two solid weeks. She could go for weeks without picking on anyone and then one person—and everyone would cry for her."

Although she saw Holm's foibles, Wessells returned in 1943, 1944, and 1945 to study and dance in Holm's productions. She said, "I went home after each summer and collapsed for two weeks; I always felt I had really grown." Wessells remembers Wilcox as an outstanding teacher and that "everybody adored Louise. We worshipped her like God."[18]

By 1941 Kloepper had a ten-year perspective on Holm's teaching style. Students in Germany were committed to discovery and to learning through improvisation, composition, and participation in choric studies—group dances in which they had to be especially sensitive to their fellow dancers and to an intended structure. Wigman and Holm had expected to implant this kind of training in America, but Holm found dancers here an impatient lot, more interested in the technical achievement offered by other leading modern dance teachers. In Colorado Holm was able to regain respect for the creative process, but in response to the competition she had faced in New York her teaching had taken on a harsh, sometimes cruel, edge. Kloepper claimed Holm had not been like that when she studied under her in Dresden.

Historian Susan Manning has described the study environment at the Wigman school in Germany as a tension between authority and autonomy.[19] This is an apt description of the atmosphere Holm created in Colorado. She encouraged autonomy by letting students create dance studies and improvise. Holm was the arbiter of their success, so although students' autonomy gave them authority over their dancing, that autonomy gave Holm an opportunity to exercise her authority—an authority the students invited as they exercised their autonomy.

In a deeper way, authority and autonomy met in the philosophy Holm delivered to her students. Her central message concerned the imperative of taking responsibility for one's choices, one's principles, and by extension, one's life. Every cohort of students was reminded that he who chases two rabbits at the same time catches neither. Holm's message thrilled young people who craved autonomy but needed an authority figure to tell them when they were keeping faith with themselves and when they were not.

A major part of the practical learning in any summer occurred in the crucible of concert preparation. Students chosen for the workshop course rehearsed every night and on weekends with

Holm's company. In 1941 ten women chosen for the workshop course were distributed over three dances: the premiere, *From This Earth*; and the lyrical *Dance of Introduction* and the comic *Metropolitan Daily*, both created in 1938. Students Shirley Brimberg, Jinx Heffelfinger, and Eleanore McDougall were trusted with roles in *From This Earth*. Frances Wessells and Elizabeth Nichols danced with Wilcox and six company members in *Dance of Introduction*; Wessells and Nichols plus Gladys DeBarry, Deborah Froelicher, Elizabeth Hayes, Vicky Hubbard, and Patty Kerr joined Holm and the company in *Metropolitan Daily*.

For the heralded new work, Harris composed for an orchestra of ten. The suite opened with "Dawn: Mother's Lullaby" danced by Holm. It was followed by "Childhood: Children at Play" for five dancers. Then came "Love: Courtship, Marriage, Festivities" for ten, including Holm. That was followed by "Work: Treadmill and Exhaustion" for three men and a small woman and the concluding "Dusk: Retrospection" for the full company.

The title of the collaboration between Holm and Harris referred to mining that had opened the region to (European) settlement and industry. *From This Earth*, recalled Kloepper, was joked about in the company as "the miners' piece." During planning sessions with Davies, Holm had heard him speak about gutsy legends of the virile gold camps of the Old West. Holm rejected this specificity and instead saw her topic metaphorically; miners' labor in bringing ore from the earth was a metaphor for bringing experience from the bowels of the self. What was proposed as a suite of dances on a regional theme became a celebration of Everyman. With this choreographic strategy, Holm resolved both the artistic and moral dilemmas her first summer in Colorado Springs had presented. By universalizing her theme she dispensed with plot and characterization and sidestepped chauvinistic regional display.

Critical response to *From This Earth* tells us that the dance touched on audiences' suppressed anxieties. Holm's maternal solo was seen as tender, but it also communicated sadness about the inevitable loss parents must face. Tedium and resignation were recognized as the implied content of the final section. In his review of the new work, Dean E.D. Hale, director of music at Colorado College for thirty years, discussed differences between unalloyed folk dance and Holm's remodeling of its ancient simplicity and power.[20] Hale found weighty expression in the work, although not by way of the vernacular dance forms he had expected. John C. Wilcox, voice teacher and father of Martha, found riotous moments of play and a spontaneous spirit of fun in parts of *From This Earth,* but his strongest impression was of the elemental and social experiences of human beings who "toil to live."[21] Holm adroitly acquainted her audience with apprehensions inherent in contemporary living.

From This Earth was created not in New York but in the middle of the country; it was presented to a regional audience that both appreciated the work and discerned its inherent message. Holm proved that modern dance could cross the boundary between regionalism and East Coast hegemony and that modernist themes could be made accessible to general audiences.

When she brought the dance to New York, John Martin gave it a long, thoughtful, and favorable review in the *New York Times,* calling it "a major composition by one of the most gifted contemporary choreographers on any terms." For Martin the work was not pessimistic, yet he felt a cloud of desperation hanging over it. He wrote, "Mere survival seems to be its own grimly won reward." His final judgment was that *From This Earth* was "deeply felt, skillfully realized, and not easy to put out of one's mind." Always Holm's champion, Martin included a cautionary note in his review. Buried in a passage about costuming, he observed of the work that "its virtues are occasionally hidden under a difficult semiliteralism."[22] Martin's prescience had identified Holm's need to negotiate tension between the universalism expected of concert dance and the specificity required of the many commissions Holm would execute during a long career ranging across theater genres. Colorado audiences would witness her response to this apparent conflict.

Martin had begun his review by observing that Holm would not give a Broadway performance that season. Modern dance companies were in the position of having to rent Broadway houses for Sunday night performances when the theaters were not otherwise in use. The expense and strain of these fast in-and-out productions led many prominent artists to find slots on concert series organized at high school auditoriums. It was on such a series at the Washington Irving High School that Holm's company performed in New York in late January 1942. In contrast, Colorado

College had given Holm leisure in which to prepare a concert, and the Colorado Springs Fine Arts Center had put a new theater at her disposal for a three-night run.

Chapter Three
THE DANCE AND THE WAR
1942–1945

Citizens of Colorado Springs made sacrifices to World War II, but they also found opportunities in mobilization. The mountain grandeur that had drawn speculators, tourists, and consumptives in an earlier period now provided relative isolation and safety for military bases. A cadre of businessmen, never short of schemes to promote Colorado Springs, lobbied hard in Washington for Camp Carson and Peterson Field. Their efforts would continue into the cold war and result in the selection of Colorado Springs as the site for the North American Air Defense Command and its Combat Operations Center under Cheyenne Mountain and, in 1958, the creation of the United States Air Force Academy north of town.

Some residents lamented that after 1942, Colorado Springs became a typical military town and lost its identity as an attractive, quiet, crime-free health and tourist resort. Yet as the city sprawled north, east, and south throughout the decades, views of the Front Range and Pikes Peak were never obscured from the porches and lawns of Colorado College. Thin air continued to strengthen lungs and soul. Those parts of the city attainable on foot were safe and proper enough. Rumors of rape circulated infrequently through the years, and they were handled with admonitions to women not to walk around town without putting blouses over their leotards. The focus of the dancers was on the dance. Almost all of them lived and ate on campus, and their explorations took them on mountain hikes, away from the war-induced commercial clutter of the new parts of town.

War gave subject and structure to the summer of 1942. The theme of the Colorado Springs Conference on the Fine Arts was "War and the Arts," and its symposia explored the relationship between war and the creative artist, war and the audience, and war and what organizers called "the center of culture." Colorado Springs saw itself in a global context, with responsibility for preserving what was at risk from war in Europe and Asia.

Hanya Holm and her company again offered a dance demonstration as a featured attraction on opening night of the three-day conference. Martha Wilcox led a luncheon discussion on dance. She was joined by Valerie Bettis, once a dancer with Holm's company and a teacher that summer at the Perry-Mansfield School. José Limón, a veteran of the Humphrey-Weidman Company, was teaching at Colorado State Teachers College in Greeley, and he joined the discussion, as did Holm's new assistant, Harriet Roeder. Uncertainty over war conditions makes understandable a decrease in enrollment in 1942, the lowest in the history of the program. Eighteen women registered, and Holm brought a company of six. Four advanced students were given the privilege of performing with Holm's company.

Once again some students came down from Denver, encouraged by their work there with Wilcox. Another student, Marion Yahr, was a ballet instructor in Milwaukee. She had studied with Wigman in Germany and formed a close bond with the great dancer and teacher, who in 1942 was a virtual exile in her own land, driven from her school in Dresden by the Nazi regime. Mary Louise Lee, a New England educator, had also taken a course with Wigman. Lee brought one of her students, Dorothy Madden, to Colorado, and Madden went on to study with Holm in New York.

Later a prominent educator and administrator in the United States and Europe, Madden contributed memories of the 1942 summer session and explained how her experience in Colorado was important to her career. That summer and subsequent study at the Holm Studio empowered her to find her own method and material for teaching. She studied all the systems of modern dance, and later, as a teacher, she remembers wondering, "Why am I teaching other people's patterns?" She reflected on her training with Holm: "I realized I had the resources to find my own material and to help others to do so."[1] In this way Holm's legacy renewed itself in succeeding generations.

Some of Madden's study with Holm was painful: "I am grateful that someone warned me that she would fasten on one person for criticism. I once became that person." The severity of Holm's criticism legitimatized the dance as a serious enterprise for students who became her victims, as well as for those who could apply her criticisms in safety. Training in the arts, built on a master-disciple model, has historically lent itself to authoritarian teaching styles, and early modern dance was no exception. Tales are told of Martha Graham's manipulative maneuvers, and Louis Horst's biographer writes that the legendary teacher of music composition and dance choreography was merciless: "Surviving each of his assignments was a significant occasion."[2] Holm student and company member Mimi [Kagan] Kim, who studied at various studios in the 1930s, compared her several teachers: "Hanya was hard to deal with, but she wasn't destructive like some others. There was some kind of family feeling always, a cooperative environment."[3]

Harriet Roeder was Louise Kloepper's replacement as an assistant teacher. Like Wilcox, Roeder was a native of Colorado, and also like Wilcox, she had been one of the students at Bennington who danced in Holm's masterpiece *Trend* in 1937. Whereas Wilcox returned to her own school and company in Denver, Roeder stayed in New York as a member of Holm's company. In 1941 she had represented Holm at Bennington, where she had also choreographed. Henrietta Greenhood, known professionally as Eve Gentry and an original Holm Company member, was representing Holm at Bennington in the summer of 1942.

Holm entrusted the first two weeks of teaching to her assistants so she could open the summer course at her New York studio. Her decision suggests the renewed importance of summer work in New York as Bennington unraveled. Gas rationing and other constraints curtailed the usual festival of performances, and there were no major new productions. It was the final year of the Bennington Summer School of the Dance; Holm's program would have another forty-one years of life.

Patriotism, regional pride, and maneuverings to place the arts in the foreground of the nation's response to world war figured in the promotion of Holm's concerts of August 8 and 9. President Davies referred to the previous collaboration between Holm and composer Roy Harris as "not the least of the morale-building art forms sponsored by Colorado College in the Rocky Mountain region." He promised, "It is to be anticipated that the new dance, which the pair will compose during the coming summer, will have in it some of the morale-building integrity of the old West."[4] The concert was presented with the cooperation of the Zebulon Pike Chapter of the Daughters of the American Revolution as a benefit for the Blood Plasma Bank. A free preview for soldiers preceded the opening.

Holm's second summer at Colorado College gave her another opportunity to test Americana as a theme for modern dance. With one work she again tried to move her patron's ideas away from the literal. A second work, however, proposed by a third artist who joined Holm and Harris, pulled her toward characterization. Arch Lauterer, stage architect and lighting designer, had been at Bennington from 1938 to 1941 where he collaborated with many choreographers, including Holm. He had given *Trend* its powerful stage set of ramps and platforms, as well as its masterful lighting. Lauterer was a theorist of the theater who sought an ideal of total art, a collaboration of all the performing disciplines. In an unpublished essay he discussed dance-drama, which he called "a new expression of theatre in America." Finding its roots in the earliest Greek drama, he followed examples through the ages and identified one twentieth-century manifestation as Mary Wigman's *Totenmal* (with which Holm had assisted Wigman in 1930). His historical survey ended, "This type of drama and theatre, which uses movement rather than speech as its principal means of expressing an action, was brought to the attention of our theatre audience by Martha Graham in her production of *Letter to the World* in 1940."[5] Lauterer had been design collaborator for the work, which took its text from the poems of Emily Dickinson.

He had become dissatisfied with works that attempted to adapt great literature, and for *Namesake,* his collaboration with Holm and Harris, he wrote the text himself—including, however, short pieces of poetry of Dickinson and Emily Brontë. In *Namesake* the dancers spoke, not as a chorus but to help develop separate characters. Lauterer's purpose was to show the actions of remembering and forgetting and to examine the states of becoming and permanence. He developed his idea by pointing to the disappearance of Christian names in the naming of Americans. Performers were dressed literally as New Englanders of a century before. His simple yet sophisticated stage set masked entrances in unusual ways and employed a range of visual textures such as monumental forms hidden behind a distressed, deteriorating space in which the dancers moved.

In contrast to the philosophically grounded, multilayered *Namesake,* Holm's other premiere was a suite of pure dance with the patriotic and Western flair President Davies craved. Harris scored *What So Proudly We Hail* for a chorus of twenty who sang wordlessly with a string orchestra. It was subtitled "Dance Suite Based on American Folk Songs," and its sections had specific song titles: "The Girl I Left Behind Me," "Western Cowboy," "Rock of Ages," "I'll Be True to My Love," and the finale, "Rhythms of Today."

The Holm-Harris-Lauterer concert at the Fine Arts Center was received warmly yet with reservation by Elizabeth Hylbom, who was troubled by Holm's move away from ideals of absolute dance: "Both the dance offerings brought a departure from what we have learned to look for in the contemporary art, the one adding strong and vital music, the second drama and speech to the already matured technique of bodily movement." She pondered whether "this fusion of the arts is to be the direction in which the dance will find its ultimate goal and usefulness; but one hopes that, however effective, the ballet will not be drawn back into the slavery in which music once held it." She concluded, "The silently danced introduction still proved that Hanya Holm's version of the art can stand on its own."[6]

Dance Observer ran a review of the Colorado program in its August-September issue. From its ebullient tone, unusual for the journal, one can guess that it was sent in by Carol Truax, exuberant new director of Fine Arts at Colorado College. It began, "When Hanya Holm takes a hand in choreography, one is assured of something to pique the imagination and to thrill the eye." The reviewer did not repeat Hylbom's concern for dance as an independent art form: "In *Namesake* the characters are developed so that every person in the group is an individual and is given the opportunity to project a personality. The characterization and the pantomime is of the highest order, and the emotional significance is unquestionable."[7]

Both new works premiered in New York in January on a recital series that included major concert dance figures Carmen Amaya, Jacques Cartier, Tamiris and Group, Martha Graham and Group, and Doris Humphrey and Charles Weidman. When Holm presented *What So Proudly We Hail* in New York she retitled it *Suite of Four Dances*, and she used new music by experimental composer John Cage. The newly titled work paralleled the first, third, fourth, and fifth sections of *What So Proudly We Hail*, and Holm named them simply "First Dance," "Second Dance," "Third Dance," and "Finale." The American folk foundation of her choreography was recognized by a New York critic, who wrote, "[the program] evidenced in no uncertain terms that Miss Holm and her company have thoroughly absorbed the idiom of this country, and in the first two parts of this concert we were shown some really authoritative Americana."[8] Holm had confirmed her American identity.

Holm repeated her program in March at Kaufmann Concert Hall, a New York venue often used by modern dance companies. Another critic wrote, "In a curious and very original way, *Namesake*, with its score by Roy Harris and its elusive, essentially wordless emotions, is a deeply moving theater dance."[9] This review suggests that Holm had reduced or eliminated Lauterer's text. Mary Anthony, who was making her first appearance with the Hanya Holm Company, remembers clearly that she did not speak. With the elimination of text from *Namesake* and with the retitling of her dance suite and its change of music, Holm tried, as she had a year earlier, to dilute the specificity expected by her regional sponsors. Ironically, her success in that maneuver was moot, as in February *Dance Observer* had accepted her work because it was an expression of America. The year ahead, however, hints at tension between convictions Holm may have harbored about a mandate for American folk traditions on the one hand and her commitment to European elitism on the other.

Dancers arriving for study at Colorado College in 1943 would have noticed many concessions to the war emergency. First, a driving force behind the summer arts programs, Thurston Davies, was not present. He had taken a leave of absence from the college to serve as a major in the marine corps, directing the Navy V-12 College Training Program for Marine Corps Reserve Officers. Naturally, one of the training programs was installed at Colorado College. On July 1, two weeks into the summer instruction, 420 potential navy-marine officers took up residence on campus and began their combined military and academic education. Davies would preside for one more summer session, that of 1946, but he never again took up leadership of the arts programs he had designed and energized. Family crises and ill health forced him to resign from the college in early 1947. He directed several high-profile arts programs in the East, and after the death of his first wife, he and Martha Hill married.

A family of adoring female students, understanding colleagues, and sympathetic audiences gathered around Holm in the war years and gave her confidence that also proved dangerous. Nineteen forty-three was at first a joyous and then a destructive year for Holm. As well as exposing an artistic dilemma with which she struggled, it revealed tensions within American dance between amateur and professional practice and mistrust between ballet and modern dance. The year 1943 also introduced one of the most colorful characters of forty-three summers, John Colman— genius musician, helpmate and friend of Holm, source of both enlightenment and torturous confusion to students, and a disciplinarian who could not finish anything.

Colman relished his friendship with Holm, and he considered it a tribute that she treated him like a European. As well as falling in with Coloradans' regional pride and displays of patriotism, Holm legitimatized their admiration for European high culture. Chauvinistic rhetoric celebrating life in virile gold camps of the Old West also reveals a sense of separation from eastern society and its continuity with European artistic heritage. When Holm turned from Americana to the European canon in the form of a Greek legend, her Colorado audience praised her even more rapturously than before; but in the first summer she did not have the enthusiasms of Davies and the Americanist music of Harris to give her subject, she failed with dance audiences in New York. Worse, *Orestes and the Furies* caused the influential New York critic Edwin Denby to question her professionalism and doubt the basis of her teaching method.

Orestes and the Furies was Colman's idea. He had previously composed music for a full production of *Eumenides* at Fordham University in New York. He remembered vividly its creation in Colorado in 1943: "I had the whole summer to work on revisions [to the score] but in the end Hanya had to lock me in a room to finish it." He confided, "Of course, we had terrible fights; we got so there was a real technique to our fights."[10] One can imagine the anxiety these friends visited on each other. Holm liked to discuss structure of a score before she started to choreograph. Colman, however, liked to see a dance before he composed. His music for *Orestes* was for two pianos, and he later confessed that he had improvised his own part.

Holm faced another crisis in preparing her new work. Lauterer had been expected to design the set and lighting for *Orestes and the Furies,* but he did not show up in Colorado. It is not known how Holm managed to have platforms and a tower constructed for her vision of the Greek drama. (For the New York performance, Lauterer was credited with lights and stage set.) With these headaches it is perhaps understandable that Holm made some questionable artistic choices in her choreography. Mary Anthony, who was in on the creation of the work, reported, "We all saw that she was being too literal, staying too close to the plot."[11]

Nonetheless, John Wilcox reviewed the Colorado performance of *Orestes and the Furies* with superlatives:

> Miss Holm created work that stands out as one of the most arresting among the fine choreographic compositions to her credit. Many who witnessed its premiere expressed the opinion that Miss Holm has reached a new height of dramatic strength and choreographic skill. . . . [Holm] moved and grouped the thirteen furies and five principals of the cast so that they frequently suggest a strongly sculptured Greek frieze.[12]

Wilcox had high praise for the dance soloists and for the music's dramatic consistency and rhythmic unity.

Hylbom treated Holm more effusively: "Hanya Holm, whose consummate artistry has made the contemporary dance a living and real and moving experience to so many of us, last night brought in one of the most compelling and finished performances of her noble career here."[13] Hylbom's adulation hints that Holm's social persona had captivated Colorado Springs. Two clusters of elite society, one the "Broadmoor crowd" living in a posh area south of town and the other "the North End set" living in stately mansions north of the campus, vied for Holm's attention and her presence at parties.

The New York dance press also took note of the Colorado premiere of *Orestes and the Furies.* The *Dance Observer* cover for

October showed a dramatically lit Paul Sweeney as Orestes and Molly Howe as Clytemnestra in strained grip atop a high platform while shadowy furies lay curled beneath them at stage level. *New York Times* critic John Martin made the inevitable connection between Holm's new work and her 1937 masterpiece, *Trend*: "The work is perhaps the most ambitious work Miss Holm has created since *Trend* and because of the size of its cast she will not be able to take it on tour with her when she sets out in December."[14] Martin hoped, however, that Holm would present it in New York.

With the expectations of New Yorkers and the adulation of the Colorado community in her ears, the ruinous critique by Edwin Denby in the *New York Herald Tribune* must have been excruciating. Denby found Holm's student furies ludicrous and reported that they inspired laughter at inappropriate places: "It looked to me like a graduation event put on by the girls' physical education department; posture work, intermediate and advanced, neatly and seriously performed." He concluded with a sneer, "But for college girls who do not aim to become professional dancers it affords a modicum of body control. And for those educators, who have to find some way of teaching 'the dance' without offending civic prudery, Miss Holm's method recommends itself too by its Nordic innocence and smooth look."[15]

Denby's piece stakes out territory on the frontier between amateur practice—"college girls"—and professional attainment. It was modern dance that was taught in colleges and universities, whereas ballet training took place in private studios and academies. Anthony's recollections underscore this issue. A scholarship student since 1940 at Holm's New York studio, Anthony accompanied Holm to Colorado in 1943; as well as dancing in three works, she was in charge of rehearsing the student furies. She was given room and board and transportation to Colorado, but she was paid nothing for her services. She found that a good bargain, saying, "Not any of us thought about money; that was not why we were doing it." Student Frances Wessells had a small but important solo role in the Colorado production of *Orestes and the Furies* and traveled to New York at her own expense to appear in the performance there ("We bombed," she recalled). She remembered long rehearsals and sleeping on a sofa in Holm's apartment: "I made five dollars with Social Security taken out. That's what we all got."[16] For many modern dancers of this period, company membership was still a volunteer activity.

Anthony remembered the creation of *Orestes and the Furies* as the all-consuming project of the summer. She claims to have rehearsed the furies every afternoon, and she attributes the failure of the New York performance and Denby's scathing review to the fact that Holm did not have the luxury of time to prepare her New York students. Colman agreed with Anthony about the reason for the New York failure of *Orestes*: "She had a terrible group of girls—awful bodies—but, you know, I think Hanya liked that ugliness." Although Colman dismissed Denby's views—"He wouldn't have liked it, he wouldn't have understood"—he confirmed that Holm was devastated: "She would never bring anything into New York from Colorado again. She was scared." The failure of *Orestes and the Furies* in New York may have been a factor in Holm's decision to disband her company after a January performance at Hampton Institute in Virginia. For the record, she cited the difficulty of financing a company in the wartime economy.

Denby's reaction to *Orestes and the Furies* and Colman's dismissal in 1994 of the critic's views demonstrate the lingering belief in the modern dance community that some critics are unable to appreciate modern dance. Two influential dance writers, Denby and Lincoln Kirstein, applauded George Balanchine's modernist extensions of ballet, but they did not support dance that did not spring from training in *danse d'école.*

Less advance publicity than usual heralded the 1944 summer session at Colorado College, explainable perhaps by the absence of Davies and perhaps by war weariness. Colorado College and the Fine Arts Center again collaborated on a conference, their seventh. One featured presenter was George Beiswanger, associate editor of *Theater Arts Monthly* and critic for *Dance and Music.* Beiswanger was also a contributing reviewer for *Dance Observer,* and he had been a lecturer at Bennington in 1935 and 1938. He described Holm's 1944 premiere in a review published in the *Colorado College Tiger* and in *Dance Observer.*

> *What Dreams May Come* is Hanya Holm's most intriguing dance
> composition in recent seasons. The idea of the piece is an
> excellent one. A sleeper restlessly stirs and begins to dream.
> Facets of her nature—the bright, the dark and the shadowy—
> dance behind and then around her, struggling for the upper

hand. Four half-human shapes in black torment her. The dream then goes deeper. It pushes through barriers into a dancer's nightmare, comic yet disturbing. People pass the dancer by in studied indifference. They form a stream against which the dreamer endeavors to swim. They gather in audience to applaud a couple of trick performers and the aplomb of a strapping ballerina, upon whose outstretched leg the dreamer hangs a huge rose and ribbon. But when she begins to dance herself, the audience leaves in disgust. The passers-by return in slow motion, more impassive than ever, then fade away as the dreamer discovers the wall again closed against her and bathed in baleful green.[17]

With a staged nightmare Holm worked through the anxiety and humiliation caused by the failure of *Orestes and the Furies* in New York. Holm's energy was sapped; *What Dreams May Come* was the only work she choreographed for her 1944 program. An Evening of Theater Arts included a one-act play staged by Woodson Tyree, director of the college drama department. Martha Wilcox and her students from Denver showed two dances.

When a student did not appear in the final concert, it was not always because Holm and her assistants did not consider her competent; sometimes she was not available for the many weekend and evening rehearsals. Hortense [Bienstock] Loeb was the youngest student in 1944, and as a condition of being able to attend the session, her parents insisted she check in every weekend with a sister living nearby in Pueblo, Colorado. Loeb knew of Holm and the Colorado program because she had studied for a year at Adelphi University on Long Island where Holm taught. Despite her youth—she was seventeen—Loeb valued the simplicity of her classes, "the paring down, the getting down to essence, the stripping away to the simplest idea." Loeb knew, she says, that there were no combinations (previously choreographed patterns taught in class) because Holm wanted students to think for themselves and understand what they were doing: "Some people didn't feel they were dancing in the classes when we walked most of the time, but those classes made me feel like I was floating." Loeb never had a problem with Holm's criticism: "I can remember her saying over and over again, 'No, Horty, strong, strong!' when I thought I was using all my force. Now I realize she was right, I didn't have much power." Loeb remembers dancing all day long and that Holm taught more than half the classes herself: "I liked improvisation. It was easy for me, but composition was new. There was also work in elements of time and rhythm, and there was some discussion and note taking." She was so entranced with the work that sometimes she would go back to her room and cry "just from trying so hard."[18]

What Dreams May Come was performed again in the 1945 summer session, restaged on a program with two new works—one a piece of Americana created in collaboration with Roy Harris. The last summer of World War II saw the composer and choreographer return to their sponsor's initial assignment to produce work on the topic of the American spirit. But chastened, perhaps by the war and perhaps by the progress of their careers, their new piece had nothing of gutsy legends of virile gold camps. They made *Walt Whitman Suite* in three sections, each based on a war poem from *Leaves of Grass*. Harris scored "To Thee Old Cause," "The Year That Trembled," and "Drums" for singers and a string quintet. He conducted a local chorus and the Seventh Service Command String Ensemble.

Holm offered as a second premiere a light number titled *The Gardens of Eden* to music of Darius Milhaud, which the Seventh Service Command String Ensemble also played. Margery Turner had a role in that dance and in the reconstruction of *What Dreams May Come*. Turner had studied for a year with Louise Kloepper at the University of Wisconsin before coming to Colorado in the summer of 1945. She returned for the summer of 1948. Turner remembered gratefully being cast in the two works. She willingly admitted, "I was the comic interlude." About *What Dreams May Come* Turner remembered that Holm repeated structure but not choreography from the previous year. She recalled that when Holm was working on a big piece, all of the cast was expected to be at every rehearsal watching attentively until needed: "She demanded complete attention and quiet, her mind was completely involved, and she didn't worry about personalities." Turner approved of Holm's hard criticism during rehearsals and when teaching: "Some students couldn't take it. They didn't realize that the ones she was hardest on were the ones she was interested in. It was the same in composition. She was unmerciful in giving crits; she never worried about people's feelings. You had to be able to use criticism."[19] Like many artists in the throes of creation, Holm did not concern herself with interpersonal relations.

Not every student appreciated her summer training with Holm. Bernice [Mendelsohn] Bronson said her encounter with Holm in 1945 was not a major factor in her career in dance and theater. Despite "all that analysis," which Bronson remembered with exasperation, she came away confused and only later learned about the technique from Mary Anthony. Bronson is still bitter about the performing situation she found herself in: "I couldn't figure out my cues, and nobody was helping me, not Hanya, nobody."[20] Another student, Edna Jane [Nesbitt] Dexter, however, who studied in the summer of 1943 and was one of the furies in the ill-fated work of that year, represents the majority of Holm's students. She marveled at Holm's ability to use the special abilities of each dancer: "When she was choreographing, she'd ask you to do something, and then she would adapt it so it was just right for you. I think that was the teacher in her; she was an excellent teacher."[21] Holm's teaching and choreographic methods differed from those of most others of her time. She did not use a codified movement vocabulary in her teaching or while creating a dance. She addressed the needs of her students as she perceived them in class, and she was adept at molding the abilities of dancers to suit her choreographic purposes.

Holm's first five years in Colorado confirmed her American identity for East Coast dance pundits and gave her the security and structure she needed to plant deep roots for a method of dance training that was unique in America. In 1945 journalist Elizabeth Hylbom allowed her admiration of Holm to bring her to terms with expectations of dance as an absolute art form. *Dance Observer* printed a dispatch from Hylbom describing Holm's concert at the Colorado Springs Fine Arts Center on August 18. It concluded, "It was interesting to observe in Saturday night's performance the development of Hanya Holm away from the abstract and toward the pictorial and legitimately theatrical, a tendency which, wisely handled, should bring the contemporary dance closer to a wider public."[22] Hylbom validated Holm's collaborative process and her first steps toward use of plot and characterization. Holm, in acknowledging her penchant for collaboration with the other arts, developed the craftsmanship she would need to succeed in the Broadway musical, an American invention in which dance fits musical structure exactly and flows in and out of dialogue and plot.

Chapter Four
CONNECTING TO THE AMERICAN DREAM
1946-1949

Holm's celebrity burst upon her Colorado friends and supporters in the postwar years. She leaped from recognition in the largely amateur world of modern concert dance to renown in the professional world of musical comedy, where she put all she had learned of American temperament into the service of an indigenous art form. By the summer of 1949 the local press could boast, "Miss Holm can now have her pick of the future stage plays on Broadway."[1] Newspapers carried reports of her successful shows on Broadway, national weeklies ran photo features of dances she staged, and she was included in national symposia on the arts and asked to judge beauty contests.

In training a Colorado audience to perceive a new art form, Elizabeth Hylbom had referred to absolute dance, an ideal that had been pursued in Germany before Holm's departure in 1931. Holm's successes in Colorado and the influx of a strong professional population after the war, however, gave her confidence to continue along another path. She experimented with characterization, text, and dramatic themes and collaborated with musicians, writers, and designers who helped to shape her choreography. Her projects in Colorado directly contributed to her success in New York with *Ballet Ballads* in May 1948 and *The Insect Comedy* that June. The competence she showed with those ventures and the contacts she made with the musical comedy world landed her the job of choreographing *Kiss Me, Kate,* a hit being restaged in the twenty-first century.

During the war, Holm's community had been a community of women. Women assisted her, and almost all her students were women. A few men ineligible for the draft had danced, but usually in supporting roles partnering women. Jerome Andrews partnered Holm in *Walt Whitman Suite* in 1945. Paul Sweeney had the lead in *Orestes and the Furies,* but Mary Anthony danced the role of Apollo, and women dominated that work as they dominated all of Holm's productions. In 1946 Holm turned from choreography for a community of women toward choreography that gave women a different stature as partners of men and sometimes, as in 1948, as background to them. She surrounded herself with a new team of teaching and production assistants, all male and largely from the East.

A press release picked up by the Colorado newspapers in the summer of 1946 ran, "This summer Miss Holm welcomes back to the dance and to civilian life five male dancers, all former professional dancers and all recently discharged after several years in the armed services." Gesturing toward the East Coast connections Holm's presence offered Colorado Springs, the newspapers assured readers that the men would continue their training with Holm in her New York studio.[2] The veterans were Alwin Nikolais, Alfred Brooks, Glen Tetley, Harry Bernstein, and Oliver Kostock.

Nikolais came to Colorado as Holm's assistant. Brooks was a guest artist. Bernstein, Kostock, and Tetley registered as students, as did two other men, Fred Berk and Norman Chelquist. Fifty-one women also registered, making the total enrollment more than double that of any previous summer. Never before had Cossitt Gymnasium been so filled with dancers.

Holm relied on Nikolais to assist her in Colorado through 1949, and he taught at her New York studio into the 1950s. Known as "Nik" by his students as well as his most prestigious acquaintances, he possessed a relaxed confidence that accounted for considerable charisma. Kostock, of sturdy build with soft brown eyes and a compliant nature, remained with Holm in Colorado for thirty-seven years.

Nineteen forty-six was the last year Holm worked with Martha Wilcox, and she did not use Wilcox in her final concert. Students from the early 1940s report tension between the two women, and in the fall of 1946 Wilcox left Colorado Springs to concentrate on her work at the University of Denver. She remained loyal to Holm and was a frequent visitor, often taking classes with Holm's regular students.

Roy Harris and Holm worked together for the last time in 1946. *Walt Whitman Suite* was repeated on the final concert in August with the composer once again conducting. In some subsequent years a major music collaborator would be found for Holm, as in 1949 when Nicolas Slonimsky conducted an ensemble to accompany Holm's choreography and play a work of his own. In other years Holm relied on her music director–accompanist to perform and compose. Later, recorded music was sometimes used, but Colorado College was serious about music, and live performance was usually a feature of Holm's productions.

Woodson Tyree, head of drama at the college, became Holm's reliable production supervisor, and beginning in 1951 drama and dance shared some concerts, as they had in 1944. Holm's son was a member of the production team in 1946, listed under his birth name, Klaus Kuntze. He assisted the designer of masks, which Holm needed for her premiere, *Windows.* Holm (he used his mother's professional name after 1946) would go on to become a successful set and lighting designer, working on Broadway and in theaters in the United States and abroad.

The number of summer programs in modern dance training around the country grew after the war, and the American Dance Festival picked up the pieces of Bennington in 1948. In 1946, however, many dancers felt Holm's program was their best option for summer training. Bernstein, a dancer with the Graff Ballet before the war, thought Colorado was the only place for him: "I had been in the army for five years, and I needed to get into shape. That summer gave me training and a chance to perform again."[3]

A college brochure announced that there would be training for the novice, as well as for advanced students and teachers of dance, and it promised that the work of every student would point toward participation in a dance production as the climax of the summer session. That promise could not be met—just half, twenty-eight of fifty-nine, performed—and the sentence was dropped from the 1947 brochure. Although the college continued to offer training for the novice as well as for advanced students, the 1948 brochure cautioned, "Participation in the summer productions is determined by the ability of the students."

Returning veterans gave Holm new choreographic opportunities, and the natural talent of Glen Tetley suggested a wider range of movement. Al Brooks remembered clearly the shift in Holm's interests in the summer of 1946: "I had been trained as a dancer entirely by Hanya, and I was the first man in her company, so it was pretty hard that summer to hear her say, 'Do it like Glen; can't you dance like Glen and Harry?' "[4]

Brooks and Nikolais, together with Maxine Munt and Joan Kruger, had worked with Holm in New York to prepare *Dance for Four,* which they performed at the Conference on the Fine Arts in July and also on Holm's final concert. *Walt Whitman Suite* was reworked to include four men—Brooks, Nikolais, Kostock, and Tetley. Nikolais choreographed *Fable of the Donkey.* It followed a narration written by Colorado novelist Lillian de la Torre about the disasters that follow a simple man who accepts advice from everyone he meets. Tetley submitted to wearing long pointed ears as the donkey for Nikolais's whimsical treatment of Aesop's fable.

Holm had treated the evils of conformity in her great abstract work *Trend,* and now, with *Windows,* she looked at the price of conformity by using specific characters. A prologue introduced office workers typing at invisible machines; the dancers wore masks of their own features. In the five succeeding sections, dancers without masks revealed repressed longings and tensions created by their routine jobs, to which they returned in the epilogue.

Dance reviewing in Colorado Springs' *Gazette-Telegraph* was taken up by Dane Rudhyar, a composer and writer well acquainted with dance. He saved remarks about *Windows* for the end of his piece, admitting "it is difficult to define exactly the nature of this dance composition, which verges on the ballet and on the pantomime; but it gave Hanya Holm the opportunity of two superb characterizations." The review, though lacking the flights of adulation produced by Elizabeth Hylbom, reminded readers that Holm had highlighted the summer season for several years and that she brought to Colorado a significant expression of trends in modern dance.[5]

The period between 1944 and 1946 may register the peak of Holm's success as a performer. For her own company from 1936 to 1944, she succeeded best with choreography of ensemble pieces. She seldom performed independent solos, and solo roles in her group dances did not garner the kind of praise awarded other American modern dancers like Martha Graham, Helen Tamiris, and Doris Humphrey. Nationally respected writers who saw her dance in *What Dreams May Come* (George Beiswanger) and *Windows* (Dane Rudhyar), however, wrote with excitement about her performances of dramatic roles. Doris Baker, another experienced reviewer, described Holm's tight, frenzied solo in *Windows* as a "magnificently performed study in frustration."[6]

Holm unleashed her gift for comedy in two group sections of *Windows.* In one, "The Spirit Moves," she created an eerie atmosphere without the use of music; performers rapped out rhythms on a table as they sat as if for a seance. Holm would later use a similar technique for a show-stopping number in the Broadway musical *My Darlin' Aida.* Baker pointed to the success of the dramatic values in *Windows* as proof of Holm's expertness as a choreographer of dance drama. She also found much to like in the reworked *Walt Whitman Suite,* calling it a dance of heroic stature.

Although the Colorado press perpetuated the idea that Holm had a professional company and that works choreographed in Colorado were later performed in New York, no choreography by Holm had been seen in New York since the ill-fated showing of *Orestes and the Furies* in early 1944. After the 1946 summer in Colorado, however, she gathered eight dancers into what she called the Hanya Holm Workshop Group to prepare *Ozark Suite,* to music of Elie Siegmeister. Mary Anthony, Joan Kruger, Annabelle Lyon, Maxine Munt, Ray Harrison, Kostock, Nikolais, and Tetley gave the first performance on May 24, 1947.

By 1947 Holm's New York City studio was attracting the attention of dancers in the professional world of ballet and musical comedy. In the 1993 winter issue of *Ballet Review,* a year after Holm's death, the dancer and choreographer Sybil Shearer wrote of her admiration for Holm and of the help she had given her favorite Bennington teacher by suggesting her classes to a friend, Annabelle Lyon, a dancer in Ballet Theatre who was frequently on Broadway. Lyon, wrote Shearer, "came under the spell of this wonderful free movement and Hanya's enthusiasm for it." Lyon passed the word to other dancers, and Shearer claims that in two years 250 dancers from Broadway were pouring through the doors of the Hanya Holm studio.[7] Although the number may be an exaggeration, it is believable that the excitement of dancers led to Holm's first Broadway opportunities; Ray Harrison, who danced in *Ozark Suite,* was the companion of Arnold Saint-Subber, a prominent Broadway producer.

Holm's first Broadway triumph was a dance opera in *Ballet Ballads,* conceived and created by composer Jerome Moross and writer John LaTouche. A single director kept its three sections stylistically allied, and three choreographers had the assignment of coping with a large chorus, actors, and dancers. Katherine Litz was in charge of "Suzanna and the Elders," Paul Godkin did "Willie the Weeper," and Holm closed the show with "The Eccentricities of Davey Crockett."

Nine New York critics reviewed *Ballet Ballads* the day after its opening. Each critic had a favorite section, and many chose "Crockett." All raved about the show in its entirety. It moved from off-Broadway to a Broadway house, making possible more reviews and a rash of feature articles in the daily press and in many weeklies, including *Saturday Review* and *Life* magazine. Because of her work in Colorado, Holm was no stranger to Americana; she had also been able to indulge her love of play and humor and had been drawn into experiments with dance drama. Because of the appeal of her teaching, she knew Broadway dancers and how to work with them.

Yet another ingredient of her success, good casting, was something she practiced in Colorado. Holm's notebook from 1946 lists all her students as they appeared in an early class or audition. Representative notes she wrote in German translate to comments like *unable; nothing from inside; not bad, keeps up well; no technique, only emotion; no inner strength; strong, good with expression; not bad, has concentration; emotional, no shape and no form; no feeling for shapes, pale; typical college dancer, no blood; blah blah dilettante; good but does not have instrument; not a lot of character; sentimental, commonplace; lush, substantial temperament; has character but commonplace ideas; bad; not a lot of character, knock-kneed; humor; strong emotion* [translation by Marianne Forster]. Despite her obvious dismay with the quality of her students, Holm chose thirteen dancers for *Windows* and an additional five for her restaging of *Walt Whitman Suite.*

In 1949 she confided to a Colorado reporter that it is just as difficult to pick a dancer for a certain number as it is to pick an actor: "It is not his dancing alone that qualifies him. Temperament plays a big part. An excellent dancer may be of a tempera-ment completely unsuited for a certain part."[8] Holm's European origins may have given her a special objectivity with which to evaluate the young Americans before her. Her Colorado note-books reveal her ability to quickly perceive their strengths and weaknesses.

A good number of professionals were among the forty-eight students who registered in 1947. It was the first year Holm staged a demonstration of modern dance technique on her formal con-cert. Holm's dance demonstrations had exhilarated audiences who saw them performed by her original company in the 1930s, and she had introduced them to Colorado Springs audiences during the first Fine Arts Conferences in which she participated. Holm's notes tell us that the 1947 demonstration began with floor work, continued through standing exercises building to falls, then progressed through various traveling steps and culminated in jumps of many kinds. Two sections from *Ozark Suite* were per-formed in conclusion. The 1947 program was also the first in which Holm devoted a section of her concert to student compositions.

As the actor José Ferrer would soon produce Karel and Josef Capek's *The Insect Play* (which he titled *The Insect Comedy*) for the New York City Theater Company, it is hard to believe he did not have something to do with Holm's selection of the work for her 1947 premiere. Ferrer had produced himself as Cyrano in the fall of 1946. To keep in shape for the demanding role he had taken classes, along with his wife, the well-known actress Uta Hagen, at Holm's studio.

Holm explained the play, which she called *And So Ad Infini-tum,* to her Colorado audience.

> The insect world is shown to be about as contemptible as that of man, a parallel being drawn with each shift of scene by a musing tramp, who, reclining in a forest, dreams of these butterflies, beetles, ants, and moths as but duplicating human passions.... Action of the scenes is choreographed and the actor not only speaks but also dances his role. The characters are created not by insect masks and costuming but rather by characterization through movement and speech.[9]

Dorothy Adlow signed a *Dance Observer* review of Holm's production: "This was admittedly an experimental piece in which the dancer becomes actor, the actor, dancer. A fascinating interchange, it proved that with discerning direction one of the allied arts can heighten and intensify the significance of the other." After praising the agility of dancer-actors and the pace and rhythm of the direction, she concluded that she had witnessed an auspicious beginning for an experimental application of the modern dance: "In this way, it can be integrated in kindred art forms, and perhaps obliterate its overcompartmentalized status in modern art. We look forward to an enlargement of this development in American dance drama."[10] A fusion of the arts that had troubled Hylbom in 1942 was now celebrated as the salvation of modern dance from its overcompartmentalized status. Holm's Colorado supporters were invited into a special audience that watched a new development in American dance.

The fact that the entire dance world did not admire Holm for stepping over the border from concert dance to dance drama is evidenced by Sharry [Traver] Underwood's memories of the 1947 summer and her opinion about the direction of Holm's career: "She deserted the concert stage, she gave in to some things she preached against." Underwood remembers Holm arguing against the ballet, and she is bitter that Holm used ballet-trained dancers in the New York production of *The Insect Comedy,* passing over modern dancers who were versatile enough to do anything expected of them.[11] When Holm turned to Broadway, it seemed like a sellout to some modern dancers, who asked how she could continue to compare herself to those who struggled in full view of the New York critical community when her own concert choreography was hidden in a summer haven in Colorado.

In Colorado this was not a problem for Holm's audience, the college, or the majority of her students. Holm's teaching and choreography there were focused on concert dance values. It was enlightenment about serious high-art principles that students took with them to their schools and colleges and their professions. Holm's concert dance credentials were well established, and her success on Broadway was seen by most as a confirmation of her craftsmanship. (Holm is not the only concert artist who worked on Broadway; George Balanchine, Helen Tamiris, Agnes de Mille, Donald McKayle, Jerome Robbins, and Garth Fagan have done so without reproach.)

Underwood was also troubled by Holm's choreographic method. A modern dancer by training and conviction, Underwood was in the road company of the musical *Bloomer Girl* when it ended its run on the West Coast in the spring of 1947. Her fellow dancer, Gregory MacDougall, recommended a summer of study with Holm in Colorado before she went back east. Holm cast Underwood in a major role as the Chrysalis in *And So Ad Infinitum*: "It took me awhile to realize that we were doing the choreography. Glen did a lot of choreography for her, so did Nik and so did everybody. We'd go off in a corner and produce the material; it was the way she worked." Underwood admitted that after a time she became pleased that Holm accepted what she did.

After her summer in Colorado, Underwood auditioned for *Ballet Ballads*. She was chosen by two choreographers, Holm and Katherine Litz, who knew her as a dancer in the Humphrey-Weidman Dance Company. She experienced the same frustrations with Holm's choreographic strategy as she had the previous summer: "Hanya seemed to come with only an open mind. . . . I never got used to that nothingness that was a part of Hanya's first rehearsals."[12]

The choreographic method Holm used and that frustrated Underwood in *Ballet Ballads* was unusual in commercial theater. Broadway dancers were used to being shown the steps they were to perform. Holm believed, however, that performers project best that which is their own rather than that which is imposed upon them. She knew how to tease from dancers authentic reactions to situation and pulse. Then she manipulated their ideas and wove them into numbers that were not generic routines but unlike any other. It is what distinguished her as a Broadway choreographer. She remained alert to unexpected reactions, even to false moves, that could be highlighted and built into something truly original.[13]

Holm came to Colorado in the summer of 1948 fresh from huge triumphs in New York. *Ballet Ballads* had opened to unanimous raves on May 9 and had moved to Broadway on May 18. *The Insect Comedy* opened on May 29. Although reviews were mixed, Holm's work as choreographer was praised. In June she consulted on a nonmusical play in the living newspaper format at Columbia University. She was on the modern dance concert scene again. Her Workshop Group performed *Ozark Suite* several times in the 1947–1948 season, once on a benefit concert for *Dance Observer* and then in a series of concerts by the New York Dance Theater—sharing programs with the other important choreographers Merce Cunningham, Doris Humphrey, José Limón, and Jane Dudley; then with Charles Weidman, Eve Gentry, Sophie Maslow, and Limón; and finally with Limón, Maslow, Weidman, Humphrey, and Valerie Bettis.

The Colorado College summer brochures had been explaining that instruction in the dance was not organized into formal courses but was designed to introduce the technique and choreographic method of Hanya Holm. In 1948 the dance curriculum was described more fully, but the topic of study remained the Hanya Holm approach to dance. One can guess that Nikolais had a hand in describing the training more explicitly. The brochure explained that in their morning class—Technique and Theory—students studied fundamentals of movement through analysis and practice of action in space, time, and dynamics. That was followed by improvisation and problem solving. Two-and-one-half hours were given over to these two modes of learning each day. Separate sections of Dance Composition met for two hours once a week. Nikolais shared technique and theory classes with Holm, while she was in charge of both sections of composition. Nikolais taught two sections of his own system of dance notation, which he called Choroscript. Kostock taught Fundamentals of Music for Dancers and Dance History. Gregory MacDougall, then on the Colorado College faculty, taught three classes for nondancers. The college began giving college credit for summer work in dance; eight units of graduate or undergraduate credit were available for those who attended the full eight weeks.

Nineteen forty-eight gave Holm the opportunity for a new kind of collaboration important in choreographing for Broadway. She had tested her mettle with musicians and playwrights and with architectural settings. Now she worked with a visual artist, Mexican painter Ricardo Martinez, who gave her costume designs and a powerful painted backdrop based on a fantasized Aztec landscape. Not long into her commercial career Holm learned the importance of visual design and costuming for setting the style of a work and even for suggesting movement choices. Kostock gave Holm a title for the dance, *Xochipili*, a word he made up. Holm featured a quartet of men assisted by ten other dancers.

The theme of *Xochipili* was the primitive pulse of mankind, indestructible and ever recurring despite the rise and fall of civilization. There is a certain symmetry in that after a summer in which Holm dealt with human rapacity and greed in a scripted vehicle, *And So Ad Infinitum,* she celebrated the pure and eternal strengths of humankind. Connection to the primitive is a theme German dance treated often during Holm's formative period in Germany. Rejecting what they saw as false gentility in the dancers who followed the American innovator Isadora Duncan, the Central Europeans looked deep into elemental forces of life. Wigman's solos often sought an ecstatic connection to the primeval, as in the much praised "Dance of the Earth" and her celebrated whirling dances.

Martinez's backdrop for *Xochipili* was one of huge geometric rocks and fleshy plant forms, which gave both weight and a feeling of upward struggle to the stage. Strong, bright spirals patterned the chests of four lead men—Leo Duggan, Marc Breaux, Kostock, and Tetley. Loincloths were individualized with bright patterns, leg coverings ended in brightly wrapped ankles, and the men's necks and heads were covered in fitted hoods spouting large topknots. Five accompanying women were draped in long heavy skirts and shawls that produced a sculptural unit to contrast the agile, crouching, leaping men. Holm and four students danced a second movement, "The Temple Builders," before the "Men of Earth" returned. *Dance Observer* reviewed *Xochipili* and ran a photograph by Fritz Kaeser on the cover. Dorothy Adlow praised the coming together of dance, visual design, and music, which she found supplemented each other to communicate the depth of primitive experience. She also remarked, "*Xochipili,* conceived, put together, executed in the few brief weeks of a summer session, was a remarkably cohesive undertaking."[14] Working speedily, essential in pressurized commercial situations, is another skill Holm acquired in Colorado.

Colorado Springs reveled in the fame of its beloved Hanya Holm, who had succeeded with two professional theater undertakings in New York before she arrived for the 1948 summer. A prominent session of the 1948 Conference on the Fine Arts was devoted to the question "Is Lyric Theater Here to Stay?"

Advance publicity for the conference may have prejudiced the outcome of the panel's deliberations and ended the debate

in Colorado between absolute dance and dance that works with
other art media. "Dancers, musicians, and actors are realizing
that a true fusion of their respective abilities can produce an
impact that no one of the three art forms can produce by itself,"
the press assured its readers. The writer introduced the two main
speakers, Daniel Rich, director of the Chicago Arts Institute, and
Virgil Thomson, music critic and composer: "Both are top figures in their fields and they didn't get there by sitting around
agreeing with people. Each holds definite opinions about the
purpose of art and music in the world and it is a matter of habit
with them to get up on their hind legs and fight when somebody
starts an argument."[15] Observers close to the scene recognize the
voice of the irrepressible Carol Truax, Colorado College Fine Arts
director, in the dispatch to the press. Apparently she had arrived
at a resolution of the second debate, pending since the 1941
Conference on the Fine Arts, over whether art has a social role.
The writer accepted a purpose for art and music in the world,
leaving exactly what purpose open to discussion and perhaps to
fisticuffs.

The state of Colorado called on Holm to judge its Miss Colorado competition on July 23. In August, just a week before her
own concerts, she judged costumes and dancers in Colorado
Springs' annual Pikes Peak or Bust Celebration. The following
winter the National Arts Club invited her to lecture in New York,
joining a roster that included notable artists George Balanchine,
Eugene Berman, Vincenzo Celli, Doris Humphrey, Virgil Thomson,
and Antony Tudor.

Between the 1948 and 1949 summer sessions, *Kiss Me, Kate*
opened on Broadway. The show salvaged the flagging reputation
of composer-lyricist Cole Porter and gave Holm national recognition. An explosion of rave reviews after the December 30 opening often mentioned the choreography. Two major New York
dance critics credited Holm's success to her skill at subsuming
the dance to the service of other art forms and the total project.
Walter Terry wrote, "There is no ballet as such in *Kiss Me, Kate,*
but there is dancing, all of it firmly integrated into the show to
contribute to the achieving of a total theatrical impression. The
dancing gives flow to the musical, it provides the means for transitions in pace or in mood or in style, it accounts for the
production's necessary flashes of physical virtuosity."[16] John Martin

remarked on the excellence of Holm's research and her faithfulness to the style of the production, and he wrote that she had "not been tempted to superimpose herself upon the production, but has given her attention wholly to bringing out and pointing up what is inherent in it."[17] One can read a not-very-subtle comparison to Agnes de Mille, who some felt did superimpose herself on Broadway shows she choreographed.

A study of Holm's choreography in Colorado reveals the process that garnered the worship of Terry and Martin. In supporting the aspirations of President Thurston Davies and working with the songs of Roy Harris, as in all her collaborations, Holm had proved herself a good team player. She was able to see the dynamics of complex artistic and personal interdependencies and to fit her craft of moving human bodies to the total project.

Capezio Dancewear Company celebrated Holm by giving over one of its advertisements in *Dance Magazine* to a citation that read: "Her versatile craftsmanship in dance-story delineation will broaden the scope of dance expression, capturing new dance devotees and extending the field of dance appreciation."[18] Holm's aligning of dance with the other arts had not made a handmaiden of dance but exalted it. Perhaps her perspective as an immigrant led Holm to see U.S. arts holistically. She did not compartmentalize dance but saw all its forms as expressions of the American spirit.

Dance critics did consider Holm a concert artist; Martin noted that her dances for *Kiss Me, Kate* retained the taste and formal integrity of the concert dance.[19] Her ability to deliver in many styles—classic ballet, modern dance, jitterbug, soft-shoe, acrobatics, court dance, folk dance—as well as the wide swings in character of her concert choreography in Colorado, are in contrast to other dance artists who refined one style in a lifetime.

In 1949 some dancers came to Colorado to study with Holm because of her fame. Murray Louis Fuchs (he used his middle name as his professional name after the summer) is representative of that group. The mercurial young man who became a performer of irresistible charm declared, "I went to Colorado *because* she was famous; I wanted to be on Broadway!"[20] Other students came from the network of modern dance teachers and schools influenced by Holm. One dancer, Gladys Bailin, came to Colorado with Nikolais and at least two others, Murray Louis and Nancy

Robb, then went to New York to study with him and dance in his company. Joan [Jones] Woodbury went to Colorado because of her admiration for the teaching of Louise Kloepper at the University of Wisconsin.

The Holm-Wigman-Kloepper connection is clearly demonstrated by Woodbury's career. Woodbury studied several modern dance methods and preferred Holm's, so she was happy in 1951 to accept a teaching appointment at the University of Utah, where Elizabeth Hayes chaired the dance department and Woodbury knew she would be in an aesthetically compatible environment. Hayes had studied with Wigman in Germany and with Holm and Kloepper in New York and Colorado. (Woodbury later studied with Wigman for a year, one of many Americans who made the pilgrimage to Germany in the 1950s.) By 1949 Holm's Colorado program was more important than her New York school in sustaining the web that connected Wigman's training to university dance programs. The web continued to expand as educators like Hayes and Woodbury advised students to spend summers with Holm in Colorado, and many of them later sent their own students.

Enrollment in dance at Colorado College was again strong in 1949. Forty-seven students came for study, and among them were many who went on to prominent careers in dance. Almost all students performed on the final Concert of Modern Dance, August 18 and 19. Four major works were prepared under Holm's direction with the assistance of Nikolais and composer-conductor Nicolas Slonimsky. Dorothy Adlow, Slonimsky's wife, was art critic for the *Christian Science Monitor*. While in Colorado she wrote for the *Colorado Springs Gazette-Telegraph* and sent dispatches to *Dance Observer*.

The first segment of the 1949 program was devoted to Nikolais's *Extrados*, which he had premiered at the Henry Street Playhouse in New York City in May. He used a score by his friend Alfred Brooks, who here used the name Alfred Pew. Nikolais's title meant the outer curve of an arch, and it referred to space beyond the finite bounds of the universe. Adlow wrote that "a narrative unfolds related to the spiritual urge towards the otherworldly, and to the personal urge towards earthiness and fleshly experience. . . . Moods of anticipation, ceremony, and release were evoked in a beautiful and spare pattern of movement by a corps of dancers who seemed imbued with the intensely emotional content."[21] Later in his career Nikolais would abandon emotional content and develop a unique form of abstract dance-theater. An urge toward the otherworldly remained fundamental to his work, however, and reveals his connection to German dance tradition.

The 1949 program continued with Slonimsky conducting his *Little Suite,* written in an intertonal idiom for woodwinds, percussion, and portable typewriter. Then Holm restaged two dances important in her career. First was Igor Stravinsky's *History of a Soldier,* which Holm had choreographed at the Schauspielhaus, Dresden, in 1929, dancing the role of the Princess. For the last work on her program Holm choreographed to Edgard Varèse's *Ionization.* Holm had used *Ionization* in 1937 as the finale, at Bennington, of her great work *Trend.* Students who danced *Ionization* in Colorado in 1949 did not know of its importance. "We were young kids," said Louis. "We didn't know about *Trend;* we were stunned by the music."

Varèse's music caused several problems. Louis remembered that Slonimsky had difficulty finding instruments for the sounds he needed, and he resorted to substituting kitchen pans. A near disaster occurred on performance night when Slonimsky conducted *Ionization* twice as fast as the dancers had rehearsed it. Louis remembered Holm in the wings on one side of the stage and Nikolais on the other side yelling counts in an effort to keep the dancers together. Woodbury confirmed, "It was crazy."[22] The dancers persevered, and the audience responded with such excitement that the whole work was repeated—this time at the correct tempo. Adlow raved, "Superbly trained dancers executed Hanya Holm's inspired concept of Varèse's music." She observed that the audience seemed "tensely vibrant with the visual and auditory experience." She took this as evidence that "modern dance achieves its fullest stature as the counterpart of music of a high and significant order."[23] Holm had brought a regional American audience to an understanding of a new form of dance that could stand with the best modern music in the Western canon.

A COMPANY OF IRREGULARS
Chapter Five
1950-1956

Excitement mounted in Colorado Springs as news spread of Holm's successes on Broadway. In this period she choreographed five new musicals, beginning with her second Cole Porter show, *Out of This World,* in 1950 and ending with *My Fair Lady* in 1956, the success with which her name is most closely associated. The others were *My Darlin' Aida* (1952), *The Golden Apple* (1954), and *Reuben, Reuben* (1955). She also restaged dances for the London production of *Kiss Me, Kate,* and just before coming to Colorado in 1950 she directed musical numbers for *The Liar,* which had no dance. In the winter and spring of 1955 she was in Hollywood choreographing the musical film *The Vagabond King.* In the spring of 1956, just after *My Fair Lady* opened, she labored in New York on direction for the premiere performance of the Douglas Moore opera *The Ballad of Baby Doe.* It opened July 7 in Central City, a Colorado boom-to-bust mining town that had transformed itself into a cultural Mecca with a busy tourist trade.

Holm proved more than competent in meeting the demands of American musical comedy. She upheld a reputation for clever, imaginative detail and continued to employ an array of dance styles and genres. As noted by critics in 1948, she designed movement that gave flow to the musical, provided transitions in pace and mood, and offered flashes of physical virtuosity. She devised ways for dance to burst from plot and song in seemingly spontaneous fashion.

Her friends noted that Holm needed Colorado to unwind and recover her bearings after the stress of Broadway deadlines and expectations. If Colorado was no longer necessary for the advancement of Holm's career, her summer work was essential for other reasons. It let her inhabit the concert world of dance for which her training had prepared her. Just as important, Colorado maintained her identity, for herself and for the world, as a teacher. It was as a teacher that she had come to this country.

As every teacher knows, it is most agreeable to have students one can count on to respond. By accepting, analyzing, critiquing, even denouncing those responses, one teaches others, and they learn how they, too, can respond. In Holm's case it was especially necessary that she have leaders among her students, for the college and community expected a production at the end of each summer session, and those productions had to materialize swiftly.

Without a permanent dance company, Holm formed a company of irregulars on whom she could count as exemplary learners, performers, and, increasingly, choreographers. She had as many as six or eight seasoned performers with her each summer. Professional dancers who came to Colorado sometimes had guest artist status, but often they registered as students and had no special billing except for notice in the local press. For example, the period was bracketed by appearances by Ray Harrison, who received no special billing in 1950 but carried heavy performing responsibilities and danced with Holm. In 1956, as a guest artist, Harrison performed several of his own solos and three duets with his partner, Katherine Litz.

The period saw the beginning of several relationships that endured for decades. Molly Lynn, who as Molly Howe had danced in Holm's company near its end, appeared in 1951. Lynn had met Holm at Bennington and later did the certificate course at her New York studio. In Colorado in the summer of 1943 she had danced Clytemnestra in *Orestes and the Furies.* Lynn would be in Colorado in the summers of 1951–1954, 1958–1960, 1963, 1966, and 1968–1971.

Calm and self-effacing, Lynn refers to herself as an unofficial assistant to Holm. She was not called upon to teach, but she aided Holm with concert preparations and was a reliable performer and choreographer. In many of the thirteen summers she spent with Holm she was not paid. She admitted that Holm took her for granted but said, "I was there to dance, and I'd do what had to be done."[1]

After the summer of 1952, Lynn stayed on at Colorado College as instructor in dance, replacing Gregory MacDougall. The *Gazette-Telegraph* carried a picture of the beaming Holm and Lynn posed against the Greek columns outside Cossitt Gym and reported with apparent relief that the arrangement would "continue the influence on the Colorado College campus of one of the great all-time dance teachers."[2]

Don Redlich—wiry, quick moving, and with a sly humor—began an enduring relationship with Holm in 1952. He had been a young student in 1949, and he went on to study with her in New York and in Colorado in 1953 and 1956–1961. He returned as an established choreographer in 1965 for a concert to honor Holm. Near the end of Holm's tenure in Colorado, Redlich and his dance company were in residence for several summers when they performed his dances and worked with Holm to create the last concert works of her long career.

Alwin Nikolais was listed as staff in the summer session brochure of 1950, but he did not come to Colorado, and Oliver Kostock became Holm's principal assistant until her program ended in 1983. A routine developed for Kostock to teach the morning technique class twice a week and for Holm to teach three times a week. In later years he regularly offered an elective course in Dance Pedagogy. With Nikolais's departure, his system of dance notation was dropped from the curriculum, and when notation reappeared ten years later the more widely used Labanotation system was offered. Music for Dance was taught by Holm's music director–accompanist: Lucille Delaney of Denver University was there from 1950 to 1953, Carlton Gamer of Colorado College filled in during 1954 and 1955, and in 1956 Holm's friend and helpmate, the intense John Colman, returned.

Steady, lovable Kostock, whom everyone called "Ollie," cherished fond memories of his summers in Colorado: "In the early years she'd go out of her way to make it special for you. There'd be flowers in your room when you arrived, and she'd make a lot of you." He remembered long evenings with Holm watching the sun go down over the mountains: "It's something you'd never do alone, but it was so pleasant just to sit and chat away with her." Kostock reported that Holm could be generous and understanding: "If I was worried because the students weren't getting something I had been giving in class she'd say, 'They aren't ready; when they are ready they will understand.'" Reminiscing about his thirty-seven summers in Colorado, Kostock returned several times to a thrilling experience in 1946 when, just out of the army, he came to study with Holm for the first time and found himself her partner in "To Thee Old Cause," a section of *Walt Whitman Suite*.[3]

Over many years Kostock also partnered Holm at glittering parties given by prominent Colorado Springs residents. He remembered a grand party on the roof of the Broadmoor Hotel. He accompanied Holm to opening nights at the Central City Opera Festival, and he recalled bonfires at the Garden of the Gods, breakfasts on Mount Manitou, dinners with luminaries, and drinks at the Broadmoor bar with Marlene Dietrich. If he was in Holm's shadow at these affairs as he was in the teaching program, Kostock did not mind. He recognized, he said, that she had a tremendous urge to be in the forefront. He put it down to her insecurity about being famous. Kostock regretted only one pattern of withdrawal. In the first years he noticed that he was not asked to participate in the annual photo sessions on the lawn, so in subsequent years, when he could have been in photo sessions, he found reasons to excuse himself. "I regret that now," he said shortly before his death in 1995.

Kostock confided that there were some annoyances in working closely with Holm: "She'd always keep track of you, wanted to know where you were and what you were doing all the time. She even kept track of Nik that way, and at the end, when Nancy [Hauser] came out, Nancy always had to be at her beck and call. It annoyed all of us, but we put up with it." From his position of long intimacy with Holm, Kostock admitted that "there were things that you could dislike in her, but there was so much charm, so much to really like. Put that together and you have a real person, not a paragon."

With her perspective of nearly forty years of intermittent contact, Molly Lynn has insights into Holm's character and the dynamics of her summer program. Although she saw things that troubled her, Lynn recognized that Holm was a genius. She extolled her unparalleled foundation in dance and her way with students, observing, "Hanya could make students buckle down and at the same time encourage them to use their instincts."

Lynn recognized Holm's annual concerts as a major part of the learning each summer: "She gave them something to hold. She could find a way to make something out of nothing."

In summing up her own experience with Holm, Lynn recalled that there were good times and also bitter times. She observed that Holm could be exploitative and that there were strange fallings-out, even with people very close to her. Holm's career changed at a dizzying speed during most of her creative life. She sometimes forgot past allegiances as she bounded from one competitive situation to another. Lynn tries to be forgiving. She knows how courageous the young Holm had been to launch a dance career during the economic and political insecurity in Germany after World War I, and Lynn is aware of the challenges Holm overcame to succeed during her first years in the United States.[4]

Lynn remembered that Holm preferred working with male students. She watched the special relationship that developed between Holm and Redlich. Redlich had such special qualities that he had to be used as a soloist, and when Holm put him in comic roles, Lynn was amazed at how he could "let go of himself." Redlich modified slightly the assertion of many that Holm preferred working with men: "What I'd say is she wasn't as hard on the men as she was on women." His special relationship with Holm began as soon as he encountered her: "I admired her from the moment I laid eyes on her. She had so much to give, and I think Colorado was the place to see that. You worked through the technique and the theory with her, she guided your choreography, and you saw her choreograph. It just wasn't possible to get that anywhere else."[5]

The fact that Colorado was less important to the advancement of Holm's career by the 1950s is evidenced by the changing format and title of her final productions. In 1950 the word *informal* appeared on the cover of her program. For the next three years she teamed with drama teacher Woodson Tyree as she had in 1944. Whereas then the college presented the "Hanya Holm Dance-Drama Production and Demonstration," a lower key sounded between 1951 and 1953 as the college presented "An Evening of Dance and Drama Directed by Hanya Holm and Woodson Tyree." Informality reached its limit in 1955, when no printed program was produced and Holm introduced dances on her workshop program from in front of the curtain in Perkins

Hall Auditorium. In 1956 Holm was back in the Fine Arts Center, with Harrison and Katherine Litz as guest artists.

Despite Holm's demanding workload in professional theater and its attendant tensions and fears, she did produce two or three dances for each of her Colorado concerts during the years 1950–1956. Some were short numbers—one section of a dance suite to which guests and advanced students also contributed—yet she did create some substantial works. As she was doing on Broadway, she tackled a range of forms: romantic duets in 1952 and 1955; intense character studies in 1953; explorations of romantic angst in 1952 and 1954; restless, anxious work in 1955; a story piece in 1951; open, welcoming gambols in 1951 and 1953; and hilarity in 1955. She created dances for men in 1954 and 1955 and occasionally returned to that format in later years.

Holm now choreographed to already composed music. Some reviewers explained her artistry with references to music. By choreographing in response to music, Holm completed her journey away from the principles she had brought from Germany in 1931. Audiences for Mary Wigman's three U.S. tours, 1930–1933, had been fascinated by the fact that music was created simultaneously with movement. The press often interviewed her on the topic, and in an essay Wigman wrote for the journal *Modern Music* she declared, "I have come to realize in a very final way, that for me the creation of a dance to music already written cannot be complete and satisfactory."[6] Holm brought this aesthetic to the New World. Once Americanized and in a secure artistic environment in Colorado, however, Holm turned to a childhood love of great music. She often heard unexpected possibilities in it, as in 1975 when she made a menagerie of sea creatures to music of Henry Brant. Her vast knowledge of musical repertoire made it possible for her to recommend interesting music to her assistants and guests. Occasionally she assigned short, simple music to her students for their composition assignments.

With reliable professionals with her each summer during this period, Holm designed each final concert with a different focus. The major works on the informal recital in 1950 were two dance suites to preclassic music, *Concert Royal* to music of François Couperin and *Five Old French Dances* to music of Marin Marais. Other dances were choreographed by Kostock and Robin Gregory, who had been a featured dancer in Holm's company. The company of irregulars had responsibility for choreographing the seven sections of *Concert Royal*, choreography Holm then molded. Holm's music director, Lucille Delaney, and Colorado College faculty musicians accompanied the dances.

As well as dancing in several group sections, Harrison performed four solos of his own. Kostock remembered that Harrison was extraordinarily prolific: "He'd bring in a beautiful jig, and Hanya would have some criticisms, so in a few days he'd bring in an entirely different jig that was just as beautiful but entirely different. He would throw out all the material from the first one and start over!" In *Five Old French Dances,* which closed the program, Holm appeared for the last time as a dancer; she was fifty-eight years old. Undoubtedly she and Harrison, who partnered her in the dance suite, spent time discussing dances for the Broadway-bound *Out of This World* on which Harrison would assist Holm in the fall.

Allen Young, reviewing for the *Denver Post,* praised Harrison's solos for their spontaneity and individual style. Of *Concert Royal* he wrote, "This approximation of rococo style in dance was an excellent display of the freshness which Miss Holm brings to the field of dance." Of *Five Old French Dances* Young wrote breathlessly that they were "perfection in dance."[7]

The next summer Holm gave her staff, special guests, and advanced students the opportunity to take on roles in a story ballet. She employed a scenario for Aaron Copland's atmospheric *Quiet City* and invoked universality in naming her characters. Paul Arthur, a dancer in the Metropolitan Opera Ballet, was "The Evil One." Rogermae Johnson, who had been on Broadway in *Carmen Jones* and *Inside USA,* danced "The Woman in the Street." Kostock was "The Stranger," and Lynn and Melvin Fillin were "The Lovers." Sonja Easterly and Alvin Schulman danced "The Innocent" and "The Fugitive." Fifteen students were "People in the Street." The program was filled out with works by Lynn, Kostock, Arthur, and a prelude by Holm. Colorado College musicians played *Quiet City.* Delaney and Julia Sutton accompanied other pieces.

The *Gazette-Telegraph* sent Andrea Di Sessa to review the Evening of Dance and Drama. (Woodson Tyree staged and directed Christopher Fry's *A Phoenix Too Frequent* to open the evening.) Di Sessa combined aesthetic theory with praise: "From the opening prelude to the final *Quiet City,* the Hanya Holm dancers used 'movement set to music' . . . [to express] emotional states and convictions often too elemental to be rationalized by words." A large audience demanded an encore of *Quiet City*.[8]

The 1952 company of irregulars danced in several works of their own. Lynn, partnered by Harrison, danced in Holm's setting of music by Jacques Ibert. Holm's other choreography was to songs number four and one of Gustav Mahler's *Kindertotenlieder,* which she set for sixteen women. Recorded music was used for the first time in Colorado. Di Sessa offered substantive analysis of Holm's choreography of Mahler's touching song cycle, finding it "a most amazing demonstration of visualized song."[9]

The first negative review of Holm's work in Colorado appeared in 1953. John Fetler found that the dances on her program fell into two moods, slow-moving and dreamlike, and short numbers he called satirical. It was *Ritual,* a large group work to piano music of Béla Bartók played by Delaney, that he found dreamlike and idealistic, whereas he was offended by *Temperament and Behavior,* a series of eight solos and small group dances Holm set to music of Bartók and Igor Stravinsky played by musicians from the college. Fetler used twelve inches of copy to question reactions of the audience and the nature of the pieces. The audience, he wrote, "seemed to get a big bang out of the portrayal, in dance movements, of neurotic individuals." He observed that the dances struck audiences as "exceedingly funny," although he suspected the choreographer had something more serious in mind. He found that when the subject of dance was pathetic, it "produced even more laughter than the purposefully humorous numbers."[10]

Sections of Holm's work had the titles "Adolescent," "Romantic," "Fearful," "Womanly," "Restless," "Mischievous," "Neurotic," and "Somnambulant." It is probable that Holm had inspired her dancers to intensify energy states suggested by the subjects. Freeing oneself from personal habit, becoming "with it"—that is, allowing oneself to totally inhabit subjects in their physical and psychic dimensions—was Holm's goal. It could be that for one reviewer, however, the dances remained too close to pantomime, which he read as satire. After more study of audience and dances, Fetler questioned "whether humor in pathetic situations can be used as a justified means to capture the deeper reactions of the audience. . . . [The program] set a person thinking about the purpose of a form of art to which the creators and performers devote a lifetime of work."

Fetler's indictment of Holm's purpose and artistic judgment was not the last word about the concert of 1953. Later the *Free Press* published "The Season in Review." The writer pulled out for special praise the very dances that had insulted Fetler. She found Redlich's solo "almost frenzied madness superbly executed." (Redlich performed two solos in the suite, "Fearful" and "Somnambulant.") Lynn's solo ("Neurotic") was "fascinatingly witty and deadly serious." The reviewer, like Di Sessa in 1951 and 1952, used her article to theorize on modern dance: "The meaning of the dance . . . is the subjective interpretation of a chosen piece of music, poetry, or allegory on the part of the choreographer through the dancers; the portrayal of a picture or mood; the metamorphosis of a sound into visual movement to the satisfaction of the audience."[11] The issue for this writer was not whether dance should stand as an equal partner to other ingredients of theater but the opposite: whether dance could give audiences a deeper understanding of the message of other arts.

Although Holm's reaction to this theorizing is not known, she never used rhetoric of portrayal or interpretation, nor were the majority of her choreography assignments based in musical structure. In contrast to the famed musician Louis Horst, who designed dance composition courses tightly organized around musical theme and manipulation, Holm gave open-ended assignments aimed at releasing imagination. Form was important in the studies students developed, but form emerged inevitably from subject and intent.

In her second decade in Colorado Holm's social persona, the success of her annual productions, to say nothing of the respect she garnered through her realization of the American dream in professional theater in the East, left her almost without critics in the West. Some doubts surfaced, as had Fetler's after the 1953 concert, but they were soon overwhelmed by voices of the persuaded, and Colorado audiences continued to follow Holm in artistic matters.

In the studio Holm also came in for criticism from a few students, although she was adored by most. The memories of two women in the 1953 course demonstrate extremes of chagrin and

euphoria. Ellen Moore had such a difficult encounter with Holm
that she tried to erase the whole experience from her mind:
"She gave me begrudging credit because I came from Louise
[Kloepper], but when I presented my first solo in comp class she
tore it to bits. I never tried to do a solo like that again."[12] Geulah
[Greenblatt] Abrahams came to Colorado with little previous training, and she credited the summer with the "beginning of allowing myself to take dance seriously. . . . I set a path." Abrahams did
composition work that Holm liked, and technique classes gave
her security and assurance: "They were about how to free the leg
and get the body forward in space. They didn't get dynamic or
emotional. They were more neutral than other classes, more cued
into the body, more pure. That summer was my first big experience." Social dynamics also contributed to Abrahams's bliss. She
struck up a friendship with Redlich and was included in some of
the private time he spent with Holm: "There was time to sit and
talk, time to take walks."[13] She recognized that Holm favored
male students, but she never felt left out.

Differences in the remembered experiences of Moore and
Abrahams are explained by Jerry [Bywaters] Cochran. She was a
young student in 1954 and, like Moore and Abrahams, went on
to a lifelong commitment to dance. Cochran described her
nineteen-year-old self as naive: "That's what she wanted to work
with. She chose me for a large group, and her first rehearsal
made us feel calm and confident. She wound ideas around in
her miraculous way. She made suggestions that made you more
courageous. We would start improvising, and she would make
something of it."[14] Holm preferred to work with talent that was
malleable, unencumbered by movement preferences. Although
she did require skilled dancers for her company of irregulars, they
self-selected. Those who liked to work the way Holm required
came back summer after summer. Being responsive, giving her
material, taking direction, and then working again were qualities Holm valued in students. In return she gave them opportunities to test their own artistry as performers and choreographers.

Cochran credited the Colorado environment with some of
the magic of her summer with Holm: "Colorado Springs changes
you mentally. The atmosphere made an impression on everything
we did." She appreciated the total immersion in dance under
Holm's leadership. Holm stimulated students to talk unself-

consciously about big issues and their own priorities. They shared
their ideas with each other. Some kept journals.

The Evening of Dance and Drama on August 6, 1954, began
with Woodson Tyree's "A Reading from the Life of Socrates" from
Maxwell Anderson's *Barefoot in Athens*. Tyree saw relevance to the
current politics of the cold war in the script. His program notes
began, " 'Sub-Committee' investigations on subversion are as old
as government." Tyree was courageous in referring to Senator
Joseph McCarthy's Un-American Activities Committee hearings
in Washington. Colorado Springs had some vocal right-wingers
in the 1950s who accused college professors of being "pink" and
tried to get certain books banned from high school libraries.

Molly Lynn was again Holm's unofficial assistant in 1954. Don
Redlich was absent, dancing for Holm on Broadway in *The Golden
Apple*. Other old-timers were not present for various reasons, but
most would return in other seasons. Holm relied on two new
students, both professionals. Norman Cornick was a former member of the Lester Horton Dance Company, and petite Dorothy
Jarnac was building a reputation as a Broadway and nightclub
dancer.

Holm choreographed three small pieces and a group dance
for thirty with Jarnac and Lynn as soloists. Carlton Gamer, Colorado College professor of music, played three preludes by
Herbert Elwell. She programmed four solos choreographed and
danced by Jarnac and a duet Jarnac choreographed for herself
and Cornick. The program ended with a group dance by Cornick.
Forty-two dancers appeared onstage. Two of them, Cochran and
Joanna [Gewertz] Harris, have contrasting views of the creation
of Holm's big work, *Presages*. Cochran found it part of the exhilaration of her first summer of modern dance. Harris complained,
"Dancing in Hanya's large work was frustrating, since we students
did so little." In retrospect, Harris wished she had spent the summer at Black Mountain College, "but who knew?" Louise Kloepper,
her teacher at the University of Wisconsin, had recommended
study with Holm.[15]

Cornick, reminiscing about his summer study with Holm, was
fascinated by her choreographic method: "She depended on
dancers to manufacture the actual movement. She would explain the idea behind a piece, and she would take a long time to
paint verbal pictures of what she wanted. Then she'd put on the

music and ask the dancers to improvise. She'd pick the things she liked from what they did." Cornick's recollections have a critical tinge, but he insisted her strategies for pulling movement out of the dancers were excellent and produced creative individuals. Cornick had an amusing story from 1955, the year he met his future wife, ballet-trained Dorothea Britt, who was a student: "Hanya explained what she wanted and then asked Dorothea to show her something. Dorothea said, 'Hanya, I came to learn from you.' Hanya was taken by surprise, and she demanded, 'You get out there and move!' Dorothea said, 'I can't, I came here to learn.' "[16] The two women worked things out.

On the basis of his background and what she saw of him in class, Holm recommended Cornick to the college to replace Lynn, who was leaving her post there. Cornick was hired and stayed on until 1984. Over the years some of Holm's students took ballet and jazz classes with Cornick, and he believes Holm thought he was interfering in her program. Despite the delicacy of their relationship, Cornick is grateful for the years he spent working and observing Holm. In his estimation she was a philosopher who enabled her students to think not only about the body but about mind and soul in relation to dance.

In the summer of 1955 the press was definite about the informal nature of the event: "Hanya Holm's summer dance students at Colorado College will present a dance workshop program featuring original student compositions."[17] No program was printed, but a well-written narrative by Kostock was published in *Dance Observer* giving a complete picture of the program.[18] Kostock explained that Holm acted as liaison between dancers and audience by appearing in front of the curtain with a brief introduction to each number or section of the program, "giving the outline of the problem the choreographer was intending to solve, or some brief insight into the intention of the dancer in creating the various works presented." He enthused, "Miss Holm performed this role with irresistible charm, wit, and aplomb, and gave added dimension to the excitement of the evening." Without question, Holm would have enjoyed the role she had perfected with the lecture-demonstrations she presented with her own company for over a decade.

Holm choreographed three dances, two in a dramatic vein and one humorous. A group dance for fifteen used Henry Cowell's

Desert Drone. In Kostock's words, it was "a dramatically moving piece, with an enormous dynamic range—a restless, anxious searching into space, charging and molding the atmosphere with excitement and tension." Holm's second piece must be the one she and Britt had come to words over. Kostock saw it as poignantly romantic and eloquently performed by Britt and Cornick. Holm's humorous contribution was a dance for six men to a Sousa march. The audience demanded an encore of the hilarious number. Kostock noted that the program brought to a close Holm's fifteenth consecutive year as director of the Colorado College Summer Dance Session.

My Fair Lady opened in March 1956, bringing Holm the kind of attention she had received after *Kiss Me, Kate.* She went directly from *My Fair Lady* to preparations for the world premiere of *The Ballad of Baby Doe.* That task, her first opportunity to direct an opera, caused her to arrive at Colorado College three weeks after the summer session began. Kostock and Cornick taught for her, and the program profited from the return of John Colman. He taught Music for Dance, composed for one concert piece, and played Hindemith, Ravel, and Debussy to accompany others. Holm had guest artists Ray Harrison and Katherine Litz with her, and Redlich was back in her company of irregulars.

Holm let Harrison and Litz carry a good share of the program. Litz was a former member of the Humphrey-Weidman Dance Company, a dancer for Agnes de Mille, and a teacher in New York. She had choreographed one section of *Ballet Ballads* and by 1956 was building a reputation for witty, finely crafted, eccentric solos. She and Harrison had teamed for concerts of duets and solos. One solo Litz performed, "Twilight of a Flower," showed an approving Colorado reviewer "sublime heights of the ridiculous."[19]

Some at Colorado College were disquieted by Holm's absence while she worked on the opera in Central City. That unease surfaced in a review of her final concert by John Fetler. Although he found the evening enjoyable and varied in content, he questioned the purpose of the event. He asked whether it was meant purely as an evening's entertainment, was designed to show what students had learned, or was meant as a vehicle for guest artists to show their choreography. Although Fetler recognized all the means of dance learning Holm was offering her students and audiences, he professed confusion. He thought the concert showed a "condescending attitude on the part of the famous choreographer, who, we understand, arrived for the summer session three weeks late."[20]

The Ballad of Baby Doe received unqualified praise in the national press, as well as in Colorado. Denver papers described the glittering social set that attended the opening night performance and a ball after the curtain came down. Colorado Springs newspapers joined the chorus of rave reviews, but it is understandable that the town may have felt a twinge of jealousy because another Colorado community had captured the artist with whom it had a special relationship.

As her work in commercial theater became routine, expectations Holm had planted for major premieres in Colorado Springs each summer could not be met. The years 1950 to 1956 were a transition between a time when Holm used Colorado to test her own choreography and the long period in which her teaching was paramount and became focused on stimulating choreography by her students.

Chapter Six
A PARTNERSHIP REAFFIRMED
1957–1965

Tensions in the relationship between Holm and Colorado College, exposed by reporter John Fetler in 1956, continued throughout the next few years. Each party to the liaison that had begun in 1941 found strain in their codependency. Holm needed Colorado for stability in her fast-paced existence and to keep concert dance a part of her artistic life. The college gained from Holm's summer enrollments and professional stature, yet in 1959 open warfare broke out over theater facilities. It may have been a lightning rod that focused disagreement and carried it safely away. In 1960 the college awarded Holm an honorary degree, and in 1961 she turned in a lavish production that satisfied the community's hunger for a piece of her New York glamour. In 1965 the college staged a joyous recommitment ceremony that reaffirmed the partnership.

Throughout this nine-year period Holm continued to reflect glory on the college with high-visibility choreography for Broadway musicals and other media. In 1957 she choreographed an NBC television production of *Pinocchio,* with music by Alec Wilder, and a Frank Loesser musical version of *Where's Charley?* in London. She also restaged the dances for productions of *My Fair Lady* in London, Israel, Australia, Stockholm, and at the City Center Theater in New York. In 1959 she directed the opera *Orpheus and Euridice* in Vancouver and later restaged it in Toronto. By the time she accepted her honorary degree in 1960, the Broadway show *Christine* had opened and closed, and she was under contract to choreograph *Camelot.* Another show, *Anya,* followed in 1965.

At first the slide toward informality in Holm's Colorado concerts continued. In some summers Holm did not choreograph, and the descriptor *workshop* was used for programs that became vehicles for student choreography and performance. The slide was temporarily interrupted in 1961, however, when a Hanya Holm Dance Concert starring famed ballerinas Vera Zorina and Janet Collins was positioned on the Broadmoor International Theatre schedule. The Broadmoor Hotel was a center of elite social life in Colorado Springs and an elegant watering hole for international travelers. The 1961 Broadmoor Theatre Season featured Carol Channing, Marlene Dietrich, and Roger Williams, as well as Holm's concert.

Since 1948, when Holm had achieved her first triumphs with musical comedy, the Colorado press had consistently identified their summer visitor with reference to Broadway. A 1957 headline in the *Denver Post* ran "Broadway Comes West: Dean of Dancers in State." The paper counted fifty-four teachers, professionals, and students from all parts of the West learning theory, history, and technique under Holm's direction.[1] An examination of students' states of origin shows that in a typical year dancers came from twenty-two states and two provinces of Canada. Sixteen states and provinces east of the Mississippi and eight west of the river were represented. Western states sent slightly more dancers in total.

About this time the practice of requiring students to report their previous training and performing experience was begun, and a review of one year shows that of forty-seven students, nine admitted to having had no previous performing experience and two listed the previous summer as their only stage experience. Five had performed in high school groups, twenty-nine in college, and two beyond college.

Holm was forthright about her shift of emphasis to student work. In 1957 she made a curtain speech, offering *workshop* as the key word for the evening. She explained that although some dancers were professionals, "these, in a sense, made new beginnings this summer, taking instruction in dance techniques different from their past."[2] Twelve students showed their own choreography. Redlich was prominent on the program as a choreographer and dancer. One piece he choreographed was a duet with Laurie Archer. Archer's own contributions to the concert that year, and in 1959 and 1960, were substantial. A fine arts major at Colorado College, she had learned about Holm in her first modern dance course with Molly Lynn. She tried the summer course with Holm in 1954 when she did not perform and later returned for three summers that redirected her life.

The philosophy Archer took from Holm's theory classes taught her much. "Sometimes," she admitted, "my eyes would glaze over; she'd get so obscure that I'd lose it, but I learned a lot of philosophy." Pressed to remember her gains, Archer spoke of the holistic sense of space she acquired. "Discipline was the main thing, though. Once in a while I'd rebel, but looking back I see how important it was; it stood me in good stead. I was her whipping girl for awhile, but I survived it, and now I know that she was trying to get me to grow up."

Archer remembered how much Holm hated sentimentality: "She'd say, 'Don't get shtuck in the flypaper.'" The dancer summed up: "We all worked like crazy, we worked our buns off. It was such an opportunity! We had [rehearsal] space, bodies [to choreograph for], no distractions." From her perspective of a number of years in Colorado Springs, Archer saw some of the social dynamic of the community. She noted how the elite of Colorado Springs loved Holm, inviting her to their "swanky" parties. Archer went on to dance in two of Holm's Broadway shows, and she choreographed off-Broadway. She also taught children's classes at Holm's studio: "For a period, she ruled my life."[3]

The pièce de résistance of Holm's 1957 concert was *Ozark Suite*, her 1947 New York success that had been the watershed between her concert dance career and Broadway. In Colorado, recorded music was used for *Ozark Suite* and some student pieces, but John Colman had heavy duty, playing Bach, Schubert, and traditional marches. A review in the *Free Press* reported a full house and fifty people standing outside hoping to get in to "a fast paced concert dominated by humor and satire."[4] This was the last review of Holm's concerts for a few years. It is a good guess that Holm asked that coverage cease, as she would soon go on record in favor of giving young artists the opportunity to grow without pressure and fear of criticism.

In 1958 seventy students worked under the watchful eye of Holm, Kostock, and Colman. Holm explained to the press that her purpose was to give students a chance to create their own compositions and that even if they fell short, they were coming a step farther in knowledge of modern dance: "This opportunity to experiment and create is something which dancers cannot find in the competitive world of New York."[5]

The speed with which Colorado had bolted into a high modern aesthetic represented by Holm's programs and Colman's musical guidance is exposed by centennials it celebrated in 1958 and 1959. The Colorado gold rush had begun in 1858, and early in 1859 a gold camp sprang up where Denver now stands. On September 15, 1859, a large shack called Apollo Hall opened with a bar and gambling tables. Colonel Charles Thorne soon arrived there with several oxcarts full of actors and properties.

Between the summers of 1958 and 1959 correspondence shot between Colorado and New York as plans unfolded for a theater season celebrating the centennial of Colorado's first theatrical bill. Holm's loyal friend, the writer Lillian McCue, produced scripts and rewrites for Holm's inspection. A New York producer became involved, and Holm began casting. Then she abruptly canceled the project. Scheduling was a problem but the biggest impediment was the state of the theater; renovations and professional management were needed.

Holm wrote to the college administration in general language about her decision to cancel the theater project and not produce her annual dance concert: "To perform ideas with efficiency one should find readiness and preparedness for such cooperative undertakings as theatre in general calls for. Knowing of the difficulties one has to cope with by using the theatre in the FAC [Fine Arts Center], I would be foolish to attempt a professional project."[6] The president of the college, Louis Benezet, shared Holm's letter with the director of the FAC and the president of the Board of Trustees. Both wrote Holm regretting her decision and asking for her specific requirements. Holm's response was firm and accusing: "My sincere complaints reach back at least five or six years, and I have spoken many times with genuine emphasis with people responsible for the Fine Arts Center." Her two-page letter mentioned the unusable cyclorama, the sorry state of the black velours, the sand-colored velours, the lighting equipment, and the proscenium curtain: "Many times my students and I have gone after these materials with needle and thread to hold together the remnants."

President Benezet responded with another request for a more precise list of necessary improvements. Holm's reply, delayed because she was in Stockholm for a *My Fair Lady* production, came down heavily on FAC's stage manager, "a fine man with all good intentions, but with absolutely no training as far as managing a theatre effectively is concerned. . . . I would suggest that he would take a course in Stage Management and Lighting at Denver University." Klaus Holm had become his mother's technical director, and he was likely backing up, if not encouraging, Holm's complaints.

Correspondence between Holm and Colorado Springs broke off in early May when Holm departed for Vancouver rehearsals of *Orpheus and Euridice,* which she was preparing for a July opening. Not only was the theater season an idea of the past, but Holm had put on record that she would not do her annual dance production. Records of the affair reveal the confidence Holm had acquired in the eighteen years since she began working in Colorado. In 1941 she had acquiesced in artistic projects with which she may not have been in complete sympathy because she needed financial security and confirmation of an American identity. By 1959 she was in a position of power vis-à-vis her sponsors, and she proved that she could be an administrative headache. The college scrambled to appease her. Awarding an honorary degree the following year may have been part of its strategy.

Because of entreaties from college and town, her students' desires, or for her own reasons, Holm did allow Colorado College to present "The Young Choreographers' Workshop under the supervision of Hanya Holm" in 1959. It ran for an unprecedented three nights in Perkins Hall Auditorium, for so much student choreography was shown that a change of program was needed to perform it all. Once again Redlich choreographed several pieces. One of them, *Passin' Through,* became a signature work when he formed a dance company. Guest artist Joyce Trisler also contributed to the concert. She had been in the Lester Horton Company and was considered an expert on the teaching and choreography of her mentor. Her own company, Danscompany, was beginning to receive notice. Trisler's presence in Colorado, and the presence of some others who became prominent dance professionals, made 1959 a year that temporarily reversed the trend toward beginning-level enrollment.[7]

The Colorado Springs press noted Holm's absence in mid-summer for the opening of *Orpheus;* she returned from Vancouver in time to supervise her Workshop concert. With Holm away during two weeks of concert preparation, Colman had been an especially strong voice in music selection. Rieti, Dello Joio, Ives, Bartók, Schoenberg, Hindemith, Riegger, and Stravinsky were used, and Colman played—or improvised—a piece of his own.

Colman is a legend to students who took his music classes over the years. Some, like Nancy Topf, remembered them with superlatives: "It was strong rhythmic training, wonderfully challenging, exciting, really fantastic."[8] She recalled big groups of dancers clapping, pounding, and slapping out patterns. Some summers, however, Colman's expectations went so far beyond the students' comprehension that his classes dwindled to two or three stalwarts.

In 1959 I was in Colorado Springs for the first four weeks of the summer session. My memories are like a pile of unmatched beads; I can remember isolated incidents, but their string is lost. Holm had her two soloists for *Orpheus,* ballet professionals, with her so she could rehearse with them. I recall Holm's presentation of a duet for *Orpheus.* It took place before choreography class in the slightly dark, wood-paneled reception room off the entrance to Cossitt Hall. I was surprised at how romantic and low-key it was, relying for effect on small-scale detail.

The same room brings up another memory from 1959. A solo I made for Composition Class was a stylized piece that made use of long lines and slow speed. I remember the feeling of getting into the structure, not displaying myself but rather the choices that revealed the dance. The assignment Holm had given surprised me because it was so general. I have found what I think were her words recorded in Kostock's notebook from another year, so maybe it was an assignment she used often: "Construct or build for me a dance—your idea of a dance. Incorporate within this problem your concept of dancing. I want to see you *dance*— and present for me very clearly *what* dancing means to you."

Holm's notebook recorded "good, interesting," and then "leaving" after my name. Casts were being chosen for dances on the Workshop performance, and I was ineligible because I would leave after four weeks. There must have been another assignment to bring in a phrase, for Holm's notebook recorded her evaluations for my class. After my name I read "phrase ok," which is better than some other comments—"phrase stiff and hard," "vague, no statement," "longer than a phrase, shallow"—but not as good as her comment "good phrase" for Lucinda Childs, who went on to become an internationally recognized choreographer.

I count more beads of memories from 1960, my full summer in Colorado. My husband of six months was with me, and Holm had arranged that Howard and I stay on campus together. I remember a lot of what Howard did and what he observed because we talked about those things that summer and later. He played Scrabble with Holm, Colman, and violist Paul Doktor. The four of them were well matched, and games went to one as often as to another. Holm became fond of Howard, and he was able to keep Colman, who had a volatile temper, in a good mood. Howard observed Kostock's overuse of the phrase *real amazing*, and later we got to calling him "Real Amazing Kostock."

I had taken some classes with Holm the previous winter, and she suggested I audition for her next Broadway musical, *Camelot*. I made all the cuts; we were to go into rehearsal in late August. Holm commented that it would be a good idea if I spent the summer in Colorado to study with her. I dutifully registered and paid my fees. The first day of the session I was surprised to hear Archer, Elizabeth Harris, and me introduced as guest artists; we were expected to choreograph for the final concert. I remember that Holm's classes were simple. I got my kinetic "high" by improvising around the edges of the room to Colman's sublime music as I waited my turn to cross the floor.

Holm suggested "Roundelay" for the title of the dance I choreographed, and I remember being impressed with her erudition. The experience of the concert is lost to my memory except for the assurance that my four-part dance went well, especially the solo I made for Albert Reid, who became a member of the Nikolais Dance Theatre and later of Merce Cunningham's company. Holm did not choreograph in 1960, for she spent a great deal of time that summer working with music arrangements for the dances in *Camelot*. Colman contributed two sections to the concert: he assembled a chorus and conducted a motet by Palestrina, a psalm by Schütz, and a round by Barr. Howard was one of his basses, as were Kostock, John Fetler, and four others.

What I remember most about my work with Holm was her speech. She was able to get to a deep level of meaning with only a few words. I was as fascinated by the phenomenon as by the message. Howard and I had both had a German American professor at the University of Wisconsin who was capable of the same effect. We wondered if it had something to do with an economy of words necessitated by a second language learned late in life, or was it something in German training and the German language?

A reporter from the *Gazette-Telegraph* was fascinated, too. He quoted her with some amusement: "But my stress now is not only the technique, but it is also the attitude. . . . To teach the people how to work—that is one of the hardest jobs. Not just tossing the movements over—this you have to do and this you must not do— understand what you do, and then it is your job to do it." The reporter commented, "She smiled, and smoothed her skirt." He went on quoting Holm's tangled sentences and interjected his own bemused comments.[9]

The tone of the local reporter tells us, as had John Fetler's two negative reviews, that the citizenry of Colorado Springs were no longer united in awe of their summer visitor. The population had grown and was no longer homogeneous. Some residents may have been marginally impressed by a small, mild-mannered dynamo with direct connections to European high culture and a funny way of talking. To her students, Holm's speech could be a source of private hilarity as they repeated phrases to each other, stressing the *v* sound she used for *w*. Often, though, her speech awakened dancers to profound levels of understanding.

Kostock recorded a string of phrases from one of her theory classes: "Earn it by giving up habit and convenience. Sand corn by sand corn you build—it falls down and we rebuild. Understand why we are doing what we do. Understand rationally and physically. Human being is its uprightness and its reason for being. We try after honesty. We are selfish—*I* want to know. Beauty is relative." Slavishly loyal to his mentor, Kostock did admit to me that sometimes he would think "oh Hanya, how can you talk so much and say so little?"[10]

Archer's eyes were not the only ones to glaze over, yet most students took an important message from Holm as they struggled to improve their dances and their lives. I believe Holm's speech worked in a poetic fashion rather than as the linear, rational argument we usually associate with prose discourse. Her talk was often a string of truisms and metaphors from which students could choose the message they wanted to hear and were capable of understanding. The kernel of her message for me was "you make yourself by doing." I arrived at that by sifting, pondering, and connecting ideas and desires that already resided within me. I suspect other students did the same, with other conclusions.

Comparing Holm with another German expatriate artist and teacher tells us something about her language use and illuminates essentials of the study environment she created in Colorado. The painter Josef Albers and his wife, who was Jewish, left Germany in 1933 when the National Socialists came to power and the Bauhaus closed rather than accept Nazis on its staff. The couple found their way to Black Mountain College, an experimental community of living and art-making in rural Carolina. Musician John Cage, who was also on the faculty, described Albers: "[He was] an amazing man because he combined the strictures of German thinking (the ability to call the whole place to order, at the drop of a hat or at the click of his shoes) and the ability to inspire people with the possibility of their own individual freedom."[11] Another observer at Black Mountain described the Europeans on the faculty: "[They] can talk democracy and to a certain extent practice the forms—but it seems awfully hard for them to really feel it. There is a certain almost inherent feeling of aristocracy and the 'I am the expert, I know best' orientation about them."[12]

At Black Mountain students recorded Albers' most frequent pronouncements: "Please keep away from the bandwagon," "stick to your own bones," "sit on your own behind."[13] Students in Colorado heard Holm use many of the same aphorisms. Some of her favorites were "you can't sit on two stools at one time" and "dig your own foundation." Holm placed responsibility for learning on her students. For most of them, this made dance study an exhilarating adventure. Her tactics seemed authoritarian to a reflective few. It was not with a click of shoes or the drop of a hat that she commanded attention but by arranging her skirt as she sat in her chair to begin, "now children."

Nancy Topf was nineteen the summer she studied with Holm in 1961. It was the turning point in her life: "I discovered a way of being that was being modern dance. The theoretical work she gave me helped me develop my own work later, it balanced the physical with [the] intellectual; there was a moment of crystallization." Topf was inspired to change colleges and take a dance major at the University of Wisconsin to be closer to theory work. Holm's authority and the autonomy students exercised under it validated the work of professionals like Redlich and propelled many others into dance careers.

The summer of 1961 had a different character from any previous summer. No student work was programmed on the final concert, a very special production in the new Broadmoor International Theatre. Feisty Carol Truax, former Fine Arts director of Colorado College and now program director of Broadmoor International Center, arranged for the college to present an evening of dance, music, and poetry directed by Holm. Holm's focus had been divided the last two summers, first with rehearsals for *Orpheus* and then with preparations for *Camelot*. In 1961 she concentrated entirely on instruction and on her own choreography. The lavish and substantial program took much coordination among Truax, Holm, and Colman. Of five heavy-hitting sections, Holm choreographed three and Colman directed music for four.

Vera Zorina, a ballerina in the 1930s and 1940s who then became a dancer-actress in Hollywood films, read Edith Sitwell's text for William Walton's *Façade*. Holm's other star, Janet Collins, had danced the role "Night" in *Out of This World* in 1950. Collins went on to present her own choreography in New York, and from 1952 to 1954 she danced in the Metropolitan Opera Ballet—its first African American ballerina. In 1961 she spent the entire summer with Holm while they worked on two solos and a septet she danced with Harris, Redlich, and four students.

Redlich remembers well the choreographic process for the work set to Virgil Thomson's *String Quartet No. 2*. He recalled that Collins had difficulty "hanging on to choreography." She danced a solo to the first movement of the string quartet, and "it was different every time we rehearsed."[14] Collins's other solo was to a Heinrich Schütz setting of six Psalms. Holm used twenty students as a dancing chorus. Colman conducted the singing chorus of thirty-two and four soloists.

Redlich had problems of his own. A duet Holm made for him and Harris did not come easily: "Hanya had something in her head and had a hard time getting at it." The three struggled diligently to get a few spectacular moments. Holm programmed a comedy for the closing number, a dance that did come together easily. She used every special effect the theater had. Redlich and Sandra Horton entered on swings: "That was hard because we were both gigglers." Comedy seemed never to be a problem for Holm. When she noticed someone in class who had a sense of the comic, she'd use him or her for a nonsense piece, sometimes creating it in the last week of the session. "They had a whiz to them," recalled Redlich.

The Colorado press outdid itself in covering the 1961 concert with ample previews and reviews. Fetler wrote a considered and positive critique. As he often did, he reported on the reactions of the audience: "With the really amusing and hilarious final dance number of modern deus-ex-machina effects the audience was well-satisfied with the evening."[15] A review in the *Rocky Mountain News* concluded, "Certainly Tuesday night's performance at the Broadmoor International Center upheld her reputation as the nation's number one choreographer."[16] Colorado College had pulled from Holm her first major concert since 1949.

Redlich suspected that the summer of 1961 put Holm under a lot of strain and that she felt she was being tested. He had heard grumbling at the college that Holm's shows there were less professional than those she did in New York. Although she had produced something of the highest professional caliber in 1961, she did so in the fully equipped Broadmoor Theatre, not at the usual site across from campus, the Colorado Springs Fine Arts Center. In satisfying her hosts, she may have been sending more than one message.

After Holm's Broadmoor success, Colorado College publicity treated her with the special reverence it had voiced when she joined the summer faculty in 1941. Her program of dance instruction was spoken of first and often in releases about creative arts workshops, institutes, seminars, and other summer offerings. College records show that throughout this period, dance accounted for more student credit hours than any other subject except education.[17] When the press interviewed Holm, the quizzical, obliquely critical tone of 1960 had vanished, and Holm's every nuance was celebrated: "She is old without wrinkles. . . . Hanya Holm is a good name for her. Brief, emphatic, hard. . . .

She teaches the dance to anyone who wants to undertake its rigors. Her qualifications in choreography are staggering."[18]

Concerts from 1962 to 1964 were again informal, almost entirely given over to material from classes. Holm choreographed only two short dances and gave herself credit for staging one closing number. Programs began with demonstrations of technique in three sections: "On the Floor," "In Place," and "Through Space." Each concert included a section on Labanotation directed by Allan Miles. Holm had added him to her staff in place of a second dance assistant, and he offered classes in the system of recording dance that had grown out of Rudolf Laban's work in Europe in the 1920s and 1930s. Holm had been an early proponent of the system in this country. It was in her studio that the Dance Notation Bureau had been founded in 1940, and in 1948 she broke ground by having her choreography for *Kiss Me, Kate* recorded in Labanotation.

Miles spoke of the demonstrations he gave in 1962, 1963, 1964, 1966, and 1968 as nightmares: "I am not good at speaking before people, but she insisted." Despite the anguish he suffered at the podium and the difficulty he had satisfying Holm with fresh ideas for each year's presentation, Miles enjoyed his summers in Colorado. He can claim several professional notators who developed out of his classes.[19]

Nineteen sixty-two was the last year until 1977 that John Colman was Holm's music director. Leonard Taffs took over as Holm's accompanist and director of music. He, too, was a gifted improviser, and in contrast to Colman, he was even-tempered and affable. Although not a musician of Colman's stature, he provided many years of good service to Holm, and the two worked well together.

Whereas the success of Holm's production at Broadmoor International Center in 1961 gave her high visibility in the Colorado press, the triumphant festival in her honor in 1965 was big news in the national journal *Dance Magazine* and the *New York Times*. Prominent artists who had been her students celebrated the inspiration they had found studying and working with her. The theme of their praise was summed up by a *Dance Magazine* critic: "The rare capacity for a creative artist and teacher to bring out the uniqueness of the talented individuals working with her was clearly revealed in the variety and range of dancers who came to pay homage."[20]

Alwin Nikolais brought his company, which was busy with New York seasons and national tours. He was extending and reformulating Holm's dance theories at the Henry Street Playhouse in New York, where he directed a thriving school for children and a professional training program. Murray Louis performed. By 1965 he was directing his own company. Nancy Hauser brought her company from Minneapolis. Holm's former student Valerie Bettis, a successful concert artist who also worked in theater, performed. Redlich and Harris, both at the beginning of independent careers, danced.

Donald Janson, who covered the dance festival honoring Holm for the *New York Times,* found that affection for Holm, "who is older than seventy but still full of bounce," had been overflowing. He quoted the artists. Bettis said, "She gave us a foundation to move in any direction we liked." Hauser added, "We were not taught restrictive patterns but the art itself." Harris said, "She never made it a cult." Student performers offered their opinions: "She's the best [teacher] I've ever had."[21]

Holm had no responsibilities for the 1965 concert presented in her honor. "Qualified summer students will be permitted to audition for participation in the festival performance," the *Free Press* teased on June 6. Three students performed a trio from Nikolais's *Sanctum;* sixteen others performed a group section. One student dancer, Gale Ormiston, soon became a member of Nikolais's company, and at least three women went on to performing careers in New York—Janis Ansley, Lauren Persichetti, and Gail Turner.

Louis danced a duet with Phyllis Lamhut and performed his solo *Transcendencies.* Bettis performed two dramatic solos, including her signature work, *The Desperate Heart.* Taffs accompanied both. Redlich performed two solos. Hauser contributed *Lyric Suite* for eight dancers. Harris danced *Before the Music Ends (a Collage).* It required a great number of properties, and the saga of her travels from California with them was heroic. Her car had broken down, and a replacement rental car had also broken down. She finally arrived in Denver by train with ladder, trunk, flag, pitchers, baskets, bells, flowerpots, and myriad other objects. The car bringing her south to Colorado Springs, thankfully, did not break down.

Soloists on the bill came in for especially high praise in the local press: Bettis's *The Desperate Heart* was "so expressive it told its own story clearly and distinctly." Louis's *Transcendencies* had an "almost hypnotic effect with its weaving and fluid motion." "Fantastic is the only word for [Redlich's] *Earthling*. Bravos called him back."[22] Of the program to which everyone contributed, *Dance Magazine* said, "The evening was filled with convincing evidence that Hanya Holm has been an inspiration and a source, a teacher who has prepared her students and then released them to fulfill their own potential, to become independent artists and to develop the security of their own uniqueness."[23]

Lamhut, a member of both Nikolais's company and the Murray Louis Company, remembered three glorious weeks in Colorado: "Nik said to me, 'I can't pay you for this, but I'll show you a good time.' And he did!" Lamhut's expenses and transportation were paid by the college, and she counts the work without salary to have been well worth it: "We stayed for an extra week, and Nik showed us Colorado. We went everywhere. It was fabulous, I loved all of it—Hanya teaching with a flower tied to the end of her braid, Oliver, the whole thing, it was thrilling."[24]

In New York preparing for her twenty-fifth summer at Colorado College, Holm had granted an interview to Jack Anderson, writing for *Dance Magazine*. He quoted so the intent of her remarks came through clearly, if with mixed metaphors: "When I teach, I try to plant a seed. While I may knock everything out from under a student, I also try to give her something to hold on to. Some students let the seed grow. Others take the seed, but don't let it grow. They clutch it until it becomes a hard, dry kernel." She lamented that dancers of the day craved to be shown and compared them unfavorably with dancers of the 1930s: "Dancers [today] want everything easy . . . they need a comfortable living."

Anderson honored Holm as "one of the most famous of living dance pedagogues," and he observed that her severe judgments were not reserved for students alone: "The time has come when each of the modern dancers of my generation *can* offer what amounts to a formula to her students. But if we do offer it, we are failing our students." Holm's words subtly compared her own teaching with that of others of her generation, with whom she still felt a keen rivalry. They had invented strong personal styles and passed them on to students and disciples. Holm congratulated herself on the variety of styles her former students had developed: "Technique is a means to an end. If there is an end in mind, then technique will develop out of an inner fire."[25] Holm's interview with Anderson was the first of many in the next decades in which she inveighed against the pursuit of virtuosity for its own sake.

Holm often said, "I don't teach technique, I teach dance." Her recipe of basic, demanding movement classes, large doses of philosophy, and opportunities for students to find their own solutions to problems she set gave many young artists the resources to discover themselves. K. Wright Dunkley, a student in 1963, 1964, and 1965, felt so empowered by the tough love Holm rendered in her filigreed speeches that he tape-recorded, edited, and transcribed her theory classes. This chapter closes with a small fraction of entries in the 128-page booklet he assembled.[26]

- If a basic knowledge of dance is mastered according to your own personality you can go anywhere you please. This basic knowledge is an island from which you can go in any direction. It is your center, your core. Without this center you are always chasing butterflies, always here, always there, and with nothing to hold on to. If you do not have a center to which you can return, you will create vagaries which will lack conviction.

- When I started in dance, the bits and pieces were not there. We had to find them. We had to find our values wherever we could find them. Now you get everything ready-made, ready prepared. It would be much better for you if you were forced to find things out and to discover them for yourself.

- You carry the responsibility for what you become. You must look within yourself for your guidance. If you will accept responsibility, you can do anything you want.

- The more you are challenged the more strength you gain. The strength and quiet you have are concentrated during conflict, and if you overcome the conflict it will buoy you up.

- Your lack of freedom is not imposed from the outside but is a jail of your own making. Accept responsibilities for your own inability.

- You can't sit back and wait until the mastery of the body strikes you. It will never come. You have to develop your temperament. You have to want to do something and enjoy doing it. Otherwise you look like sour grapes. You make sour faces, and if your teacher tells you to lighten up your spirits you fall apart.

- That you didn't feel good is no excuse. That your foot hurt is no excuse. That the floor wasn't level is no excuse. That a fly buzzed past your nose is no excuse. If you do a movement half-heartedly a miracle will not happen. You are the miracle, and there are no kudos to be gained because you did a movement right once. Do a movement right every time you do it.

- Don't let anything go by without questioning it. Hidden symbolisms come out of little things which are not explainable.

- The difference between the artificial and the real rose is the difference between manufactured and life. This is an immense difference. You can keep on learning and learning until you are ninety-five, as there is no limit, but your questions will only be answered if you can keep in contact with life.

- Art is living. It is not just craftsmanship. It is the flow of love. There is that meeting place of the body and the soul and the spirit that gives you control.

Chapter Seven

DANCING INTO THE BOOM
1966-1974

The dance boom of the 1960s and 1970s was a bubble-up phenomenon ignited by strong regional hunger. Ford Foundation grants in the early 1960s helped to support it, and the National Endowment for the Arts (NEA), founded in 1965, also helped. NEA's Dance Touring Program, initiated in 1973–1974, helped even more. Dance professionals were hired to teach and perform in colleges and universities as higher education became the livelihood of many dancers and supported dance companies formed by disciples of an earlier modern dance generation. The artists who gathered at Colorado College in the summer of 1965 to honor Hanya Holm are examples of the phenomenon. Most of them depended, and would continue to depend, on regional sponsors to help them sustain companies and create new work.

With its long-standing summer arts program, the heritage of philanthropy in the 1930s, and the vision of college president Thurston Davies, Colorado College could rightly claim itself a leader in regional dance activity. Holm's program drew hundreds of dancers and aspiring dancers for rigorous summer study, and dozens went out to energize university dance departments, dance companies, and festivals around the country.

The affluence of the 1950s, which had reached universities and colleges by 1960, led to building programs—in 1962 Colorado College celebrated the opening of Olin Hall of Science and the Charles Leaming Tutt Library—and new instructional programs in all areas. In the very special community of Colorado Springs, however, there was a countercurrent to the national affluence of the 1950s. We had a glimpse of it in the 1958–1959 controversy over using the Fine Arts Center (FAC) for a theater festival. The FAC Board of Directors saw a serious problem in raising money for the renovations Holm required for the project. Furthermore, a theater festival would have made it necessary to cancel weekly film showings that guaranteed a certain income, no small consideration to the strapped FAC.

Colorado Springs, once a town of millionaires, was beginning to struggle with finances and agonize over priorities like communities that had never known the comfort of reliable largesse from their prominent citizens. John Fetler, the reporter who had given Holm her first negative review and then joined her praise singers in 1961, was an old-time newspaperman who watched the changes in Colorado Springs over sixty years: "The founders made the arts their amusement, but in a couple of generations the millionaires died out and the taxman came. With their fortunes gone or tied up, the elite could maintain a certain social life, but it was separate from the cultural activities of the town."[1]

Holm's introduction to Colorado Springs had come soon after the building of the Fine Arts Center and the creation of the El Pomar Foundation to further the arts. It was a period of confidence and excitement in cultural growth, but it was the beginning of the end of that period. Davies succeeded in linking the philanthropy of Colorado Springs' founding families to the college, but he also moved Colorado Springs into a patriotic pro-military posture that fueled its next stage of growth. Military money and the commerce it spawned became important to the overall economy just as the big fortunes of the elite families became restricted.

Colorado College, like colleges everywhere, did see revenues creep upward through increased enrollments, certain government programs like the GI bill, and foundation and individual giving. In 1962 the Ford Foundation awarded the college a $2.2 million challenge grant. It took effort to scare up private philanthropy, but in a three-year campaign the challenge was met. El Pomar Foundation and Bemis-Taylor Foundation were among twenty-eight national and local foundations whose combined donation was $2,902,697. Alumni gave a generous $1,231,731. Parents and other individuals gave $969,064. Business and industry threw in a little over $500,000.[2]

In the nine-year period from 1966 through 1974 the dance boom brought dancers in unprecedented numbers to the college. Enrollment in Holm's summer program spurted upward throughout the 1960s, reached 119 in 1972, and stayed near 100 until the end of the decade. Gilbert Johns, extroverted professor of psychology, took over as dean of the summer session in 1966. He claimed Holm's program carried the summer financially for many years.[3] Johns was a factor in bringing the young energy that invaded the campus during the dance boom; he was as skillful a publicist as Davies had been in the 1940s.

Johns introduced another dimension of Holm's artistry to Colorado Springs in 1971 by inviting her to direct operas for the newly formed Colorado Springs Opera Festival. He also maintained stability within Holm's program. As would be expected in this period of student unrest, Holm and her staff occasionally confronted what Oliver Kostock characterized as "bonfires of discontent that the administration had to put out." Johns often watched dance classes and made it clear that he appreciated Holm and her program. Kostock said, "The kids just knew they weren't going to get very far with him."[4] The majority of students, however, were completely within Holm's thrall.

Kostock and Molly Lynn were witness to the transformations hundreds of young people experienced. Holm empowered the students; she taught them endurance and how to develop mental and spiritual stamina. Lynn confessed that she fed off some of that herself. Kostock found it difficult to separate the program from Holm: "She loved it. She came to be refreshed, and she had something to offer." Her two assistants were sometimes horrified by the way Holm treated some students. "She'd go at them for things they could do nothing about," said Lynn.[5] Kostock recognized that Holm had a talent for sensing a person's weakness, but he marveled, too, at her ability to spot talent: "She could get them to perform beyond their capacities."

Tom Kanthak, who studied with Holm for three summers in the early 1970s, explained how Holm changed his life: "We were looking for gurus, and she popped up. She talked about life, and she talked about dance, and we're saying, 'This is for me.' The movement had failed—the peace-love movement—and she filled a need. Every day was an awakening."[6] In the 1960s and 1970s Holm demonstrated certainty to a seeking generation that was confronting relative values in a confused society. Her speeches about digging foundations and sticking with principles alerted them to the possibility of truth and certainty. The discipline she enforced may have been what they craved in a period of national questioning when modern dance itself was undergoing radical change.

The dominance of modern dance pioneers with neoromantic, expressive styles had led to a formalist backlash, and that segued into questions about the very nature of dance. "No to spectacle, no to virtuosity . . . no to moving and being moved," declared Yvonne Rainer in 1965.[7] In New York, choreographers presented ordinary people doing ordinary things and called it dance. Holm, however, continued to insist on mastery over the body, choreography for the proscenium stage, and performing to great music.

During the summer of 1966 a new theater that would free the college from its dependence on the poorly maintained facility in the Fine Arts Center was under construction. Holm had to make do with Cossitt Gymnasium for her Student Workshop performance. She arranged seating as if before the fourth wall of a proscenium theater. Student work and demonstrations from class filled the program. The next year Holm's Workshop was presented in a well-equipped 800-seat theater in Armstrong Hall. The new venue inspired Holm to choreograph her concert's closing work. In 1968 a redesigned printed program hinted at renewed formality. Neat offset printing on colored stock with a soft photograph or sketched portrait of Holm on the cover replaced the homemade look of earlier programs. The title of the event subtly changed each year until, in 1972, the word *Workshop* disappeared and the title *Hanya Holm Dance Concert* became the norm. One must suspect the suave Dean Johns of maneuvering these changes. Two-performance runs also returned in 1972; workshops had just one midweek performance.

Among the 100 or more students who registered each summer were a small group of experienced dancers, a handful of clumsy beginners, and a wide range in between. Holm and her assistants faced the challenge of stimulating the best while inspiring the not yet ready. Composition classes were divided according to the students' potential, but technique classes included all skill levels.

Two students who were near-beginners in 1969 went on to prominent careers in dance. Lanky Jessica Sayre was in her sophomore year at Oberlin College when a guest teacher staged some multimedia improvisatory events called happenings. Sayre was excited by her participation and wanted to do more. Her teacher saw that she lacked the necessary movement experience and suggested study with Holm to get some of the basics. Sayre remembered the teacher saying, "You'll like it, just go." She laughed, "I was just a hippie kid; I was still wearing underpants under my leotard." The night before the placement audition for Composition Class, an advanced student taught a warm-up class.

> I went, and I learned first position and second position. Somehow I looked credible. They put me in the advanced comp class, and I aced my first assignment. Then they all trashed my second assignment, but Hanya assigned me some music and a group to choreograph something for the concert. That was hard, and Hanya had to help me. She wasn't nice, but I did learn. Hanya respected my premise; she didn't make me throw out my ideas. I learned a lot.[8]

Sayre was eager to talk about what her summer with Holm represented: "I learned that dance is a profession and a life experience, and I learned how much I loved it. I was vitally challenged." At the time, Sayre was in the process of transferring to Yale; she was a member of the first small group of women who integrated the all-male college. All she wanted to do, however, was dance: "I called Hanya and asked if I could come down to see her. She said, 'Please come.' She advised me to stay in school— 'You don't know yet who you are.' So with my tail between my legs I went back to New Haven and finished." After graduation from Yale, Sayre went to study in New York City. Her special qualities led Alwin Nikolais to take her on, and she became a featured soloist in his company.

Chris Burnside was recommended to Holm by Frances Wessells, Holm's student in the 1940s. Wessells took Burnside to New York to meet Holm, and he received a full scholarship for the summer. But it was difficult for him to go from the nurturing environment of his study with Wessells to Holm's structure. "I had a rough time," he confessed. That year Holm assigned places in line, and dancers were expected to stay in those places in every class. Burnside remembered, "I was behind a broom of a guy, and I began to realize that I was picking up on his movement." He played a trick to get his place in line changed, and then he could move more fully. Holm found a lot to criticize, however, and she often reminded him that he had terrible habits. Burnside persevered, and he believes Holm began to appreciate him. She chose him to dance in the piece she choreographed: "Sometimes she'd get so mad, she'd get livid, and I'd calm her down. I think we developed a mutual respect for each other."[9]

Both Sayre and Burnside remembered the environment. In the beginning they felt a little debilitated by the altitude, but soon it became exhilarating. Both found a supportive group of students with whom to socialize. Burnside became pals with Gretchen Phillips, a prominent student choreographer in 1969 and two subsequent years until she became Holm's assistant in 1972. Sayre went to parties at the off-campus apartment of an older student: "We all crowded into her place to watch the landing on the moon."

We hear in their reports that a year after the student protests of 1968 and while the country was agonizing over the war in Vietnam, Sayre and Burnside were seeking a place for themselves. The comfort of friends and the interest of teachers may have been especially necessary for young people at the time. Holm gave them more—confirmation of their career desires. The severity of her demands was something to fight against at times, but it also valorized the dance and intensified their commitment to it.

Nineteen seventy was an unusual year. After student compositions and two pieces by Lynn, half of Holm's program was given over to a reconstruction of a sixteenth-century spectacle staged for the Medici court in Florence. *The Descent of Rhythm and Harmony* was meant to be a tribute to Holm on her thirtieth year of continuous instruction at Colorado College. Holm recruited the musicologist Julia Sutton for the reconstruction project, which was funded by the National Endowment for the Arts. Sutton, a respected authority on Renaissance music and dance, had been in Louise Kloepper's classes for children at Holm's studio in New York; she considered Holm her fairy godmother: "Hanya recognized that I wouldn't be a dancer and she told me so, but I wanted it, and I kept on trying." When Sutton turned to music Holm suggested that she study music at Colorado College in the summer so she could take technique classes. Sutton did so in 1949 and some other summers. Holm allowed her to stay in class for just an hour because she knew Sutton didn't have the strength for more. "She was right," the musician said.[10]

In 1970 a lengthy program note provided historical background to the spectacle a sixteenth-century audience of 3,000 in the Uffizi palace in Florence would have witnessed—an experience uniting all the arts in a "joyous assault upon all the senses." Preparations for the twentieth-century reconstruction in Armstrong Theater were tense, difficult, and bitter. Lynn, who danced, remembered that Sutton and Holm had different agendas: "There was a lot of bickering and a disquieting rehearsal situation." Sutton understood that she had been brought in to stage the production, but Holm expected to have control. The relationship became so strained that Sutton threatened to withdraw from the project, and Holm softened her posture somewhat. Sutton admitted that Holm had impeccable eyes: "Hanya could give exact directions to the dancers to achieve what I wanted. I have to love her for it."

Sutton saw why dancers came to study with Holm in such numbers and were transformed by the experience: "Students were dancing all day—just what they wanted—and she knew her business. She took up a different set of muscles each week, and by the end of the week you really felt them, you knew how they worked."

After her experience with early-dance reconstruction, in 1971 Holm returned to her usual, calmer format of student dance studies, and she choreographed a large group work, *Forces,* to music of Edgard Varèse. It was a year of potential among the students. At least nine went on to high-profile careers as performers or educators: Arthur Bridgeman, Jennifer Donohue, Carey Erickson, Richard Haisma, Gary Lund, Gerald Pearson, Sara Pearson, Gretchen Phillips, and Marcia Schramm.

Nineteen seventy-one was the first year of the Colorado Opera Festival organized by Johns and music director Donald Jenkins. Johns spoke gleefully of his success in recruiting Holm to direct the world premiere revival of Tommaso Traetta's early-nineteenth-century *Il Cavaliere Errante:* "I flew her in for a reading. She sat with her hands folded through the whole thing, and then she said, 'I do it!'" Johns claims he went to all of Holm's rehearsals: "It was kind of fun to watch her work." He was especially entranced by Holm's comic strategies. For example, to indicate the passage of time she had a minor character knit a bright red-and-white striped scarf. When each new scene opened, the scarf had grown longer.

In 1972 Holm directed Ravel's *The Spanish Hour* and *The Child and the Sorcerers*. The following year she directed Rossini's *The Italian Girl in Algiers,* in 1974 Gilbert and Sullivan's *Iolanthe,* in 1975 Mozart's *The Abduction from the Seraglio,* in 1976 Puccini's *Gianni Schicchi,* and in 1977 she choreographed Verdi's *Aida*. The three Colorado Opera Festival productions each summer were polished. Soloists were brought in from the New York City Opera; directors and conductors were experienced. Klaus Holm was set and lighting designer. Holm often came to Colorado well before her dance teaching began to rehearse.

In every season she directed for the Opera Festival, Holm also choreographed for her annual dance production. Johns encouraged this by providing special musical stimulation. His musical interests shaped Holm's summer concerts while he was dean. In 1972 he brought in the American Brass Quintet, and Holm choreographed to the group's performance of four sections of Bach's *Art of the Fugue*. She used music of Ravel played by two trumpeters for a second piece. Phillips, now Holm's assistant, choreographed the concert finale to Poulenc played by the quintet. Student pieces in 1972 all used acoustic sound. Two members of Festival Winds played for three Holm pieces the next year.

In 1969 Holm had replaced "Demonstrations of Technique" with "Entrances" at the top of the program and "Exits" to close. In 1972 she combined the two. She rehearsed her entire student body to within an inch of their souls for "Entrances and Exits." Dancers were positioned in each of the wings on stage right, and four entered together, followed in four counts by four more, then four more, and so on. Upon exiting, the dancers ran around the back of the stage and waited their turn to enter again and again. A seemingly unending parade of young people passed before the public.

Holm's notebooks reveal that she gave much thought to planning all aspects of the student portions of her concerts. She listed "Entrances and Exits" in fifteen sections one year: "forward; tiptoe; sideward; undercurve; skip forward; hop steps forward; overcurves; bounce; running leap; turn hop; step leaps; step step leap; side slide; slide *tour jeté*." For the last section, "everybody runs in to get ready to jump." Then, "groups sit in a semicircle and solo jumpers stand." Solo jumpers were listed.[11]

Material was different in other years. Step kicks were introduced, hop turns and slide turns, scissor kicks, and can-can. A finale that became traditional was the cakewalk. Holm selected men she could trust to cross the stage leaning back and kicking high forward with a springing step. It brought down the house.

Holm made serious business of selecting student choreography. For most of her dancers, Composition Class was the highlight of the week. In these high-enrollment years, the course was divided into two or three sections, each meeting once a week. Each class could undertake seven assignments. If a promising product emerged, the choreographer or choreographers were obliged to work on it and show it again and again. Holm made lists and noted precise timings and accompaniment to draw up a program of the best pieces and best dancers. Each concert moved efficiently and had good production values thanks to Klaus Holm. Students realized they were participating in something important.

Mimi Kim, a member of the Hanya Holm Dance Company from 1937 to 1941, became Holm's unofficial assistant in 1973. Phillips was Holm's official assistant, with Kostock, but the fact that she and Johns had married troubled Holm. "I don't want policy made in the bedroom," she told Kim. She was there, Kim was sure, so Holm would not have to depend on Phillips.

From her five years as a company member and occasional contacts over the years, Kim knew Holm's foibles, but she also saw how brilliant Holm was at getting things out of people.[12] While she was in Colorado Kim comforted a few tearful dancers, but she remembered that one weeping girl, whom she had quieted during the evening, knocked on her door late at night to say "you know, Hanya is right." Kim believed Holm's program worked so successfully because she had an instinct for what people wanted. It could be a crescendo of release in a technique class, tearful self-examination, or real self-discipline.

One hundred five students had an opportunity to see a profound example of self-discipline when they arrived for the first day of classes in 1974. Tom Kanthak has written about it:

All . . . of us aspiring dancers entered the sky-lit gymnasium of Cossitt Hall to the sight of an old woman sitting perfectly erect and serene on a long wooden bench, flanked by Oliver Kostock and Gretchen Phillips, the two associate teachers for the summer. Hanya, the old woman, waved a hand in the air—a sort of beckon to us to sit on the floor in front of her—and began to speak. Her words were difficult to understand, not only because of her peculiar quasi-Germanic accent but because part of her face was paralyzed. As she talked she explained that because of a recent stroke part of her face was propped up by surgical tape and she was having some difficulty walking so it was necessary to use a cane for at least part of the summer. We were not to worry, however, because there was much work to do and there was little time to talk about difficulties.

Within a few short weeks we were all astounded by the miracle woman, Hanya, dancing around that huge gymnasium floor. We gathered at her feet at 8:30 in the morning and ended rehearsals with her at 9:00 in the evening. In between were classes in dance theory, technique, composition and improvisation, as well as many student composition rehearsals. She did not stop and she expected us to not stop either. I remember clearly the end of a particularly long and strenuous technique class. The weather that day was incredibly hot, the movement combination was so simple it was nearly impossible to do, and to top it all off the old woman then expected us to run-run-leap until I thought I was going to die and then I slowed down. As soon as I stopped to catch my breath, I heard this screech from Hanya, "Don't stop now, you must keep dancing!!!" So I continued, and ran-ran-leaped until I thought I would die again, and then a remarkable thing happened. I felt as if I was flying. I felt pure, unbound ecstasy. For the first time, I had the experience of complete joy in moving—the sense that I could do this forever.[13]

Despite the near catastrophe of a stroke, Holm completed her direction of *Iolanthe* and directed her own dance concert in which the Festival Winds participated. She choreographed a duet for Phillips and student Jim Kelly and let Phillips show three works. Kim was guest choreographer again, and a generous amount of student work was shown. As was now routine, "Entrances and Exits" opened the show.

Students were inspired by Holm to commit their days and nights to dance. Reflecting on his summers in Colorado, Kanthak discovered the reason for his motivation:

With the front range of the Colorado Rocky Mountains as a backdrop, I spent a total of three summers at the feet of Hanya listening to her philosophize about dance—or was it dance? Was she talking about life or was she talking about dance? As I continued to listen, it was clear to me that one could never really separate the two. "You have to go down to go up." "You have to go through it to do it." We would spin for an hour and some of us would get sick from the motion. She would say, simply, "Stop resisting the motion and become part of it. If you resist the inevitable, it will make you sick or it will overtake you. Let go." So often she would remind us that we were a part of something bigger than us.[14]

Another young man had a life-changing experience of a different kind during this period. Lindsay Fischer, a native of Colorado Springs, was recruited for the opera *The Child and the Sorcerer,* which Holm directed on a double bill in 1972. He was one of three boys and eight girls playing Numbers and Tree Frogs. Seven of Holm's summer students appeared as Shepherds, Frogs, and Moths. Fischer went on to become a principal dancer with New York City Ballet, perhaps the highest rank to which an American dancer can aspire. He credits Holm with having made it possible for him to follow a career in the arts. "She made it easier for my family," he said. Fischer's grandmother was a first-generation German on the edge of the social set that had once ruled Colorado Springs cultural life: "Hanya was able to move in those social circles, the old elite, without any apologies for the arts. She was a wonderful example. She made my grandmother understand that the development of a great artist is the same as the development of a whole person." Holm recognized talent in the young boy and urged that he attend a professional school. She talked with the family about the importance of a complete education along with good dance training. On her recommendation he was allowed to enroll in the National Ballet School of Canada in Toronto.

Fischer's career, however, was suspect in his hometown: "The Family Value Movement was beginning, and artists were under suspicion. It really wasn't until I brought my wife and kids back to Colorado Springs that I was accepted and my family's trust in Hanya, and me, was vindicated. They could relax."[15] Hinting at homophobia in Colorado Springs, Fischer thanks Holm not only for having recognized his promise as a dancer but also for

possessing the social poise with which she made a potentially suspect profession an honorable one.

Holm's granddaughter, Karen Trautlein, described her grandmother as a "great schmoozer." Said Trautlein, "She was completely comfortable in the most elegant social situations, and she
could also get down."[16] The photographic record confirms this.
Holm saved pictures of dinners with Broadway producers at the
Stork Club, glittering parties at the Plaza Hotel, and negotiations
with the elite of dance and theater. Other photos show an easy
familiarity with both men and women. She built human pyra-
mids at beach parties and embraced companions in moments of
wonder and exhilaration.[17]

Students trusted Holm because she was uncompromising, and
they adored her because she was fun. The flower at the end of
her braid, the jolly banter she could initiate before class, her concern for boyfriends and girlfriends, her interest in their mountain hikes—as long as they didn't interfere with rehearsals—en-
deared her to young people. No matter how enraged she became while teaching, she dropped her anger at the end of the
lesson. She had favorites in class, but she treated everyone the
same outside the studio. "She could charm the pants off them,"
grinned Kostock. Although she loved families, she also accepted
homosexuality. "Be yourself," she was heard to tell one prominent student whom she saw was having difficulty with his sexual
orientation.

As dance fashion in the nation changed with the iconoclasm
of the 1960s and 1970s, Holm held her course. Student work
and her own choreography were presented with traditional theater values. A few experienced students found her work dated,
but she dismissed any hints they were rash enough to drop. The
period gave expression to experimentation in East and West Coast
centers, and those experiments were copied across the country,
but before Holm's death in 1992, respect for a master creator
and skilled use of resources of the theater had returned to modern
dance.

The dance boom needed a teacher like Holm who made
demands for mastery and pointed to connections between dance
and life. Her constancy and the discipline she enforced anchored
many young people wandering through unsettled times. Between
1966 and 1974 almost a thousand young people attended Holm's

summer courses. Some went on to careers in dance; all discovered the possibility of greatness if they could be true to their principles.

dance concert

August
7-8-9

by Hanya HOLM
and her dancers
Orchestral Music by ROY HARRIS

FINE ARTS CENTER
COLORADO SPRINGS

Reserved Seats at 5 E. Pikes Peak Ave. Phone M 1285-1286
August 7; $3.00 and $1.75: August 8 and 9: 75¢, $1.00, and $1.75
$1.50

Presented by COLORADO COLLEGE

© PHOTO BY KNUTSON

DENTAN PTG. CO., COLO. SPGS.

Poster announcing the first Hanya Holm summer concert at Colorado College, 1941. Photograph of Robin Gregory, Jinx Heffelfinger, and Louise Kloepper by Loyde Knutson. Courtesy Dance Division, New York Public Library.

Hanya Holm, pianist Johana Harris, and composer Roy Harris touring the Rockies, 1941. Photograph by Loyde Knutson. Courtesy Dance Division, New York Public Library.

Posing as cowgirls, 1941. *Seated left to right*: Hanya Holm, Martha Wilcox, Louise Kloepper, Barbara Hatch, Robin Gregory, Shirley Brimberg, Eleanor McDougall. Photograph by Loyde Knutson. Courtesy Dance Division, New York Public Library.

Posing on the lawn of Colorado College was a tradition. Here Hanya Holm and composer Roy Harris confer as dancers from the Hanya Holm Company look on, 1941. Photograph by Loyde Knutson. Courtesy Dance Division, New York Public Library.

Robin Gregory and Kipp Kiernan of the Hanya Holm Dance Company, 1941. Photograph by Loyde Knutson. Courtesy Dance Division, New York Public Library.

Hanya Holm directing her advanced students, 1948. Photograph by Fritz Kaeser. Courtesy Dance Division, New York Public Library.

Orestes and the Furies, 1943. *Left to right*, Mary Anthony as Apollo, Paul Sweeney as Orestes, Molly Howe as Clytemnestra, with Furies at stage level. Photograph by Fritz Kaeser. Courtesy Dance Division, New York Public Library.

Hanya Holm entering her nightmare in *What Dreams May Come,* 1944. Photograph by Loyde Knutson. Courtesy Dance Division, New York Public Library.

Hanya Holm performing her solo "Alone" in *Windows,* 1946. Photograph by Loyde Knutson. Courtesy Dance Division, New York Public Library.

Glen Tetley, Leo Dugan, Marc Breaux, and Oliver Kostock with accompanying women in *Xochipili*, 1948. Scenery and costumes by Ricardo Martinez. Photograph by Fritz Kaeser. Courtesy Dance Division, New York Public Library.

Hanya Holm's students, 1951. Holm sits *center* with her arm over the shoulder of Melvin Fillin. *Right of her* are Martha Wilcox, guest artist Paul Arthur, Molly Lynn, Jim Ray, Oliver Kostock, and Sonja Easterly, *standing*. Guest artist Rogermae Johnson is second from left in top row. Al Schulman sits in the front row in white shirt. Beside him in striped shirt is Jeff Duncan. Photograph by Dick Hill. Courtesy Dance Division, New York Public Library.

Don Redlich, 1953. Photograph by Stanley L. Payne. Courtesy Pikes Peak Library District.

Hanya Holm with choreographers for her 1960 concert. *Seated left to right,* Elizabeth Harris, Claudia Gitelman, Holm, Laurie Archer; *standing,* Oliver Kostock and Molly Lynn. Photograph by Knutson-Bowers. Courtesy Dance Division, New York Public Library.

Hanya Holm teaching in Cossitt Gymnasium, 1960. Photographs by Myron Wood. Courtesy Pikes Peak Library District.

Hanya Holm and John Colman, 1961, the year of their collaboration on a gala concert at Broadmoor International Theatre. Photograph by Bob McIntyre. Courtesy Dance Division, New York Public Library.

Valerie Bettis, Alwin Nikolais, and Hanya Holm backstage in 1965 during the concert honoring Holm's twenty-fifth consecutive summer of teaching at Colorado College. Photograph by Benschneider. Courtesy Ben Benschneider Estate.

Hanya Holm posing two dancers, with the American Brass Quintet accompanying, 1972. The August 4, 1972, issue of the Summer Session weekly newspaper *Clarion,* edited by Dean Gilbert Johns, captioned this photograph "The Hanya Holm Dance Ensemble and Cardiac Monitoring Unit." Courtesy Special Collections, Tutt Library, Colorado College.

Sara and Gerald Pearson performing their "Magnetic Rag" in the 1971 Hanya Holm concert. Photograph by Benschneider. Courtesy Ben Benschneider Estate.

Hanya Holm and a van carrying students from Minneapolis to Colorado College, 1974. Photograph by Tom Kanthak. Courtesy of the author.

Hanya Holm conducting a composition class with her assistants Gretchen Phillips and Oliver Kostock, 1974. Kostock's dog Tessie rests in his lap. Photograph by Tom Kanthak. Courtesy of the author.

Hanya Holm conferring with Mimi Kim, a former company member and Holm's unofficial assistant, in 1974. Photograph by Tom Kanthak. Courtesy of the author.

Claudia Gitelman and Terry Kaelber in Hanya Holm's *Homage to Mahler*, 1976. Photograph by Tim Davis. Courtesy Dance Division, New York Public Library.

Student dancers in Hanya Holm's *Homage to Mahler*, 1976. Photograph by Benschneider. Courtesy Ben Benschneider Estate.

HOLM ON THE *front* RANGE

The Hanya Holm 40th Anniversary Festival

June 16 - August 7, 1980
Colorado College, Colorado Springs, Colorado

Program Book for 1980 festival marking Hanya Holm's fortieth consecutive year as director of the Colorado College Summer School of the Dance. Courtesy Special Collections, Tutt Library, Colorado College.

Two student duets from the 1980s. Photographs by Benschneider. Courtesy Ben Benschneider Estate.

Members of the Don Redlich Dance Company in Hanya Holm's *Jocose*, 1983. Kathryn Appleby, *foreground*, Don Redlich, *left*, and Jim Clinton. Photograph by Benschneider. Courtesy Ben Benschneider Estate.

Hanya Holm's last bow at Colorado College, 1983. Flanking her are her assistants Nancy Hauser and Oliver Kostock. Photograph by Benschneider. Courtesy Ben Benschneider Estate.

Chapter Eight
ESCALATION AND REFLECTION
1975–1977

From 1966 when he had become dean of Summer Session, Gilbert Johns transformed Colorado Springs' summers with an escalation of arts activities that became frenzied by the end of his tenure in 1981. Hanya Holm was a major focus of his energy, and in 1980 he arranged an orgy of performing arts activities in her honor. The grandeur of his visions, however, ultimately contributed to the demise of Holm's program. When budget discussions came, a combination of other factors—Holm's loss of empathy with her students, the age and fatigue of her staff, a new college president, and advice from clear-eyed but inexperienced new performing arts faculty—focused to kill the summer school of instruction and dance production that had endured for forty-three years. The ending scandalized the dance community nationwide and infuriated Holm's audience in Colorado Springs.

In 1975, however, Holm's program seemed eternal. Johns's enthusiasms were making the summers exhilarating, profound, off-balance experiences. That year, when I returned to Colorado for the first of three summers as Holm's assistant, the session had three operas and concerts by the American Brass Quintet and the New York Chamber Soloists. Two afternoons of music in the library offered Spanish folk songs of the Southwest and French piano music of Debussy and Satie. There was a lecture on the architects Louis Sullivan, Frank Lloyd Wright, and Mies van der

Rohe. Theater in the library offered plays by Pirandello, Stoppard, and Pinter. There were two film festivals. The summer would have been giddy were it not for the job to be done. Nearly 100 dancers needed training, and a concert had to be prepared.

I had come to the attention of Holm again in 1972. I had left the cast of *Camelot* in 1961 after one season and joined my husband in Boston, where we began a family. Back in New York by 1971 and with all three of our daughters in school, I was thrilled to accept an invitation from Alwin Nikolais to teach at the huge professional school he directed with Murray Louis. The next year the two invited Holm to give a master class once a week, and her "Wednesdays" became an institution within an institution.

After Holm engaged me as a teaching assistant, we met in her Greenwich Village home to listen to tapes of the New York Saxophone Quartet, which Johns had arranged to accompany Holm's 1975 concert. Holm had chosen the quartet's performance of Henry Brandt's *Bach Menagerie* for her choreography. She told me about her plans to use long blue-and-green silks manipulated from the wings by unseen dancers to create the appearance of ocean waves. She would choreograph a menagerie of sea creatures. I chose the short *Blues* by Eugene DiNovi and began to give thought to its choreography.

I remember the warm welcome I received in Colorado from Oliver Kostock. I can still see his wide grin, feel his strong hug, and watch the love in his hands as he fondled Tessie, his Yorkshire terrier and constant companion. When we got to discussing the work ahead I was surprised to hear him say, "Hanya has lost empathy with the human body." His chuckle made me wonder what I would face.

Holm was in Colorado ahead of Kostock and me directing the opera *The Abduction from the Seraglio,* and she was facing a crisis in the musical end of her dance program. Her lovable accompanist and music director, Leonard Taffs, had told her late in the game that he could not be with her for the summer. Holm's friend Bessie Schönberg, director of dance at Sarah Lawrence College, recommended someone from her staff. But Marilyn Rosenberger could not be in Colorado until the second week, so a young man from the college was hired to fill in. Poor Paul Petersky! He was a good jazz improviser, and he accompanied laypersons' dance classes at the college, but Holm found nothing in his music she could use. His clean-cut good nature somehow absorbed her rejection and abuse.

Rosenberger, when she arrived, fared little better than Petersky. She knew plenty of music theory, and she poured out her frustrations to me in talk of chord progressions and keys that she was trying in vain to suit Holm. She studied scores of Holm's Broadway shows and found melodies she thought would please. Holm heard nothing that satisfied her. She had developed a symbiotic teaching relationship with Taffs and, before him, with the brilliant John Colman. Adapting to a new musical personality was a perturbation she had not expected or wanted. She resorted to beating a drum for some exercises.

Rosenberger and I marveled at Holm's power over the students, and it is she who described the phenomenon most accurately and graphically: "Why is it that when I give my students this much [she held her hands out framing about a foot of space between her palms] they give me back this much [the space between her hands shrank to about 3 inches]? But when Hanya teaches, she gives this much [the same foot of space framed with her hands] and her students give her back THIS MUCH!" Marilyn flung her hands as wide as her arms could reach. We watched the gymnasium full of young people transfixed, some nearly catatonic with the strain of trying to do as Holm asked. Something in her manner internalized discipline. They tried because they thought they should be able to do what it was they now expected of themselves.

Nineteen seventy-five was Holm's thirty-fourth summer at Colorado College. To *Denver Post* reporter Pat McGraw she demurred about her age, admitting only to "60 plus." Actually, Holm was eighty-two. By now it was difficult to see the blond in the tip of the braid wound up and fastened at the back of her gray head. In a gesture to deny the wrinkles of age, she wore a scarf around her neck. Black tights instead of bare legs reached from under her black skirt. Her small body was straight, firm, persistent. Her attention was everywhere. She moved across the campus in slow, aristocratic determination—stopping to cluck over a patch of roses, noting the snow line on the Peak, greeting students, chatting with staff, and never arriving even a minute late for her classes.

In early years Holm had taken her meals with her staff and students in the college dining hall, but by the mid-1970s she had regular summer use of a sorority bungalow. Her son was stage set and lighting designer for the Opera Festival and for Holm's concerts, and as his three daughters became teenagers he found jobs for them in the costume shop or put them to work helping him in the scene shop. Holm kept house for her son and granddaughters, planning and preparing their meals and keeping track of the girls' schedules. Thus while she was in daily rehearsals for the opera and, after its opening, for her own choreography, she taught every day and managed a household as well. On one occasion when Kostock and I were included on a social outing with Holm, I found myself marveling to myself, "She's the youngest one among us." Her stamina impressed me, and so did her curiosity about experience.

Holm taught fewer technique classes—Kostock and I taught two each week to her one—but she took over most theory classes. With her decorative speech Holm continued to mesmerize students with talk of purpose, the need to understand, and the liberation that comes with discipline. Theory classes were like what early students spoke of as "review," in which Holm would pursue dancers' understanding of a simple mechanism—the knee bend, for instance. Sections of her technique classes were static, but she could also get the dancers moving. She roamed the space near the piano, and the muscles of her body tensed with exhortations and commands. Occasionally she moved among the dancers with sharp gestures and appeals. When the class was organized to travel across the floor, Holm always sent them across from one side only, letting them find their way around the edges of the studio to regroup at the side whence they came. Kostock used this system as well, but I used the organization of most dance teachers. I expected dancers to reverse the pattern they were doing, leading with the opposite side of their bodies as they came back across the floor to their starting positions. Holm later expressed disapproval of my method.

Students were divided into two sections for composition class, each meeting on a different afternoon once a week. Kostock and I sat with Holm to participate in the evaluations. Holm's standard introductory assignment—dating back at least to 1967—was to create three short studies using symmetrical, asymmetrical, and parallel design in duets or trios. Assignments that followed were for larger groups. After explaining each assignment, Holm let the dancers choose their groups, and then she wrote down names, making sure everyone was accounted for and committed. Her expectations of a product were palpable, and dancers worked long hours to prepare their studies. The final concert program was in the air from the first day. Once the strong dancers had been identified, they were given pieces of music—in 1975 either one of the short *Dances for Children* by Carl Orff or music by Elliott Carter in the repertory of the Saxophone Quartet.

Without Taffs, who would have improvised music for "Entrances and Exits," which by then was traditional (the press had announced it), Holm settled on some fife and drum music with which I was familiar. I sat with her over the tape recorder for long afternoons, counting out bars of music so she could plan exactly the traveling steps that would build up into the men's final cakewalk. Holm was a show-woman; every aspect of her programs received her full attention.

Although Johns was publicizing her concerts as formal events, to her students Holm spoke of *workshop*. She wanted them to understand that they were amateurs. Breaking the word down into its French meaning, she explained that they were lovers of dance. With a theater sense honed throughout many decades, Holm capitalized on their refreshing naïveté. Because students were dancing material they had crafted, it was within the range of their abilities, and they were assured—never self-conscious or pompous—in their performance.

As it had from the first year of her program in 1941, a great deal of the summer's learning occurred in the crucible of concert preparation and in that special state of being that is being connected to an audience. Townspeople who came—and more came during Johns's years as dean—especially loved the humor Holm included in each program. Well into the 1990s, Colorado Springs residents were still chuckling over moments they remembered. "Her program was what the summer was all about," one total stranger told me as I roamed the campus.

Although the general level of the students was low, there were good dancers who knew the value of doing simple things well. I saw all of them, experienced and beginning, grow as they rose to the opportunity Holm proffered. Many students from 1975 found careers in dance. As was now usual, a group came from Minneapolis. Of them, at least Wendy Ansley and Tom Kanthak have had long careers as dance educators. A group came from Sarah Lawrence College, encouraged by Bessie Schönberg. Victoria Marks is one who became a well-known choreographer. Among other students Susan Blankensop, a beginner in 1975, impressed instantly with her potential, and she became a dazzling technician of the Merce Cunningham persuasion, and Margaret Morris became a brilliant performer in the Murray Louis Dance Company. Steve Grey, a Colorado College student, and Dale Thompson, a Rutgers University dance major, both went on to dance in the Nikolais Dance Theatre—Thompson for an extended period. John Munger, a Harvard graduate, was inspired by seven summers of work with Holm to give up a career as a prep-school teacher of English and devote his life to choreography and dance administration. (I mention just a few whose careers are known to me. Appendix One lists all of Holm's students over the years.)

One of Johns's first acts as dean had been to revamp the Summer Session's weekly bulletin. A staid, stapled assortment of announcements became the *Colorado College Clarion,* an eight-page summer session newspaper with drawings, photographs, and lots of humor. "People actually read it," an old-timer told me. "We waited for it to come out."[1] As might be expected, Holm was a frequent subject of reportage and of a fair amount of the humor. She saved the *Clarion* review of her 1975 production of Mozart's *Abduction from the Seraglio.* It was written by Visiting Professor Charles Milligan, who delighted in revealing the true significance of the work—simulated group therapy. A shadowy photograph of naked men and women dancing in a circle dug at the author with the caption "Milligan conducts a group therapy session." His article explained the plot, motives, and characters in pseudo-psychological jargon. Holm penned at the bottom of the two-page review, which treated her direction favorably, "This is the college paper and the professor wants to be funny."

The cover of the last 1975 *Clarion* showed both sides of an Indian-head penny; the profile of the Indian was Holm's. Two pages of copy about her concert augmented three snapshots taken in Cossitt Gymnasium. Two showed Holm in front of a class, one of them captioned "Hanya displays drum" and the other "Hanya plays drum." The third snapshot showed me leaving the studio carrying the drum and was captioned "Claudia steals drum." Holm was not pleased.

Nineteen seventy-six was another breathless summer of performing arts activities at Colorado College. Besides opera and
dance, the New York Chamber Soloists and the Fine Arts String
Quartet performed. Theater was represented with plays by Joe
Orton and Peter Nichols. There were film series, exhibitions by
the Photography Institute and the Architecture Institute, and a
number of distinguished lectures. Four 1976 issues of *Clarion*
mentioned Holm, three for her direction of Puccini's *Gianni
Schicchi* and one for her dance concert.

Schicchi was paired with *The Soldier's Tale,* choreographed by
Gretchen Phillips, who performed the role of princess. As well as
being a prominent contributor to the dance program for seven
years, Phillips had helped Holm with opera direction. Phillips
usually intuited what Holm wanted of the singers and helped
them achieve it. Johns told me he heard Phillips tell the singers,
"Don't give her what she asks for, give her what she wants."[2] The
singers did not view improvisation as the same kind of opportunity Holm's dancers did, and they had little patience for her seemingly endless rehearsals.

Holm's choreography for the 1976 Summer Festival of the
Arts gave me one of the greatest artistic experiences of my performing career. Johns had engaged Jeanne Piland to sing Gustav
Mahler's touching song cycle *Kindertotenlieder* (Songs on the Death
of Children). Piland, a mezzo-soprano with New York City Opera, had sung during two seasons of the Colorado Opera Festival.
Holm planned the first and fourth of Mahler's five *lieder* for seven
short dancers, representing children. She worked with them several nights each week and sometimes on weekends, scolding and
humiliating them when they could not give her what she expected. Nonetheless, they felt honored to have been chosen to
be in her dance. The movement vocabulary of the two group
sections was simple, and the constantly changing groupings were
always interesting. Holm displayed her famed ability to move dancers through space.

She asked me to dance a solo for the second movement and
a duet with advanced student Terry Kaelber for the third. Holm
never completed the cycle; perhaps she felt she did not have the
right dancer for the difficult, turbulent music of the fifth song.
Holm's work on my solo began with what seemed to me unending
talk. She translated the German text over and over, explaining

every phrase many times, working out the metaphors, and expressing in other ways the profundity of Friedrich Rückert's poetry. I yearned to get started on the dance, but she talked more. When we finally went into the studio, the dance came together in just three rehearsals, and I realized that Holm had been preparing herself for the inevitability of the choices she would make. The duet was also finished in three rehearsals.

As Kaelber and I worked on the dance in the weeks leading up to the concert, Holm changed nothing and allowed us to work out for ourselves the mechanics of footing and contacts. She was unrelenting, however, with exhortations that we understand the monumentality of the poetry and music. Any hint of sentimentality in our performance was damned. I had trouble in my shoulders, and she detected wobbles in my runs, and these technical deficiencies were soundly criticized, but her exhortations to be "with it" were unremitting. If we were with it we couldn't make a mistake, she assured us.

The dances were exquisite, long phrases of great poignancy. Holm's choreography called on two influences. One was her training in German dance of expression. She used angularity, an inner muscular opposition to the direction indicated by gesture, dynamic extremes like strains upward that collapsed downward, reaches into space, and pushes against it. The other early influence Holm brought to her choreography was her love and understanding of great music.

The content of *Homage to Mahler* was grief coupled with faith in reunion after death. She insisted that this be communicated not with "mugging" but through the tension of the shapes she designed and the dynamics of the movement. Holm's aesthetic was a belief in the possibility of communicating the essence of experience through movement. This aesthetic was rooted in her artistic formation in Germany in the 1920s, and it was the dominant aesthetic of the modern dance world in which she worked when she came to the United States. It produced countless masterpieces by dance artists in the first generation on both continents, many of which have been, regrettably, lost, but some of which are still cherished in restagings and re-creations.[3]

Homage to Mahler had a life beyond Colorado. I had arranged to co-produce a concert in New York in January 1977, and I asked Holm if her solo and duet could be performed. She agreed. The downtown venue was hardly adequate for the elegance of the work, but I gave an especially "with it" performance, garnering a good review from Rose Anne Thom in *Dance Magazine* and notice from Murray Louis in one of the *Dance Magazine* essays he collected in his book *Inside Dance*.[4] The director of the Riverside Dance Festival saw the performance and was so impressed that he opened his spring calendar for a repeat of the program. A *New York Times* critic who came to the concert was unimpressed with Holm's choreography, and I felt guilty for having shown Holm's work to poor advantage.[5] Had I known then that it was the first time any of Holm's Colorado choreography had been shown in New York since 1943, the year she was scared off by the reception of *Orestes and the Furies,* I would have been nearly suicidal.

Holm and I never discussed the bad review. She allowed me to perform her work again, involving herself in rehearsing it and supervising the construction of a new costume. From 1975 onward the Don Redlich Company performed dances Holm was creating for them, and through Redlich's efforts Holm's name was reunited with those of the "Big Four" who had remained in the concert dance world when Holm turned to Broadway.

In 1977 Colman was Holm's music director again. He was a vibrant colleague, and he became a friend. He made the air in the dining hall ring with the crack of his laughter and never passed up an opportunity to let a difference of opinion become a test of wits. He had an excellent eye for movement. He could become testy if he detected a teacher using an inappropriate meter for some phrase or exercise; I still remember one such sword-crossing experience with him. His first class with Holm put her in excellent spirits.

Performing arts offerings of the Colorado College Summer Session escalated again that year, and the opera season was especially resplendent. Mozart's *Così fan tutte* was followed by Stravinsky's *The Rake's Progress.* Then Johns and music director Donald Jenkins pulled out all the stops and programmed Verdi's *Aida.* Holm did not direct but choreographed *Aida.* She used dancers from her program for the many movement opportunities. Don Borsh, Stephen Koester, John Munger, Eddie Martinez, and Keiko Romaguera were cast as the gods Osiris, Anubis, Seth, Thoth, and Horus. Others were used as Priestesses, Acrobats, Entertainers, and Helpers. With all her resources focused on *Aida,* Holm did not choreograph for her final concert. She chose material from composition classes and staged her traditional opening "Demonstration." My dance, *A Suite for Players,* closed the show.

Holm and I had many conferences in New York about my role of Isis, and Holm gave great attention to the costume. Frank Garcia, who executed costumes for Nikolais and Louis, met with her many times over fabric selection, color, construction, and design. Building on a white Egyptian sheath, he created the many-colored wings Holm wanted. Another feature of the costume was that my breasts were bare.

The choreography did not come easily. Tall, good-looking Don Borsh, dancing Osiris, and I sat for hours with Holm while she told and retold the story of the sibling gods. None of us found the kinetic imagery the dance needed, and each rehearsal was a struggle. I was unable to satisfy Holm with a backward-curving walk she wanted. The duet became tight and muddy. Nonetheless, I was looking forward to performing it, and my injury was tragic for me and for Holm. While rehearsing my own piece for the dance concert, my knee snapped. By evening it was the size of a pineapple and unable to bear any weight. *Aida* was days away. Our student Rachel Brumer was my size, and she was capable. Borsh and Holm taught her the dance. Of course the breasts had to be covered. In my opinion Brumer gave a fine performance, but Holm was glum, disappointed more, perhaps, because of the costume modification than by the performance. Typical of her, she was especially solicitous of me, gracious to an extreme, but we both knew I had let her down, and neither of us expected I would return to Colorado the next summer.

The injury was not the only reason, for we had had two little disagreements. Holm had complained that I expected the dancers to "reverse" rather than run to the other end of the gym to repeat their material from the same side. I heard her say sotto voce that I was ruining "Entrances and Exits" because the dancers would not have the habit of running around the back of the stage to prepare for their next entrance. We also had an uncomfortable exchange over a rehearsal schedule.

Some of Holm's most loyal students were enrolled in 1977. Articulate John Munger, with his wife, Katie Schmitz Munger, kept a daily journal. Here are some jottings of an enthralled young couple whose lives were changed because of Holm:

Analysis of the walk forward and backward with special attention to the problems of going backward. Analyzed and practiced transferring of weight from foot to foot while walking in first [position]. Great attention paid to straightened legs. It was an exhausting class in a way that only Hanya can create. She insists that you bring all the energy and that you invest completely in order to get anything out of it.

Hanya worked on two things: isolation and vibration. We isolated the hips, the ribs, the knees. We did a long vibration in place which included a sternum arch and some weight shifts. Across the floor we used the internal vibration while walking with isolation, walking fast and smooth and then built up to the Hanya chug [a fast sideward galloping with the dancers leaning forward, fists pumping up and down at knee level].

Hanya started her part of the class by talking for about fifteen minutes. The key was the idea of *control* vs. ignorance and habit. She said that she sees many habits that we aren't even aware of, and that's deadly—you have to know what you are doing and you must have decided to do it that way. She talked specifically about control as it pertains to verticality. She said that the "plumbline" doesn't exist—you can't point to where it is since every time we move it shifts. She said that we have 4 sources of energy: the spirit, the mind, the heart, and the body, and that we have to keep track of all of them all the time. . . . Across the floor: Walk forward. She nailed the class for stepping "on" the beat instead of stepping "with" the beat. She said that John Colman creates a pulse and we don't step *on* that. We create our own and through human will, the two coincide.

The Mungers also recorded some of Holm's pithy statements, calling them "tidbits."

- Dances without purpose have false starts and stops.

- Showing off the body or the emotion is tacky.

- Loud landings kill the magic of elevations.

- Faces are delicate.

- Simplicity is a delight.

- If you try to put your head through the wall, you're the one with the bloody head and the wall doesn't care.

- An atom takes up very little space but it can set the world afire; so can you.[6]

Although Holm's words puzzled and amused some dancers, Munger represents those who recognized the quality of mind behind her words. Princeton graduate Jim Kelly, a student in the same period as Munger, is another. After summers in Colorado, he moved to Minneapolis and danced in the Nancy Hauser Company before he chose another path and went to law school. After securing a job in a leading banking firm in New York, he renewed his acquaintance with Holm, visiting her often with his wife and young son: "I was always taken with her far-ranging mind. She was curious about every topic, astronomy, geography, any subject. It was a genuine mind, a very impressive mind."[7]

Glen Tetley, one of Holm's students who achieved international recognition, also revered her intelligence. Tetley had embarked on a crash course to acquire technique to take advantage of opportunities that came his way as a beginner just after World War II: "Hanya could explain the basics to me, the *plié*, for instance, in a way I could understand. I had done a pre-med degree before the war. Hanya knew anatomy. She could explain how the opposing muscles worked. She made it possible for me to understand all the other training I was getting."[8]

Although some students were able to articulate reasons for their worship of Holm, many did not know exactly why they loved her. In 1976 some students lit what Kostock called a "bonfire of discontent." A litany of complaints about classes—they were too large, there were no levels, we don't get enough combinations, and so forth—ended with "we don't get Hanya often enough." It amazed me (it was real amazing to Kostock) that some students complained about Holm's choices of structure and about Holm's teaching, yet they wanted more of her. I pointed out the apparent contradiction to a leader of the protest, and he blurted out, "She's so cute!" Clearly, learning in Colorado centered in Holm, the person.

The dance boom that began in the 1960s crested by the mid-1970s, and 1975 was the last year Holm's enrollment exceeded 100. It remained high for some years and then went down gradually. One student was a close observer of the last sixteen years of the program. Edward Martinez, a young man from Colorado Springs, studied with Holm every summer from 1967 to 1983. Martinez saw that "Hanya was losing it with the students by the mid-1970s."[9] A cataract operation had not turned out well, and

Holm had to wear painful contact lenses and glasses as well. With amazing willpower she was able to disguise the resulting tunnel vision and dizziness. Johns created a special scholarship for Martinez to be Holm's escort. He took her shopping and ran errands. As her eyesight and strength declined further, he walked with her across campus. He was at her side at all times by 1981.

Martinez told me twenty years after my last summer with Holm that she had formed the idea that I wanted to take over her school. A lack of deference and circumspection on my part, an innocent exuberance for a job I liked, had been misread. "This is my school," she huffed to Martinez. My relationship with Holm had been complex since 1959, when I took some class at her studio on the corner of Forty-ninth Street and Sixth Avenue in Manhattan. It had taken resolve to stand up to her criticism. I now wonder if the anger I saw her direct toward students in Colorado masked a deep anxiety about failure. Her early life in Germany had been difficult, and her successes in the New World had not been won easily, but she had refused to capitulate. Perceived failings in others may have threatened her assurance.

"Hanya couldn't delegate," Martinez observed in 1996. Her inability to delegate and compromise undoubtedly contributed to the anguished ending of her program in 1983. There were sensational years before then, however. Johns made special arrangements for the summers of 1979, 1980, and 1981. He spent lavishly to capitalize on the presence of a colorful national figure whom he admired and the community adored. In doing so, he built a palace in which the Hanya Holm–Colorado College Summer Program of Instruction and Dance Production would expire.

Chapter Nine
HOLM ON THE RANGE AND OTHER AMUSEMENTS
1978–1981

"*For her dual contribution to modern dance* and the American musical theater as pioneer, choreographer, superb teacher and inspiration for three generations of dancers," Hanya Holm was honored with the 1978 Capezio Dance Award in New York in April. The award, given by the maker of dance shoes and dancewear, is one of three major national awards for contributions in dance. Holm received the other two slightly later.

The curtain came down on the first night of Holm's 1978 Colorado concert to a special award ceremony in which Holm was presented with a Medal of Distinction in the Fine Arts from the city of Colorado Springs. Thus her thirty-eighth year in Colorado began and ended with national and regional recognition. Cooperating with the mayor and city council to make the local award was the Colorado Springs Dance Theatre, a nonprofit organization that was bringing as many as three dance companies to the city each year. A regional dance audience had been built and sustained.

To commemorate her Capezio Award, Holm sat for a photo session with dance photographer Jack Mitchell. Dressed in her black teaching costume, she sat in a simple wood chair with her chin tilted up and neck stretched to obviate the need for a scarf. She laughed with her teeth parted and her small fists in a clench of delight and affirmation, her pose and animation belying her eighty-five years. Two of Mitchell's photographs graced the program cover of the 1978 Hanya Holm Dance Ensemble concert.

Holm was, as always, a headliner on the college's performing arts roster. Summer Session dean Gilbert Johns relished his role as impresario. Orchestrating the summers' arts activities had become his greatest delight and principal occupation. Much like the great Russian American impresario Sol Hurok, he coddled his artists, treating them to postconcert dinners at the best Colorado Springs restaurants. He gave parties with fine cuisine and wine. Spending went unchecked because there was slight connection between Summer Session and the regular college administration.

Total college summer enrollment during the 1970s was high, and as many as twenty-six programs were offered. Dance continued to enroll more students and account for more credit hours of instruction than most others, generating almost twice as many tuition dollars as were needed to pay the direct costs of the program. As well as admiring Holm as an artist and educator, Johns must have been grateful to her for the financial base she provided. Letters of contract show that throughout his administration he rewarded Holm with salary increases and increased scholarship money for her to distribute. A typical letter began, "It is with great pleasure, gratitude and fondness that I will confirm our arrangements concerning your participation in our summer program."[1]

In 1978 Holm's final concert was low-key, a breath before the frenzied last three years of Johns's administration. He ratcheted up his summer performing arts festival in 1979 and gave it the name "Estimable Festival Estival." The *Gazette-Telegraph* answered the inevitable questions about the title: "First, it's the tongue-in-cheek creation of Gilbert Johns, dean of Colorado College's summer session. Second, and more important, it's the most unusual and elaborate musical summer to be presented at the college—perhaps in the city—in many years."[2] Johns centered Holm in much of the publicity he generated. "Hanya was great copy," he said. "She gave reporters a combination of transcendental statements on dance and good German kitchen philosophy."[3]

In 1979 Johns's roster of concerts ran the gamut from erudite (Mozart, Mendelssohn, and Schubert by the Primavera String Quartet and Babbitt, Schönberg, and Wolf by soprano Bethany Beardslee) to tongue-in-cheek ("Irish, Not Stewed," an Evening of Ancient and Modern, Authentic and Show Business Irish Songs with Louisa Kerry). The eleventh annual trivia bowl was squeezed into a swollen schedule of events that concluded with Holm's concert. Holm also agreed to an evening of reminiscence during which she showed film clips of Mary Wigman and films of her own 1963 choreography for *Dinner with the President.*

It had taken the New York journal *Dance News* a year to print a feature celebrating Holm's Capezio Award, but it was a long, thoughtful article—"Hanya Holm: Young Octogenarian." Writer Tobi Tobias, who visited Holm in Colorado, quoted her about the wonders of the environment: "In such a tremendous, open universe you must find out exactly where you stand." Tobias analyzed the connection between Holm's concert career and her work on Broadway. Recognizing Holm's flexibility of mind and inquisitiveness, she wrote, "It is not as astonishing as sober-minded modern dance acolytes of the time found it, that she would have turned her choreographic talents to musical comedy." That turn, which had always been glorified in Colorado, was now accepted by a respected national critic. Many in the concert dance field had castigated Holm for turning to commercial theater, but the Capezio Award, given for her dual contributions to modern dance and musical comedy, had vindicated her choice.

Tobias watched Holm teach and noted the philosophical speech with which Colorado Springs readers were familiar: "With the physical energy and prowess of the body, there must be in proportion energy of the mind, thinking, and of the heart, feeling, emotion, if you will, but never emoting. When you dance I want to see all three energies, a whole person. Be *with* it." Tobias's article ended:

> She has a sturdy belief, confirmed perhaps by her own experience, in the power of will. "I see the body is riddled with fear, but not determination," she observed to a soloist with haunted eyes. "Don't say, 'I can't.' Say rather, 'I won't,' and then I believe you. But if you want to, you can. You just have to find the way to do it. And there comes the hard work and the changing that you are so terrified of. But if you will accept that, no, you cannot move Pikes Peak perhaps, but you can surely shift smaller hills."[4]

As the finale to the Estimable Festival Estival, Holm offered a restaging of *The Insect Comedy,* seen in Colorado in 1947 as *And So Ad Infinitum* and produced in New York by José Ferrer, bringing Holm praise for her choreography just after she had triumphed with *Ballet Ballads* and before she choreographed *Kiss Me, Kate.* Holm reminded readers of the *Colorado Springs Sun* that *The Insect Comedy* is a story about the forest life of fascist ants, capitalist dung beetles, hoarding flies, lovesick butterflies, an idealistic chrysalis, and a hobo who moves away from the teeming city to find those miserable creatures: "There is such a thing that people are different. Each one is doing what they think is right in their own realm, and it makes for differences, that's why we have society."

For her new production Holm enlisted the help of the Colorado Springs writer Lillian McCue to shorten and update the script. McCue changed the high English of the original translation from Czech to colloquial speech, making its delivery easier for student performers and more comprehensible for audiences. Holm explained her strategy: "We try to keep it light as we can. You laugh at the exaggeration, you see the ants' idiotic stubbornness of blind obedience. It becomes ridiculous, not 'ha ha' funny, but hits some irony." She explained the significance of the role of the chrysalis, originally played by Sharry Traver and now by William Harren:

> The chrysalis constantly speaks to prove her existence—"I am born, I will be born, I have great ideals! Something should happen to the world. Just wait until I come!" It is the promise of idealism versus materialism. She has the potential to lift Mr. Average out of the average, out of the stillness of being frozen, of having blinders on. But the chrysalis dies immediately after emerging from its cocoon. Unless you nourish it, and give it life, idealism dies.[5]

Holm helped her audience to appreciate the social satire of *The Insect Comedy.*

Student Stephan Koplowitz performed the part of a blind ant, a disappointment to him because it involved little more than counting. He was surprised that Holm dedicated so much time to a project that involved little dancing, but he admitted that she did not start rehearsals until well into the summer and that she worked swiftly. Koplowitz, who became a prominent choreographer, had a love-hate relationship with Holm. He tried to fasten on positive aspects of his two summers of study with her: "It was all business out there. There were lots of beginners—I was a beginner—but she was not about beginning. She assumed everybody was into it."

Koplowitz analyzed the mechanics of Holm's success and why students strained to win her approval: "She was withholding. She didn't give praise and she was tough, but she was one of the three women pioneers of modern dance, and she happened to be standing in front of you . . . people wanted to touch history. She was not user-friendly, but no one doubted her stature." Pressing Koplowitz, I was surprised to hear rather negative statements coming from my genial friend: "The program didn't have any diversity; it was monolithic, boring. There was no curriculum, and people saw through that. The only thing that kept it interesting was Composition."[6] Koplowitz admitted that it was important to his career that Holm took his early efforts at choreography seriously. Although by 1979 some students were having trouble with Holm's instruction, aspects of her program worked magnificently. The wheel of autonomy and authority, perhaps squeaking and lurching a bit, gave dancers a great woman's attention to their efforts and inspection of their choices. And, Koplowitz assured me, there was a lot of fun to be had along the Front Range.

Holm preserved a letter in praise of her 1979 concert from Glenn E. Brooks, dean of the college: "My family and I attended your presentation last evening, and once again we realize how lucky we are to have you with us at Colorado College. I want to thank you now, as I am sure I will thank you many times in the future, for your distinguished contributions."[7] Brooks's remark about the future can be read as a gracious gesture toward Holm's eighty-six years. The community of Colorado Springs and Holm had reached such a level of codependency that neither could envision an end to their relationship.

Johns capitalized on the community's rapture with Holm in 1980 by making the entire Summer Arts Festival a celebration of her fortieth anniversary. He called it "Holm on the (Front) Range." It was a high-profile affair. "I had the cover of every magazine in the state," he boasted. As with her twenty-fifth anniversary year in 1965, the 1980 Summer Arts Festival brought to the college prominent dance companies directed by former students. In addition, Walter Terry, who had won the Capezio Award a year after Holm, came from New York to lecture on "200 Years of American Dance." Jack Mitchell honored Holm with an illustrated lecture, "A Photographer Looks at the Performing Arts." William Bolcom, composer and pianist, and Joan Morris, mezzo-soprano,

paid tribute with a recital, "The Golden Age of Musicals." Violin-
ist Sergiu Luca and pianist Anne Epperson played "A Celebration of Music Inspired by the Dance." Dancing tributes were given
by Nikolais Dance Theatre, with two performances and a
lecture-demonstration; Murray Louis Dance Company, also with
two performances and a demonstration; Nancy Hauser Dance
Company, with a performance; and Don Redlich Dance Company, with a demonstration, a concert, and a program shared
with Holm's students.

Johns left ample proof of the pleasure he took in putting the
summer together in an appointment letter to Holm dated March
5, 1980.

> The Hanya Holm 40th Anniversary Dance Festival promises to
> be as spectacular an artistic event as Colorado has ever seen.
> One can't help but think of the Christo curtain that was put
> across the [mountain] pass at Rifle, but then that only lasted for
> a few hours and I expect that we'll all be flapping in the wind for
> eight weeks. Your appointment to the 1980 Colorado College
> Summer dance faculty will be as:
>
> Visiting Professor of Dance and Director of the Dance Program.
>
> Your duties in the dance program are, of course, well-known to
> you: namely to plan, direct, teach and choreograph in the most
> successful and important dance program in the world.

He named her staff, including not only her teaching assistants
but all contributors to the festival.

Colorado Springs' merchants saluted Holm with advertisements in a festival booklet that doubled as a program for each
event. Capezio Ballet Makers bought the back page to congratu-
late Capezio Dance Award recipients Hanya Holm and Walter
Terry. The booklet contained a rapturous essay by Colorado novelist Lillian de la Torre: "Forty years ago, Colorado captured Hanya
Holm. For keeps." She described Holm as independent, fearless,
full of fresh curiosity, and richly creative, "as ever she was." De la
Torre ended her essay, "And Colorado, she's ours!"[8]

There were countercurrents to the community's delirious
admiration, however. The college administration had begun to
question Johns's overspending, and during discussions about it
Johns threatened to resign on more than one occasion.[9] A decline
in Holm's health came at a time when university dance departments, which supplied most of her students, were focusing on

professional preparation. Many young dancers craved a prowess they interpreted in ways Holm and her staff did not. Furthermore, Colorado College was about to acquire a new president and a new performing arts faculty, none of whom were acquainted with the legacy of Holm's long association with the college and the respect she enjoyed in Colorado Springs.

Holm's Colorado audience knew nothing about these festers. The press turned out exuberant features and interviews that reflected the community's pride in its summer resident artist. Holm took advantage of several interviews to express gratitude for the support the college had given her during the lean years of World War II. The region had been a sanctuary from rough times, a place for joining with other artists who shared common aims and goals, she said. Thurston Davies lived in spirit in Holm's words. She probably felt once again cherished as Davies had cherished her when he included her in his ambition to build a center of culture in the Rocky Mountain region as "the torch of the spirit" was passing from Europe to America.

Johns, like Davies, put his summer arts initiative in a global context; his letter of contract had laid out Holm's duties toward "the most successful and important dance program in the world." The jocular tone of his hyperbole notwithstanding, he believed in Holm, and after the vicissitudes of the next years he remained her admirer and friend. He visited her in New York, and his sons paid calls. In 1984, when she won the Scripps American Dance Festival Award, he traveled to Durham, North Carolina, to be with her on that auspicious occasion.

During her festival year, Holm again explained to the press that her teaching was aimed at getting students to solve their own dilemmas, understand themselves, and decide what principles they espoused. She compared the foibles of her current students with those of forty years before. Dancers in the 1940s, she remembered, were overly emotional, and she had difficulty protecting them from their abandon. "Now it's mechanization," she fretted. She claimed dancers of 1980 were afraid to use their emotional power. They were afraid to be themselves and covered their fear by decorating themselves with movement. She aimed for a balance.[10]

The visiting choreographers reveled in the means she had given them to be themselves. Most identified Holm as a philosopher rather than the initiator of a method or technique. Nikolais reversed the terminology, however, and argued that Holm's was the only true technique in modern dance, the only training that proceeded from principles that could be built upon. Hauser turned discussions to the concept of space. Hauser had been particularly influenced by Holm's fascination with circles and curves. She said Holm's architectural theories of space were an unlimited source of inspiration. Awareness of invisible but knowable trajectories that connected dancers to other dancers made the stage space alive and electric. Space was their partner, Holm often told students.

The full series of concerts that comprised the festival "Holm on the (Front) Range" was well reviewed in Colorado. Glenn Giffin, dean of the region's dance critics, came frequently from Denver. Giffin was well-read in dance history. He compared Nikolais's trademark marriage of costumes, props, and masks to transform dancers into denizens of another world with the work of Mary Wigman and Oskar Schlemmer in Germany. He found Nikolais's work manifested their shared theories with the greatest success.[11]

During the festival Holm was busier than in most summers. She taught, supervised the preparation of student work for her final concert, choreographed for student dancers, and worked on a major piece for the Don Redlich Company. In New York that spring she had begun choreography to Maurice Ravel's *Sonata for Piano and Violin*. During the summer she finished two sections of the three-part dance that would become *Jocose*. Redlich's company performed it frequently after its full premiere in 1985, and it had another life in the 1993 program of Mikhail Baryshnikov's White Oak Project, touring the world to acclaim. Giffin fastened on the word *sly* in his review of the work. With "sly innuendo," he wrote, she showed that "there is fancy as well as fact to the art and science of dance."[12]

All the embellishments of "Holm on the (Front) Range" were making the 1980 Colorado College Summer Session a financial disaster.[13] Johns must have known that, but he was unable to restrain either his enthusiasms or his wit. Looking ahead, he allowed himself two inches of copy in the program book:

> 1981 will be Hanya Holm's 41st consecutive summer at Colorado College. Hanya will continue her legendary Dance School at the

College. The Summer Program in the Arts will continue to make use of her genius. Modesty, sanity and self-preservation restrain us from promising you a program for 1981 that includes the Alwin Nikolais Dance Theatre and the Murray Louis Dance Company and the Nancy Hauser Dance Company and the Don Redlich Dance Company and Bolcom and Morris and Walter Terry and Jack Mitchell and Sergiu Luca and Anne Epperson. However, we will promise you a Summer Program in the Arts once again marked by quality, unusual programming and high entertainment value. Thank you for celebrating Hanya's 40th with us. It has been a summer to remember.

The following March, Johns's letter of appointment began, "Now that we have the 40th Anniversary behind us, we have no choice except to arrange the 41st Hanya Holm Anniversary Festival." He once again laid out her duties "in the most successful and important Summer Dance Program in the world." Johns reminded Holm that they had already agreed that she would be a major contributor to a Bartók Centennial Festival, working with Don Redlich and his company on choreographing Bartók's *Cantata Profana*. Redlich and his company would be in residence for the last four weeks of the summer, and he would teach, along with Holm and Kostock. Hauser and Kostock would assist Holm for the first four weeks. Holm's salary was again increased.

Sixty-four dancers registered for instruction in 1981, down just seven from the preceding year. Twelve of the most prominent students from 1980 returned, probably on scholarship. An entire concert was given over to student work; "This Is My Work" was its empowering title. Holm's *Cantata Profana* premiered another night in a concert with the Don Redlich Company. The 1981 festival, modest after the gargantuan "Holm on the (Front) Range" festival, was substantial nonetheless. Johns named it "Bartók and Other Amusements." He continued to treat his artists well, although more of them were local. As he had done several times before, he offered his resignation when budget discussions came, and this time the college accepted his offer. The 1981 Summer Session was his last as dean, and "Bartók and Other Amusements" was the last festival he directed.

Choreographing *Cantata Profana* was a big undertaking; some observers compared it to Holm's masterpiece, *Trend*. Like *Trend* and her 1943 *Orestes and the Furies*, it used professional soloists and a chorus of student performers. Also like *Trend* and other large-scale works Holm had created, it employed a large stage set of platforms, stairs, and ramps, designed in this case by Holm's son, Klaus. A high platform stage left connected with other structures stage right to form a bridge that had symbolic meaning. Holm moved dancers in the space under the bridge, as well as in front of the construction and on the stairs. Joan Finkelstein, who took the lead part, ran, leaped, and posed on the highest towers.

Bartók had based his cantata on a Romanian folk ballad in which he heard universal themes of passage into manhood through search for the ideal. Unwieldy scoring for full orchestra and double chorus made it necessary to use recorded music for the twenty-minute work. Redlich was at Holm's side throughout the project, and during interviews he often fleshed out his mentor's ideas, explaining that the stags (some dancers wore antlers on their heads) represented freedom of the individual and release from the bounds of traditions.

Cantata Profana was not an unqualified success. Irene Clurman of the *Rocky Mountain News* found Holm's treatment overly literal:

> Movement carefully echoed the words of the Cantata, with its emphasis on lunges and muscular arm sweeps. Holm adeptly moved a huge cast up and down a stage set of steps and platforms, and the lighting by her son Klaus Holm beautifully sculpted the herd of horned animals into a coppery mirage. However, the work's simple blocking and mime too often made the effort look like an elaborate school pageant.[14]

Giffin refrained from evaluative statement in his review but instead pointed to Holm as one of the few choreographers who had the "bigness of conception" to understand choral movement. "It's something of a lost art in dance circles," he wrote.[15]

Although Holm had risen successfully to the challenge of monumentality many times in her career, *Cantata Profana* was an undertaking too ambitious for the eighty-eight-year-old master with failing eyesight. Eddie Martinez, the student hired by Johns as Holm's escort, described 1981 as the summer Holm's limitations forced her to depend on others as never before: "Don became her cane and her eyes; he really finished the piece for her. I was an unofficial rehearsal assistant, so I saw it happen. There was one day when it all stopped. Don took over. She couldn't see."[16]

Martinez was piqued at not having been chosen to perform in *Cantata,* but that slight does not change the awe and gratitude he feels for Holm. He credits her with his happiness in life: "She made you responsible for yourself. She helped you persevere, she made you go beyond what was not important to get to where you had to be." Martinez confessed that Holm was sometimes hard on him and that at times he blamed her for his confusions: "She could be destructive, but it was a way of making you grow up. I truly love her for that." This often overweight, openly gay young Latino, marginalized by society, adores Holm for having taken him seriously and for helping him to cross a frontier of maturity and self-knowledge.

In 1981, his fourteenth summer with Holm, Martinez saw the unraveling of her program. A newly hired college dance instructor hoped to give classes of her own during the summer, and a territorial dispute erupted instantly. Cossitt had been Holm's for forty summers, and sharing it was a notion out of her ken. Kostock and Martinez watched one of the new professor's classes, and Kostock charged that she was teaching a style to people who had not danced before. It was a sinful pedagogic strategy to Kostock, who believed Holm's teaching, and his, was innocent of style. Meanwhile, some students were criticizing Kostock's classes as mere exercise.

Martinez was aware that problems that should have been addressed were not: "At the end Hanya had no idea of what the body could do. There should have been some intervention, but Hanya wouldn't have allowed it." It did not help that *Cantata Profana* was less than a triumph. The newly appointed president of Colorado College, Gresham Riley, gave an after-theater supper to honor Holm, Redlich, and his dance company. Riley; James Malcolm, the new director of theater; and the new dance instructor were undoubtedly cordial, but it is logical that they questioned the place of Holm's program in their vision of performing arts at Colorado College.

Chapter Ten

CURTAIN
1982–1983

Seeing a declining enrollment, hearing complaints from students, and wanting a summer dance program that integrated with the year-round program he wished to build, President Gresham Riley, who took office in July 1981, summarily dismissed Holm after the 1983 summer. Almost everyone connected with the college agrees that Riley mishandled the situation. Colorado Springs historian Judy Finley is one who recognized that Riley misjudged the strength of local opinion: "He was new, and that one act put him on the wrong foot with the community. It took a long time for him to regain the trust of those who cared about the arts."[1]

An institution that had helped to contribute a regional modernism to dance, prepared one of Broadway's best choreographers, helped make the dance boom possible, launched careers, inspired thousands of dancers, and educated many thousands to modern dance died an ignominious death when Riley sent his new summer school dean, Elmer Peterson, to New York to give Holm the news. The dance world was outraged, and Holm was devastated. Bessie Schönberg, herself an immigrant, was sensitive to the special rootless feeling of that status, even after many years: "It's hard to describe how tough that can be, losing your home."[2]

Vitality had been injected into Holm's summer program with the hiring of Don Redlich as a teaching assistant in 1981 and the installation of his company on campus for part of each summer.

Redlich, whom Holm considered her artistic inheritor, was known nationally, and he was a master teacher in the same pedagogic style as Holm. A possible solution to the impasse between the college and Holm would have been to involve Redlich in a larger way in the instruction. Redlich claims Peterson raised the issue of a larger role for him at Colorado College and that he would have been willing to discuss it but that Peterson never brought the subject up a second time.

Peterson had been associated with Summer Session for a number of years as director of the French Institute, and he was a respected and admired faculty member. His March 1982 letter of appointment to Holm lacked the flamboyant touches of Johns's letters, but it was just as cordial: "Seeing you and your students here and just being close to the great educational experience they receive is, and always will be, a great boost to me."[3]

Thirty-five students registered in 1982, and their work in choreography class filled a program at the end of the session. Redlich and his company gave a concert on July 8, the first event of an abbreviated Colorado Summer Festival of the Arts. The company premiered *Ratatat,* the most recent work Holm had choreographed for them, and also performed Holm's 1980 Ravel ballet, *Jocose.*

The summer before, Redlich and his company had been in residence for the final four weeks to prepare *Cantata Profana* for the Bartók Festival, and Nancy Hauser had taught the first four weeks. Hauser's daughter Heidi says her mother and Redlich bargained for the opening weeks of the summer because preparation of the students' final concert had become trying. Redlich won the bargain in 1982 and 1983.

Another inside story, this one painful for me to relate, is that by 1982 Oliver Kostock felt betrayed by Holm. Eddie Martinez heard him complain, "You're always introducing Nancy and the great Don, but you never bother to mention me—after I've stood by you and helped you all these years."[4] Conscientious, supportive Ollie was loved by many students, but his classes were coming in for increased criticism. Among Holm's papers are notes he made while watching Hauser's classes, suggesting that he was aware his teaching needed refreshing.

James Malcolm recalled his first years as head of the Department of Theater and Dance at Colorado College. He says the

Holm productions he saw were superb: "I never felt that her work suffered because of her age." Malcolm insisted that he had no part in the decision to end Holm's program after the 1983 summer, but he supported Riley's move because he was disturbed, first, that Holm's program had no connection to his department, second because it was not paying its way, and only last because Holm was elderly.[5] Others at the scene believe Malcolm directly or indirectly instigated the dismissal. He had reshaped his department, firing some faculty and making others uncomfortable enough to resign. Norman Cornick, Holm's student in 1954, whom she had recommended to the college as head of dance, implicated Malcolm in the firing. He stayed at the college until 1984, but, he said, "we had a terrible time after Malcolm came in."[6]

Holm's forty-third summer at Colorado College began as all the others, with expectation of hard work, learning, growth, and fun. The Don Redlich Company danced on June 24, four days into the summer session, once again performing Holm's *Jocose* and *Ratatat* along with two works of his own. During the last four weeks of the summer session, Hauser assisted Holm and Kostock with instruction and with preparation of the Hanya Holm Dance Concert of student work.

The student body of twenty-nine began the concert with solutions to Holm's by now traditional assignment in symmetry, asymmetry, and parallel design. The most substantial group of studies was called simply "Spaces." Holm assigned stage designs to advanced students, giving them floor plans and models prepared by her son, Klaus. Holm was revisiting with her students the architectural editing of space that had been of keen interest to her throughout her career. In German-derived dance theory, the human figure is in constant dialogue with its spatial environment. Every gesture and move reflects the dynamic of space, and as dancers respond sensitively to space they take on resonance and quality. When space is reconfigured with columns, ramps, platforms, other stage devices, and light, the interrelationship of dancer and space becomes insistent and powerful. Many of Holm's classes in technique, improvisation, and composition were aimed at sensitizing dancers to their place in a spatial universe of forces and possibilities.

As the summer of 1983 progressed, a camera crew was on campus capturing material for a video documentary, *Hanya: Por-*

trait of a Pioneer. A testament to Holm's entire career, it aired on Public Television in 1985.[7] Footage from the 1983 summer in Colorado showed Holm leaning on her cane in the doorway of Cossitt Gym watching a class taught by Kostock and also speaking to a group of students sitting at her feet. The video ended with a diminutive black-clad Holm, feet well turned out, strolling across campus away from the camera flanked by two young people. The unmistakable message of the last image was of the eternal renewal of dance. Outtakes from the taping in Colorado give views of Holm and Redlich watching and commenting on student compositions. They also contain interviews with students, who beam with enthusiasm for the training they are receiving. The camera was kept running through a party in Holm's bungalow celebrating the end of shooting. The film crew paid homage to Holm with a mixture of awe and familiarity. Clearly, they had enjoyed their assignment and had grown to love the woman.[8]

The finished videotape contains archival images of Holm and her company dancing on the Colorado College lawn in 1941. Unwittingly, therefore, the producers, Marilyn Cristofori and Nancy Mason Hauser, framed Holm's forty-three-year partnership with the college. When they captured Holm in 1983 they did not know, nor did she, that President Riley would cancel Holm's program and that 1983 would be her last summer of dance instruction and production. After Riley made his move the dance world erupted in protest, and the Colorado press and public denounced his decision.

Peterson was embarrassed about the role he was forced to play as the messenger of bad news. He remembered that as soon as he became dean in 1982 he had tried to work it out so that Holm could leave gracefully. He is certain he had more than one conversation with Redlich about taking on a bigger role but that Redlich declined: "I think he was a little afraid of Hanya; everybody was a little afraid of her. Maybe Gil [Johns] was a little afraid, too. After the 1980 summer, the Front Range Festival, it would have been a perfect time for her to bow out but somehow Gil couldn't arrange it."[9]

Redlich saw that the program was in trouble because of the number of students. His respect for Holm, whom he calls "the lady," restrained him from taking a proactive role: "With the lady, you just don't take over. All she did was ask me to teach. The invitation came from her, and since we had her dances, of course I wanted to do that."[10] Like adult children who misread the moment at which parents, who have been their caregivers, require care themselves, Redlich and the college were paralyzed. It is true that at ninety years of age, Holm was still a force. She may have diminished in physical size, but her personality and determination had not shrunk. She was quick-witted and an excellent conversationalist. Her stamina awed everyone.

In New York Holm was teaching at the Nikolais-Louis Dance Lab and at the Juilliard School. As in Colorado, her enrollments were dropping, yet she refocused many young lives in both schools. An experienced French student was brought up short by Holm at the Nikolais-Louis school. "She put up a mirror," Luc Peton said. "She demanded me to know why I was there and why I was dancing." He credits Holm with his rededication to dance and with a willingness to yield to new ways of moving.[11]

Some Colorado students in 1983 were not serious, but, as always, many had life-changing experiences. One was Valda Craig, who pursued her fascination with Holm to a thesis that earned her an M.A. from George Washington University. With a good ear she captured Holm's verbal style in notes that reveal the colorful, ever-changing images Holm used to convey her message about dance and life.[12]

- There is no short cut—wishful thinking will not do.

- Don't be afraid to grow up. Once you get over the hump, there is so much inspiration. It is wonderful.

- Don't kill the flame, emotion—control it at your will—but it must be there. Have some passion. Want something.

- Let your little fire come up—don't dampen it. Learn to master it.

- Are you pleasing someone who asks you to do something? It's not enough.

- Don't give up. Don't get discouraged. The bubble can burst. It can happen. It might be tomorrow, it might be next week. It might get worse. Don't be afraid—you'll get through.

- Have responsibility. Nobody wants to hold you back, destroy, criticize to make you feel bad, but some live in delusions of grandeur that have to be broken.

- Get all these stimulations together—the miracle happens. A new form, a new experience happens, an amalgamation process. Something strange happens, something floats in and it becomes real—it's elusive. Allow, so the little miracles can happen.

- We use the physical, we are matter. We have a relationship to time and space but it is not just physical education, it is art.

Colorado College's decision to fire Holm became known to the community by means of an article in the *Gazette-Telegraph* in September. The writer implicated Peterson in the decision and quoted him about the difficulty of the choice and of substituting any other program for Holm's. Peterson asserted that the decision was made solely on the basis of enrollments and explained that enrollment in all arts programs had been declining as young people turned to more practical classes like basic economics and computing. Others at the college and in the Colorado Springs arts community had their say. All were saddened and distressed by the rupture, but some agreed that times do change. Others found the college's decision abrupt and unexpected. One woman who had been a student of Holm's was quoted: "Hanya is just the master. She's generations beyond most of us."[13]

Editorial comments quickly followed. Former Summer School dean Gilbert Johns, now critic-at-large for the *Gazette-Telegraph,* headed his weekly piece "Dance Suffers a Discouraging Week." He reminded his readers of their privileged position as spectators at the world premiere of *The Ballad of Baby Doe,* which Holm had directed at Central City Opera House in 1956, and of the many operas she had directed for the Colorado Opera Festival in Colorado Springs. He reminded them of the forty-three years of exciting, inventive dance she had shown them and of the four major new works she had recently choreographed: "I must not give the impression that the curtain has fallen for Hanya Holm. She is alive and well in New York, witty, feisty and wise."[14]

Glenn Giffin's denunciation of the dismissal and how it had been accomplished was strident: "Forty-three years down the drain. A 43-year loyalty dismissed." Giffin had talked with Holm by phone and quoted her: "It was very abruptly, very ugly done. . . . It was not friendly. There are ideals established with the amount of years. That is a life-time. One doesn't just say 'close the curtain.'" Giffin also phoned Riley, who asserted that Holm's dismissal in no way indicated a change in the college's attitude toward the arts. He cited waning interest and enrollment and his desire to establish a closer tie between the academic program and the Summer Session.

Giffin questioned Riley's explanation:

> Now what seems clear in all this is that the Colorado College administration has no idea of Holm's importance in the dance world, or it wouldn't so lightly throw away that 43-year association. The real reason seems to be mere academic convenience. It has, furthermore, seriously called into question the college's support of the arts, despite president Riley's disavowals of the same. When a major creative artist (she choreographed "Kiss Me, Kate" and "Camelot" on Broadway, her "Trend" is a part of all modern dance historical accounts, her teaching of Alwin Nikolais, Murray Lewis [sic], Don Redlich and other notable dance-choreographers) is turned out so abruptly, the dance and art world sits up and takes notice. The notice is not to Colorado College's credit.[15]

Giffin penned a note to Holm on a computer printout of his story: "Sheer stupidity must be substituting for intelligence."[16]

Letters of outrage flowed in to Riley. Martha Hill, who had brokered the liaison between Holm and the college and was now director of the Dance Division at the Juilliard School in New York, expressed the shock in the dance world: "One can only conclude that Colorado College has seceded from the ranks of those institutions which support the best in American education for the arts and, further, has little realization of the supreme value of its most creative major figure, Hanya Holm." Margery Turner, who had been Holm's student in Colorado in the 1940s and now headed the Dance Department at Rutgers University's Mason Gross School of the Arts in New Jersey, told Riley he had created a nationally recognized error in judgment. Carolyn Brooks, a dancer in Holm's company in the 1930s, asserted that Holm was not diminished by Riley's action, but Colorado College had been. Holm's supporters within the college and in Colorado registered disgust with Riley for not having consulted anyone, least of all Holm herself. Invidious comparisons were made with past administrations.

Martha Wilcox, an important agent in the success of Holm's early years at Colorado College, wrote what she called "a sizzler." The body of Riley's reply to these letters ran as follows:

I regret that you have interpreted in the way you have my decision to cancel the Hanya Holm Institute of Dance. Contrary to
what you may believe, I value very much the numerous and
historic contributions made by Hanya to both Colorado College
and the world of dance. By means of an honorary doctoral
degree as well as an entire summer's College-sponsored celebration (1980) of the fortieth anniversary of Hanya's Institute,
Colorado College has publicly acknowledged the value it places
on Hanya's artistry.

James Malcolm also received mail. From the West Coast came
stinging criticism of the college's action and of a job description
Malcolm had circulated for new dance faculty.

For a college dance program to "let go" a person of her rank in
the world of art is shameful. Holm might have informed you that
anyone claiming to be able to fill your job description—able to
teach technique at all levels, ballet, jazz, modern, history, composition, music—will teach *all* of them poorly, and that any dance
program that offers training based on this kind of administrative
ignorance is fraudulent.

Early in November Riley wrote to Holm. He said he had heard
from friends of both Holm and the college about the disappointment and unhappiness his decision had caused, and he had
learned that Holm felt betrayed. He apologized for any personal
hard feelings created by his decision: "It was never my intention
to cause an affront. I, as well as the entire Colorado College community, value and appreciate the many contributions which you
have made to both the College and the world of dance." He repeated the list of tributes the college had given her, and he ended
by hoping he and his wife could meet with Holm during a visit
they were planning to New York to see if better feelings about
the matter could be developed. Intuition tells me the meeting
did not take place.

In the early 1940s Holm had made uncertainties about an
unknown art form evaporate. With momentum from Thurston
Davies's vision for a center for the arts in the Rocky Mountain
region, audiences had accepted modern dance along with modern music and exhibitions of new visual art. Colorado audiences
were shown serious choreography that validated their craving for
high modernist connections. In stepping nimbly across a frontier
of regionalism Holm had satisfied eastern critics' unease about

her nationality. By adapting to collaborative art making she made an enduring contribution to musical comedy, an American folk art.

With insistent reiteration of a philosophy of responsibility and control, Holm escorted students into territory that linked dance practice to the construction of personal identity. Her students experienced frustration and shame, and they joked about her and collected "tidbits" and "Hanyaisms," but all of them grew under her tutelage. During four decades of teaching in Colorado, Holm used the exhilaration of movement to take young people beyond the frontier of what they expected of themselves. Through them, the Hanya Holm–Colorado College Summer School of the Dance continues to propel America's dance culture.

Chapter Eleven
AFTERMATH

Elmer Peterson wrote to Holm in a grieving tone after he returned to Colorado from his mission in New York: "You have been the life and soul of the summer program here and this is a case in which no sort of transplant or substitution will match up to the distinction which you brought for forty-three years."[1] His words were prophetic. With ground cleared for Colorado College to design a summer dance curriculum that would integrate with the academic program, become solvent, and bring young dance vision to Colorado, all three missions failed. An instructor of dance for children in the college's adjunct program, one of the long-time teachers who ran afoul of James Malcolm, said, "They threw her out because she wasn't attracting enough students, and then they couldn't attract anybody—not anybody."[2]

There was no summer dance at Colorado College in 1984 or 1985. Then the college organized a three-week workshop co-directed by its faculty and Bill Evans, a nationally prominent choreographer and teacher based in the West. The project ended in 1987. Not until 1996 did it seem the college would have a national summer dance presence again. The Daring Project, a ballet group in which Lindsay Fischer had a role, was in residence for two summers, and that segued into a summer Ballet Intensive that attracts scores of young people who receive thorough classical training. Riley dismissed Holm in part because he saw no connection between her institute and the college's Department of Theater and Dance, but the Ballet Intensive does not relate to the college's program, which is focused on modern dance.

Colorado Springs did not forget Holm. The press gave ample and gleeful coverage to her selection in 1984 for the Samuel Scripps American Dance Festival (ADF) Award. She was the fourth recipient of that prestigious national award in dance. Stephanie Reinhart, codirector of ADF, asserted that the selection of Holm in 1984 was not connected to the slight she had endured from Colorado College the preceding fall: "We were recognizing her lifelong contribution to modern dance."[3] The citation read as follows:

> To Hanya Holm, dancer, choreographer, educator, whose originality, vitality, and uncompromising individualism has made an indelible mark on the history of American modern dance.
>
> Though trained in her native Germany, Hanya Holm embraced her new country, bringing to it Rudolf von Laban and Mary Wigman's concepts of time, space and energy, which she molded to fit and enhance the American spirit. With her passionate dedication to the art form, she has affected the lives of generations of dance artists.
>
> The lyricism, wit and humane social commentary that illuminate her modern dance choreography continue to profoundly affect audiences, critics and young artists. As one of our most original choreographers, her fresh vision has also inspired important innovations and brought new energy to the Broadway stage.
>
> Her persistent idealism, artistic innovations and achievements as a teacher and choreographer continue to be an inspiration to us all.

A full evening's program in Holm's honor at ADF included the premiere screening of excerpts from the video documentary *Hanya: Portrait of a Pioneer* and a performance of *Jocose* by the Don Redlich Company.

When news reached Colorado of Holm's death on November 3, 1992, the lengthy *New York Times* obituary by Jennifer Dunning circulated among Holm's friends, and Colorado newspapers published their own obituary with photographs.[4] The *Gazette-Telegraph* identified Holm first as founder of the influential Colorado College Summer Dance Program, then recounted her achievements in modern dance and her status beside Martha Graham, Doris

Humphrey, and Charles Weidman as one of the "Big Four" who taught at Bennington. It listed *Trend* along with her major Broadway successes. The newspaper numbered at 5,000 the students who had studied under her at Colorado College. The unknown reporter was not restrained from remembering some of the "pithy instructions" for which her students remembered her. "Feel it, children, don't schlep it" was one. The article quoted several of Holm's statements of dance philosophy: "Dance is not a temporary thing. It is sacrifice. Pursuing dance . . . is really a conquering of the body in relationship to the art you serve."[5]

Holm reached the age of ninety-nine, and instead of the usual memorial service, a one hundredth birthday party was organized in New York on March 3, 1993. We knew Holm had wanted to live to be a hundred and that her other great wish was to have had a great-grandchild. On what would have been her one hundredth birthday her oldest granddaughter announced that she was expecting a child; it was a birthday gift nonpareil.

Many people with connections to Colorado attended the crowded birthday celebration. Louise Kloepper came from Wisconsin. Glen Tetley spoke, as did John Colman. John Munger traveled from Minnesota to read some of the "tidbits" he had recorded in his journal.[6]

After birthday cake and a champagne toast, Don Redlich played a brief tape recording of his mentor speaking about the importance of sticking to one's principles. The voice of the diminutive, uncompromising woman who had been our taskmaster and our amusement brought the community of celebrants together. Silently, we united in resolve to improve our lives through self-knowledge and purpose. We understood that the principles to which Holm held herself and all of us accountable were not rules and regulations but tools of understanding with which to manage life. Everyone agreed that Redlich had chosen a perfect remembrance of a remarkable individual whose revelatory teaching will always inspire dancers and their audiences.

STUDENTS ENROLLED

IN THE HANYA HOLM/COLORADO COLLEGE SUMMER DANCE PROGRAM,

1941–1983

1941 Dorothy Alexander, Shirlee Brimberg, Nadine Buck, Bluma Caldwell, Frances Davies, Gladys De Berry, Deborah Froelicher, Hilda Gumm, Dorothy Guy, Alice Hayden, Elizabeth Hayes, Daisy Hedges, Jinx Heffelfinger, Vickery Hubbard, Patty Kerr, Eleanor MacDougall, Aileen McAllister, Nancy Martsolf, Rossa Blair Mosher, Elizabeth Nichols, Catherine Proudfoot, Mary Lou Randall, Cathryn Risch, Betty Sheffer

1942 Mary Washington Ball, Shirley Broughton, Martha Childress, Deborah Froelicher, Berte Gray, Ida Howland, Eileen Keegan, Marjory Kinney, Lucy Lampkin, Mary Louise Lee, Sally MacGregor, Dorothy Madden, Louise Musman, Jean Reed, Barbara Ripley, Kathleen Schroeder, Margaret Lee Thomas, Marion Yahr

1943 Dulcy Amter, Tanya Bogoslovsky, Lois Daubert, Frances Davies, Norma Davies, Evelyn de la Tour, Teresa Gushurst, Ruth Jacobs, Mildred Kaeser, Patricia Kerr, Carolyn Meyer, Elizabeth Mitchell, Mary Morison, Margaret Murphy, Louise Musman, Edna Jan Nesbitt, Adele Novotny, Nora Ravsky, Vera Sieradz, Joy Sylvester, Theodosia Wons

1944 Dulcy Amter, Hortense Bienstock, Joan Brodie, Mary Carrigan, Lillian Covillo, Frances Davies, Marilyn Frederick, Mary Geppert, Beatrice Gottlieb, Maizie Gusakoff, Marie Hanse, Batya Heller, Ruth Jacobs, Mildred Kaeser, Anna Lee Manson, Jessica Nixon, Florita Raup, Jeanne Roberts, Jeanne Rogers, Dorothy Sellner, Vera

Sieradz, Virginia Stoeckle, Alice Taylor, Patricia Urner, Frances Vanderkooi, Eunice B Veazie, Doris Wilk, Helen Young

1945   Mary Adair, Louise Anawaty, Lena Belloe, Louise Carroll, Eileen Fezler, May W. Fitzpatrick, Clara C. Haley, Virginia Harris, Tilla Hevesi, Caroline Jackson, Joan Kruger, Marian Levinsohn, Frances Lutes, Anna Lee Manson, Elizabeth Mason, Betty McCord, Bernice Mendelsohn, Lois Miller, Phyllis Ongley, Florita Raup, Mary Ellen Rouse, Edna Schiff, Elizabeth Schneider, Margaret Thomas, Margery Turner, Linda Verrill

1946   Leah Aberson, Georganne Abramson, Bebe Alpert, Rebecca Balaban, Fred Berk, Katya Berk, Harry Bernstein, Sonia Borenstein, Louise Carroll, Norman Chelquist, Barbara Chifos, Ruth Collins, Margaret Covert, Thelma Dodson, Lois Ensign, Ann Gibson, Betty Grathwohl, Nancy Gregson, Eleanor Hamilton, Martha Howe, Philomena Joy, Patricia Kerr, Oliver Kostock, Ruth Kriehn, Joan Kruger, Dorothy Latimer, Marjorie Lehman, Paula Levine, Jacqueline McMahill, Catherine Mendum, Margaret Mercer, Lucette Moulin, Ada Mounton, Dorothy Mueller, Maxine Munt, Leonora Nelson, Christine Neubert, Elizabeth Nichols, Nora Nugent, Mary O'Connor, Katherine Peters, Elva Peterson, Barbara Quirin, Myta Rom, Eya Rudhyar, Elain Sarnoff, Jean Schweitzer, Madelaine Schwer, Jean Sharp, Diana Smith, Eve Smith, Glen Tetley, Patti Utgard, Barbara Voichick, Vivian Watkins, Marian Watson, Chen-Hua Yang

1947   Antoinette Beck, Warren Boudinot, Dorothy Briant, Elizabeth Brooks, Margaret Bryan, John Castello, Penelope Corya, Diane Cotton, Jane Denham, Marian Edmonds, Evelyn Freed, Donna Glick, Elaine Golden, Dorothy Gotterer, Sybil Gramlick, Gertrude Green, Sara Jarvis, Miriam Jerabek, Oliver Kostock, Esther Kraft, Laura Kratz, Rosemary Kriegel, Joan Kruger, Charles Loubier, Kathryn Lowry, Jacquelyn McMahill, Mary Miller, Jack Moore, William Murphy, Patti Musson, Edna Nahon, Anne Neprud, Mary O'Connell, Friedann Parker, Margaret Pataky, Anita Siegel, Mildred Solez, Lene Struckmeyer, Julia Sumberg, Glen Tetley, Sharry Traver, Barbara Voichick, Helen Waskowich, Marian Watson, Elisabeth White

1948   Sarah Aman, Ursula Angell, Patricia Barrett, Marian Bassett, Antoinette Beck, Marc Breaux, Cornelia Cerf, Nancy Connable, Calvin Cook, Jackie Cooper, Leo Duggan, Barbara Dwyer, Joy Eckley, Janice Ford, Jean Harper, Alice Horne, Ruth Irish, Carl Jones, Mildred Kaeser, Oliver Kostock, May Marcus, Elisabeth Meyer, Mary Miller, Zane Miller, Randy Moman, Jack Moore, Jeanne Murdoch,

Patti Musson, Anne Neprud, Francene Nethercut, Della Parker, Barbara Pfeiffer, Suzanne Pressey, Jeanne Riley, Nancy Robb, Hannelore Robinson, Hanna Rubin, Sonia Savig, Peggy Schaper, Mimi Schoemberger, June Sebree, Richard Shade, Pearl Shinn, Patricia Shuey, Stewart Snyder, Mildred Solez, Shirley Spachman, Audrey Swanson, Glen Tetley, Margery Turner, Carol Walgenbach

1949   Kathryn Adams, Marshall Amerman, Myrtle Anderson, Bladys Bailen, Marian Bassett, Joan Castator, Deborah Choate, Colleen Cook, Patricia Cooper, Mary Crosby, Blaine Dixon, Melvin Fillin, Joseph France, Murray Fuchs, Murray Gitlin, Karen Goldberg, Hayden Griffin, Frederic Handschy, Calvin Holt, Martha Howe, Joan Jones, Mildred Kaeser, Elisabeth Landi, Celia Lischner, Frances Lober, Mary Lundbeck, Billie Mahoney, Margaret Miller, Randy Moman, Marilyn O'Neill, Arlene Ongley, June Owen, Donald Redlich, John Reese, Jane Reynolds, Maxine Rice, Faye Richards, Nancy Robb, Sylvia Senter, Marjorie Spitznagel, Alfred Srnka, Betty Toman, Linda Verrill, Janet Westlund, Claire Williams, David Wood, Doris Yurstenberg

1950   Donald Brown, Barbara Byrne, Marjorie Calhoon, Judith Callaway, Zora Cernich, Katherine Cockey, Grace Cohen, Martha Cornick, Doris Coulter, Jeff Duncan, Melvin Fillin, Sara Fitspatrick, Jay Griffith, Phyllis Hamilton, Patricia Harley, Judith Haskell, Raymond Huff, Mildred Jentsch, Leonore Landau, Martha Lyon, Beverly Malstead, Mary Miller, Evelyn Nash, Catherine Planche, Elizabeth Reel, John Reese, Dorothy Robinson, Julie Sanford, Edith Schelberg, Christine Schumacher, Jane Shank, Patricia Sullivan, Thomas Turner

1951   Rebecca Ball, Edward Bedno, Paul Chambers, Charlotte Cole, John Copland, Rhoda Dentan, Jeff Duncan, Sonia Easterly, Melvin Fillin, Donna Gillett, Katherine Haak, Virginia Howe, Anne Ingram, Natalie Jaffe, Rogermae Johnson, Clifford Kirwan, James Metcalf, Patti Musson, Shirley Nelson, Karla Olsen, Patricia Piepho, Grace Rapaport, James Ray, Alvin Schulman, Patricia Scott, George-Jean Sperry, Marilyn Wood, Jean Zahorsky

1952   Mary Allen, Fannie Aronson, Jane Austin, Katherine Brown, Grace Butler, Kaliope Candianides, Paul Chambers, Jeri Crowther, Martha Culbert, Sonja Easterly, Joanne Finkelor, Naomi Goldberg, Vera Goldsmith, Faith Gulick, Julie Hamilton, Jane Hauser, Waltrand Herrmann, Mary Hooper, Barbara Horgan, Katherine Hutchinson, Clifford Kirwan, Loretta Li, Virginia Liese, Caroline Loring, Barbara Mills, Judith Philipp, Janice Rabinowitz, Geraldine Ratliff, James Ray, Donald Redlich, Jeniel Reeves, Ann Ritterbush, Joyce

Rutherford, Joy Sallick, Penelope Simmons, Maxine Solow, Jere Stevens, Lois Tomlinson, Barbara Turley, Beverly Webster, Carolyn Wilcox, Marilyn Wood, Doris Wuestenberg, Persis Zentmire

1953   Pat Ablett, Fannie Aronson, Peggy Barclay, Mildred Barnhart, Barbara Bench, Kay Brown, Kaliope Candianides, Norma Carter, Paul Chambers, Ann Choate, Lois Christianson, Ivy Cole, Royce Colon, Jeri Crowther, Diane Diener, Anna Fulton, Beverly Gee, Leon Gersten, Betty Godwin, Geulah Greenblatt, Zuzana Gyulai, Dolores Hammond, Helen Harris, Virginia Harris, Elaine Hess, Doris Hysler, Mary Josephson, Mildred Kaeser, Clifford Kirwan, Roberta Laughlin, Arthur Leath, Virginia Leise, Marilyn Maycock, Peggy Merle-Smith, Barbara Mills, Ellen Moore, Marquel Pettit, Jim Ray, Donald Redlich, Betty Sawyers, Don Sobieske, Jere Stevens, Janie Vaughn, Jo Zaccaro

1954   Patricia Ablett, Margaret Barclay, Nancy Berquist, Evelyn Binz, Anne Bogart, Margaret Bolton, Jerry Bywaters, Susan Cary, Norman Cornick, Elece Cox, Jo Crail, Yvonne Crittenden, Denise Dewan, Margaret Fox, Joanna Gewertz, Howard Girvin, Barbara Grant, Julie Hamilton, Teres Hancock, Janie Harnack, Virginia Harris, Mildred Hobbs, Florence Howard, Linn Howard, Jeanne Hurley, Marie Hysler, Dorothy Jarnac, Joyce Jensen, Marilyn Jones, Sue Katzenber, Bruce King, Melvin Kingston, Delores Koster, Joan Lenivson, Virginia Liese, Maxine Loeserman, Katherine Mackenzie, Gayle Madson, Dorothy Maxwell, Erin McQuaid, Valda Mock, Sylvia Mocroft, Bernadine Muller, Shirley Nelson, Rita Parr, Joan Penman, Marianne Pettit, Rita Poehling, Mary Reardon, Marlene Saldin, Dora Sanders, Ruth Schubach, Sophie Sieniewicz, Martha Spann, James Stasheff, Jacqueline Thom, Wylma White, Martha Williams, Jane Woodbridge, Dora Wylie

1955   Patricia Abbott, Olga Acar, Pamela Battey, Dorothea Britt, Juanita Broberg, Janet Brof, Sonia Bronskin, Anna Brown, Betty Brown, Kay Cardwell, Paul Chambers, Lee Cooper, Geraldine Culp, Barbara Farr, William Faulkner, Nancy Gardner, Howard Girvin, Mary Heworth, Laramie Hitchings, Judith Jaffa, Joyce Jensen, Joy Kenneway, Clifford Kirwin, Stanley Klir, Carol Kluss, Jo Lechey, Marilyn Maycock, Valene Mayrick, Carol McClug, Joyce Millward, Jean Morrison, Currie Pederson, Bette Phillips, Marina Sandaval, Lunora Sauders, Lena Simpson, Stanley Sobiesko, Mary Stukey, Charlen Thomas, Mary Von Wippel, John Waller, Carolyn Way, Florence Wehrli, Robert Wiegand, Mary Willis, Tommye Yates, Sharon Yenney

1956   Pamela Battey, Clare Becker, Margarette Bobo, Mrs. Robert Bonio, Katherine Brown, Julia Carver, Yvonne Crittendon, Geraldine Culp, Evelyn de la Torre, James Dromie, Mary Emmert, Mary Fairchild, Florence Farrell, Jo Fields, Releigh Fleming, Elsbeth Geisert, Lynn Gerstenfeld, Toni Glatter, Ingeborg Gupler, Lynore Hamilton, Sally Hanson, Mary Harrington, Ray Harrison, Ann Hersey, Valeta Hershberger, Helen Keith, Rosemary Kilgore, Carol Kluss, Margaret Land, Ralph Lee, Marilyn Leibovitz, June Lelodia, Mario Lelodia, Katherine Litz, Philip Massina, Evelyn Minks, Marilyn Muegge, Sally Nash, Alexandra Nelson, Pola Nirenska, Rita Parr, Martha Patterson, James Ray, Don Redlich, Cheryl Richardson, Ann Robertson, Nola Ruspini, Marina Sandoval, Lathan Sanford, Joan Setzer, Norma Spieth, Jean Stearns, Peggy Stone, Frances Taylor, Janice Tenney, Lee Wagner, Susan Watson, Judi Wisdom, Jane Yosepian, Mary Young, Olga Zampos

1957   Ann Amter, Laura Archer, Barbara Bierner, Loabelle Black, Betty Bryant, Paul Chambers, Barbara Davidson, Kenna Dayton, Terry Dolson, James Drowns, Alida Dureau, Chloe Ellis, Carol Fried, Emily Gamboa, Ursula Gray, Karen Grimmett, Lawrence Hayward, Karen Hobbs, Linda Howard, Margaret Hyden, Cynthia Jones, Normandie Karr, Clifford Kirwan, Greta Knight, Jeannine Koeher, Michael Matohie, Michael Maule, Hatty Mitchell, Hans Muller, Christine Nicoloff, Nona Paulsen, Arlene Pelagrove, Donald Redlich, Marian Reynolds, Catherine Richards, Thais Roberson, Ruth Rose, Thomas Ruh, Joan Rundell, Nola Ruspini, [?] Rust, Susan Salem, Lathan Sanford, Joan Schwartz, Esther Shulman, Harriet Slaughter, Sally Snead, Marjorie Stuart, Amanda Taylor, Vera Thalrose, Harriet Vermilya, LeeAnn Wagner, Judith Willis, Evelyn Woerheide

1958   Ann Amter, Florence Armstrong, Julie Axelsen, Robyn Baker, Toni Beck, Harriet Berg, Barbara Bierner, Mary Billehus, Peggy Blackman, Molly Boswell, Ray Braussard, Anne Brown, Terrance Brown, Larry Burgoon, Paul Chambers, Paula Chartok, Sandra Cohen, Dan DeNett, Linda Duboff, Dick Foose, Sarah Ford, Carol Fried, Maybelle Garrard, Patricia Grover, Judith Hagan, Nancy Hall, Lela Harkrader, Elizabeth Harris, Jane Higgins, Sandra Hopkins, Janet Hoyman, Marilyn Itz, Mary Josepheson, Normandie Karr, Dorothy Kiester, Clifford Kirwan, Jeannine Kocker, Karen Larsen, Jere Lowry, Molly Lynn, Bernadine Madole, Edythe Marrow, Dorothy Masursky, Michael Matchie, Edilia Maytorena, Mary McNamara, Jefferson Miller, Mary Montague, Carol Muir, Teressa Oliver, Hal O'Neal, Susan Perkins, Jayne Poor, Elizabeth Rasumny, Don Redlich, Beverly Rhodes, Ann Ritterbush, Nola Ruspini, Nancy

Rydman, Neal Scheenreck, Anne Sillman, Susan Smith, Martha Sutcliffe, Margaret Swindell, Jimmie Talcott, Vera Thalrose, Nancy Thysell, Jacquelyn Toman, Donald Walker, Linda Walker, Suzanne Weininger, Sally Wengert, Helen Weser, Judith Willis, Ann Willumsen

1959   Mary Anderson, Shirley Appleman, Laura Archer, Homer Bailey, Robyn Baker, Marcia Barratt, Elizabeth Bramen, Ray Broussard, Kathrine Brown, Larry Burgoon, Bessie Caldwell, Norma Carter, Paul Chambers, Lucinda Childs, Joan Cooper, Barbara Davidson, Fern Davies, Irene Dean, Barbara Dilley, Diana Dunagan, Sandra Faxon, Claudia Gitelman, Alice Hankins, Claudia Harding, Janet Harns, Elizabeth Harris, Sally Hatfield, Lawrence Hayward, Richard Hittson, Judith Hogan, Jane Howbert, Elizabeth Jones, Clifford Kirwan, Jeannine Kocker, Mary Luck, Julia Maguire, Carol McCue, Roberta McCue, Annelise Mertz, Jefferson Miller, Jane Morrow, Beverlee Patton, Gretchen Petty, Marya Randall, Don Redlich, Rose Rochman, Sharon Rushing, Nola Ruspini, Rosalind Schmuts, Marja Seron, Judith Skwiot, Lois Slaughter, Geraldean Smith, Sally Snead, Don Steele, Vera Thalrose, Joyce Trisler, Peggy Turner, Robert Windsor, Sandra York

1960   Laura Archer, Kay Ashcroft, Julio Axelsen, Susan Biageier, Evelyn Boggs, Shirley Boyce, Elizabeth Braman, Jeannine Bramwill, Carol Brooks, Mary Brown, Larry Burgoon, Sarah Burnhum, Joan Carey, Diana Dunagan, Sue Farmer, Nancy Gitbert, Claudia Gitelman, Richard Goldberger, Barbara Griffith, Patricia Grover, Elizabeth Harris, Delia Helstrom, Elizabeth Hiller, Billie Hutchings, Sally Inge, Mary Kerns, Mary Kohlhaas, Karen Laruch, Linda Laurence, Ruby L'Herisson, Molly Lynn, Julie Maguire, Anna Marquez, Patricia McConnell, Cynthia Molkenbur, Janet Nielsopp, Katheyn Posin, Lynne Powell, Mary Quinn, Albert Reid, Sharon Rushing, Iris Selimann, Josephine Semotan, Patricia Speir, Denise Stephens, Richard Toews, Robert Twitchell, Deborah Waters, Toby Wiley, Robert Windsor, Lucretia Wray

1961   Virginia Adams, Gloria Armstrong, Kathryn Aschenbrener, Ina Begerow, Susan Brehm, Karin Bundesen, Mitchell Byron, Julie Chatham, Louella Clennen, Grace Collier, Ferial Deer, Joan Ditmere, Deveda Erikson, Joan Ernst, Phyllis Haskell, Heidi Hauser, Nancy Hempill, Roberta Herbison, Sandra Horton, Sally Howell, Billie Hutchings, Jan Ihrie, Rebecca Jenkins, Heather Jensen, Kathryn Karipides, Barbara Karl, Theodore Katz, Patricia Kinnel, Julia Maguire, Diane Mazanek, Patricia McConnell, Myra McIntyre, Mary McKinley, Judith Osborn, Beverlee Patton, Lorraine Powlus, Jane Robbins, Emily Roberts, Barbara Rutherford, Maynard

Sebranek, Sharlyn Smoot, Mary Sweazey, Nancy Topf, Robert Twitchell, Joan Vosbrink, Margaret Wabb, Sheila Wheeler

1962   Anne Averbuck, Wilson Barrilleaux, Susan Bass, Marjorie Boetger, Seece Boyce, Rima Brodie, Beverley Brown, Jane Brown, Winifred Burgman, Julian Burwell, Christine Clark, Lillian Cochran, Carole Cody, Elissa DeWitt, Vicki Dils, Susan Dunn, Charles Everett, Robert Fletcher, Trudi Galloway, Mary Guinn, Heidi Hauser, Ruth Heike, Martha Hixson, Loren Johnson, Rosalie Jones, Donna Kerness, Marilyn Lowen, Marsha Mayer, Lorene McAfee, Nancy McDonald, Pricilla Miller, Julie Philpott, Jean Pinkerton, Lois Rathborn, Robert Roth, Linda Scarbrough, Judith Shelby, Betty Shuford, Susan Sindall, Spencer Snyder, Charlotte Stone, Karen Stronach, Robert Tandy, Harriet Ulmer, Toni Urso, Jeffrey Way, Sandra Williams, Alcine Wiltz, Joan Wohlstetter, Barbara Zakarian

1963   Wilson Barrilleaux, Seece Boyce, Madeline Bryant, Mary Byrum, Paul Chambers, Christine Clark, K. Dunkley, Mary Emanuel, Charles Everett, Antoinette Fanning, Dodie Foland, Gayle Frankes, George Freelove, Elizabeth Harris, Joan Harrison, Robin Inman, Judy Johnson, Betty Kalezi, Patricia Kallien, Dwan Kaskay, Clifford Kirwan, Nancy Kolodney, Margaret Kurz, Judith Morton, Harry Mossman, Alice Olds, Pamela Olson, Linda Osborne, Eleanor Otto, Patricia Peterson, Terrie Reeves, Myra Rollins, Elizabeth Sacks, Carole Sahlstrand, Gretchen Schneider, Otho Seward, Pamela Smithlin, Margot Starr, Gail Turner, Merrily Vincent, Barbara Waddill, Diane Walker, Mary Woodcox, Regina Wray, Sally Yengo, Barbara Zakarian

1964   Judith Annis, Nina Bellak, Donna Busby, Beverly Cook, Chardelle Cooper, Shelia Corbitt, Jacquueline Davis, Sheila Donaghe, Claudia Dryer, K. Dunkley, Charles Everett, Mary Gallagher, Nancy Green, William Hansen, Donald Heinselman, Marianne Holstrom, Lucy Huddell, Diana Johnson, Sharon Jones, Patricia Kallien, Carol Kidwell, Lothian Langhorst, Charlene McDonald, Nina Pauff, Lauren Persichettit, Roberta Ramstead, Cecelia Rose, Diane Rose, Diane Sandys, Gretchen Schneider, Samuel Tapia, Alta Townes, Susan Webb, Mary Woodcox

1965   Janis Ansley, Wilson Barrileaux, Karen Bender, Joan Brown, Madeline Bryant, Frances Buchner, Cynthia Carlisle, Mary Cerney, Ida Chadwick, Carleton Chard, Beverly Cook, Diantha Davis, Veronica Demsey, Leonore deSylva, Susan Duling, K. Dunkley, Greta Flodquist, Mary Freese, Judy Friedlander, Erlinda Gonzales, James Hathaway, Heidi Hauser, Thomas Hustvet, Alan Iverson, Patricia Kallien, Carol Kidwell, Margaret Kurz, Irina Lasoff, Alice

Leib, Alma Martinez, Diana McKelvey, Marilyn Moran, Gale Ormiston, Linda Osborne, Lauren Persechetti, Susan Richenthal, Gretchen Schneider, Sam Tapia, Gail Turner, Catherine Vandertuin, Emily Wadhams, Penny York

1966   Jane Abramson, Roberta Armstrong, Joan Baker, Mary Bird, Chris Brandt, Lucy Brooks, Ruth Clugston, Dianne Damro, Nadine Emerald, Penny Fray, Alice Frost, Gilda Gant, Nancy Goss, Fleus Greene, Marsha Hale, Sandra Harris, Susanne Haynes, Jim Julian, Gary Masters, Jean Milane, Kathleen Morris, Judith Novak, Enid Obee, Pamela Olson, Ruth Onato, Milani Pirrie, Pamela Pleasant, Alice Reyes, Patricia Rogers, Linda Ruzich, Kathleen Seymour, Judith Sonnek, Kathy Stelly, Josephine Sutlive, Catherine Vandertuin, Cornelia Von Oettingen, Patricia Wehner, Regina Wray, Arlene Zuefle

1967   Mary Anderson, Rachell Astian, Betty Bowman, Cathryn Cornelius, Saundra Dugan, Esther Geoffrey, Phyllis Grant, Kalah Guller, Holly Hajjar, Toby Hankin, Suzanne Hellmuth, Barbara Joyce, Maureen Kinney, Denise Lapaglia, Sheila Laughlin, Daphne Mantis, Joseph Martinez, Sandra Massour, Drelene Matich, Helen McCandless, Patricia McConnell, Barbara Miller, Deborah Miller, Jerald Miller, Karen Mueller, Teru Osato, Linda Osborne, Gerald Pearson, Suzzanne Pierre, Jane Quentin, Alice Reyes, Natalie Richman, Cherly Rogers, Robert Scott, Prudence Serl, Tahlma Shingerland, Beverly Sonen, Shelly Stark, Karen Steele, Terry Stoner, Susan Suhrke, Toni Thomas, Melissa Upton, Kathleen West, Sara Wiener, Marie Winckler, Corrine Windus, Regina Wray, Ruth Young

1968   Gail Abbott, Peggy Anderson, Charlotte Barker, Margo Bassity, Virginia Bingham, Alexa Brill, Jane Brown, Judith Carnell, Mary Cerny, Diana Cole, Evelina Dearborn, Sandra Dexheimer, Trena Folkers, Nancy Foster, Marie Foyse, Penelope Fray, Gayle Graff, Harriet Hanger, Jane Huffman, Elaine Ivaldy, Jorja Jahrig, Eilif Jespersen, Lillian Koppin, Susan Krohn, Frances Labarre, Denise Lapaglia, William Marsh, Joseph Martinez, Janet Monninger, Joan Muckenhirn, Dolores O'Connor, Tricou Petit, Gretchen Phillips, Natalie Richman, Helen Roberts, Robert Ross, Mary Safire, Joanne Saltzman, Mary Sebastiani, Doris Smith, May Steels, Gail Turner, Carol Wilkinson, Nancy Wulk, Earlaine Young

1969   Christopher Burnside, Diana Cole, Eileen Danville, Nancy Davis, Linda de Lissovoy, Sarah Fincke, Carolyn Foyse, Joan Friedman, Joan Frisius, Connie Hamner, Suzanne Helmuth, David Herz, Charlotte Hildebrand, Patricia Hodges, Edward Holloway, Anne Howbert, Paul Jarocki, Jean Jennings, Robin Johnson, Susan

Kaufmann, Sharon Kelly, Susan Lane, Carol Lo Castro, Debra Loewen, Sarah Mangelsdorf, Carol Manners, Tempe Manners, Joseph Martinez, Elaine McHugh, John McVay, Creighton Miller, Kathleen Morris, Dolores O'Connor, Gretchen Phillips, Gwenda Pollack, Syby Reese, Alita Robnak, Joseph Rocha, Gladys Roman, Susan Sandler, Jessie Sayre, Marchia Schramm, Frederick Sherwood, Susan Smith, Varya Soudakoff, Cinde Switzer, Edward Sydow

1970   Karen Arlen, Charlotte Barker, Pamela Barnett, Sonja Berthrong, Kathryn Biesanz, Jeannine Bramwell, Lise Brinton, Barbara Burnham, Penelope Burr, Patricia Callahan, Joan Dake, Rosanne Drillich, Claudia Edwards, Cathy Einhorn, John Fischer, Carolyn Foyse, Deborah Fritz, Nancy Frost, Joanne Gabbs, Elizabeth Garren, Amy Grossman, Jacqueline Hand, Barbara Hanson, Martha Harpstrite, Mary Hauserman, Jeana Hibbard, Karen Holt, Ann Hooker, Mary Horner, Marya Huseby, Sheri Ille, Elaine Ivaldy, Ellen Klein, Gwenda Klein, Gabrielle Lawrence, Isabel Lee, Kristin Lindley, Marianne Livant, Eddie Martinez, Patricia Massoth, Kathleen Morris, Sandra Mulford, Joan Munday, Alice Niemeyer, Dolores O'Connor, Teru Osato, Judith Page, Patricia Petzar, Gretchen Phillips, Deborah Pleskow, Vicki Pollack, Sylvia Poole, Mary Powell, Allison Price, Deborah Quinn, Judith Ragir, Nancy Rhea, Joseph Rocha, Judy Sazama, Lauren Schuler, Nancy Stern, Edward Sydow, Barbara Thornburgh, Leslie Tily, Deborah Vacha, Charles Van Wert, Lawrence Wilson, Susan Wilson

1971   Wendie Abend, Nancy Allyn, Ann Arends, Barbara Bennett, Paula Bluebaugh, Arthur Bridgeman, Donald Chamberlain, Deborah Collins, Eileen Cooley, Timothy Crafts, Susan Crate, Leslie Cunningham, Dallas Dexter, Jennifer Donohue, Eugenie Doyl, Diana Drake, Diane Ellis, Carey Erickson, Anita Feldman, Wendy Freed, Carol Friedman, Jane Friedman, Ferris Frost, Nancy Frost, Amy Grossman, Leroy Gurga, Richard Haisma, Martha Harpstrite, Sandra Hendrick, Sheri Ille, Sara Kieth, Jonette Lancos, Gabrielle Lawrence, Hilary Leibsohr, Patricia Lillis, Leslie Litin, Ann Little, Gary Lund, Eddie Martinez, Lucy Marx, Constance McKeon, Lyn Miller, Edna Muller, Eileen Nemeth, Colleen Nepstad, Craig Neustaedter, Christina Nichols, Gerald Pearson, Sara Pearson, Lea Peterson, Constance Pfitsch, Gretchen Phillips, Margaret Pierpont, Debra Powell, Ellen Rafel, Jeanette Robertson, Patricia Rockwood, Howard Sabatt, Mary Sames, Pamela Samuel, Holly Schiffer, Elizabeth Schlosser, Gretchen Schneider, Marcia Schramm, Sallie Shepardson, Anna Taffs, Deborah Vacha, Patricia Ward, Elinor White, Lawrence Wilson, Kenneth Yoder [compiled from list of participating dancers in final concert]

1972   Heidi Alford, Joan Andrus, Diane Bearman, Dawn Beattie, Cyndie Bellen, Elizabeth Binder, Dennis Breeze, Lowell Britson, Dena Brown, Jane Bulger, Penelope Burr, Joan Burroughs, Sara Burstein, Louise Cadle, Susan Carlson, Carol Chapman, Elizabeth Clements, Nancy Coburn, Ethel Coe, Helene Conway, Lauren Cotton, Timothy Crafts, Janice Cronin, Martha Dains, Kathryn Davis, Laurie Dill, Maria Drake, Lucinda Durham, Janis Dybdahl, Nancy Ekberg, Ann Ellison, Patricia Ethridge, Kay Evans, Jeannde Ford, Pamela Francis, Barbara French, Merrill Fuchs, Enid Gifford, Carol Ginsberg, Gloria Goodale, Sandra Gookin, Donna Gregory, Alan Hadley, Elizabeth Hager, Ann Hammack, Rebecca Hansen, Venecia Harder, Eric Haskell, Susan Hawkins, Sara Hicks, Joseph Holloway, Susan Hostetler, Helen Hunt, Christine Jenkins, Elizabeth Johnson, Eve Kahn, Pamela Kariotis, Vicki Katz, Steven Keith, Wendy Kennan, Barbara Kerr, Barbara Kieft, Ann Kilduff, Victoria King, Carolyn Klismith, Tamar Kotoske, Ruth Lebrun, Roberta Levine, Richard Linowes, Gary Lund, Pamela Magrill, Edward Martinez, Lana Matthews, Susan McDonough, Theresa McGuire, Robin McNelly, Patricia Merritt, Lyn Miller, Kathleen Morriss, Susie Muir, John Munger, Clair Nagel, Jonathan Neale, Laurel Near, Sharon Ogg, Perry Patterson, Nellie Perret, Barbara Peterson, Karen Petrie, Margaret Pierpont, Cheryl Pleskow, Allison Price, John Rankin, Patricia Rockwood, Mitchell Rose, David Rotholz, Catherine Rusoff, Beverly Ryan, Virgina Sarber, Lana Schwarts, Gordon Shepard, Sallie Shepardson, Dinah Smith, Robbe Sokolove, Carol Soleau, Janice Stafford, Mary Steel, Jana Steele, Nancy Stern, Amy Targan, Judy Thompson, Paula Traktman, Catherine Turocy, Donald Van Hoon, Judith Van Wyk, Claire Wolfowitz, Jessica Woody

1973   Fern Bartner, Dawn Beattie, Sylvia Blaustein, Dana Block, Marcia Breit, Pamela Budner, Jeremy Burton, Linda Cohen, Catrina Cramer, Janice Cronin, Julia Cushing, Kristin Darnell, Joyce Davidoff, Betsy Davidson, Patricia De Lee, Cynthia Dean, Douglas DeWitt, Roberta Diamond, Pricilla Doernbach, Janine Egert, Leanne Eldrige, Judy Fischer, Pamela Francis, Barbara French, Ferris Frost, Irma Fyfe, Carol Ginsberg, Diane Goldman, Sarah Grimes, Mary Gruber, Kathyanne Guy, Elizabeth Hager, Elizabeth Hefelfinger, Kathleen Higgins, Sherry Hilding, Mary Hoagland, Charlene Hummel, Helen Hunt, Jan Isaacs, Jane Jacobson, Michelle Javornik, Mary Jewett, Lisa Judge, Janie Kahan, Dana Keeler, James Kelly, Wendy Kennan, Nina Kolesnick, Donald Ladig, Jacqueline Lang, Phoebe Lawrence, Frances Leffwich, Richard Lillehei, Andrea Lovato, Jacqueline Low, Valerie Luiz, Nancy Madden, Edward Martinez, Nancy Merkel, Kate Michaels, Ceceli Miranda, Paula Momii, Audrey Montano, John Munger, Carole

Nicol, Gwen Noel, Sherry Ogg, Kristin Olson, Perry Patterson, Sara Pennington, Margaret Pierpont, Marlene Pitkow, Phyllis Pollack, Allison Price, Deborah Ray, Jara Reed, Andrea Reichlin, Renee Rockoff, Jane Roeder, Beverly Ryan, Betty Schneider, Glenn Shinn, Geraldine Smith, Sandra Smith, Tamar Smith, Varya Soudakoff, Nancy Staun, Maila Strauss, Mary Stroud, David Struthers, Molly Sumner, Constance Swisher, Samuel Tucker, Klasina Vanderwerf, Cynthia Vollmer, Linn Walker, Devon Wall, Ceil Walsky, Debra Weiss, Sally White, Clare Wolfowitz, Karin Wood, Thomas Yarnel

1974   Richard Abbott, Deborah Allton, Jane Amerson, Judith Anderson, Mari Anixter, Wendy Ansley, Larry Aranda, Teresa Bain, Dawn Beatie, Dana Block, Nori Bowman, Joann Boyle, Heidi Burkle, Jeremy Burton, Mary Burton, Patricia Campbell, Ellen Carey, Pamela Colgate, Carol Corbus, Yvette Cornelius, Leslie Cox, Allison Davis, Eleanor Day, Douglas DeWitt, Pamela Elder, Leanne Eldridge, Kristin Eliasberg, Deborah Ellis, Elaine Evans, Janet Fattore, Barbara French, Robert Gappa, Margaret Gibbe, Deborah Gibson, Steven Gray, Karla Hackstaff, Jean Hannum-Pulos, Paula Harrington, Heather Harris, Elizabeth Heffelfinger, Caroline Herter, Rochelle Holt, Jenel Hopper, Elizabeth Huebner, David Hughes, Thomas Kanthak, Matia Karrell, James Kelly, Susan Kennedy, Mona Ketchersid, Barbara Koenig, Betty Kolner, Carolyn Kruse, Donald Ladig, Brett Larson, Lola Lee, Louise Lefevre, Terry Lehman, Gail Lewis, Barbara Lippman, Diane Malik, Edward Martinez, Suellen McAndrews, Linelle McCune, Ellen McLarty, Cynthia Merrill, Cindy Meyer, Thomas Michel, Cecile Miranda, Edward Myers, Emily Odza, June Panagakos, Perry Patterson, Lynn Perkinson, Janet Perry, James Pogue, Allison Price, Linda Priest, Patricia Ratcliffe, Deborah Ray, Kathryn Redman, Susan Roebuck, Elizabeth Rowland, Beverly Ryan, Maria Schaefer, Kathleen Schweizer, Judith Shapiro, Linda Shook, Julia Sides, Phyllis Spiegel, Danny Spinuzzi, Michelle Stevens, Sandra Strahan, David Struthers, Lee Sweetland, Anne Tantillo, Denise Terandy, Vera Thalrose, Andrea Torrice, Carla Wagner, Pamela Warvel, Leslie White, Maria White, Carol Willis, Eula Yancey, Lillian Zamora

1975   Wendy Ansley, Dawn Beatie, Margaret Bender, Emily Benenson, Anne Berkeley, Mary Bessison, Susan Blankensop, Barbara Bolt, Katherine Brann, Marcia Briet, Stephanie Brooks, Anne Bryan, Jeremy Burton, Sandi Cannon, Gail Casson, Alice Cleveland, Betsy Cohen, Elaine Dorsey, Susan Dunaway, Pamela Dvore, Catherine Elliott, Richard Flippin, Nancy Frost, Lisa Gordinier, Steven Gray, Charles Gross, Marilyn Guadagroli-Dubitsky, Gretchen Gudelfinger, Heidi Gundlach, Trina Hardy, Linda Harkavy, Maragret

Hartcell, Brenda Hassenbein, Salley Heyward, Marjorie Huebner, Deborah Jelin, Carl Kaelber, Thomas Kanthak, James Kelly, Antoinette Keyser, Amy Klein, Kathleen Kromka, Carol Kuyper, Donald Ladig, Brett Larson, Heather Lee, Lola Lee, Gail Lewis, Ellen Lippman, Betty Mahaffy, Charon Marco, Victoria Marks, Eddie Martinez, Merle Matsunaga, Elizabeth Matteson, Margaret McGough, Cynthia McKee, Linda Medland, Joyce Mills, Margaret Morris, John Munger, Nancy Nelson-Smith, Jill Novascone, Deborah Olin, Caren Paul, Linda Peacock, Donna Pelle, Kristin Peterson, Patricia Peterson, Judith Pettet, Harriet Pierce, Winston Pierce, Katherine Pincoffs, James Pogue, Dianna Rawnsley, Karen Ritter, Janet Rollinson, Joann Schmitz, Jo Schneider, Sue Schroeder, Carol Scoville, Judith Silverman, Cathy Sims, Chris Small, Varya Soudakoff, Kay Tani, Anne Tantillo, Dale Thompson, John Tobin, Carl Watley, Wendy Weiss, Julie Williams, Bonnie Wilson, Dim Winternitz, Sarah Winton, Karen Wolman, Emilie Zonsius

1976   Julia Allen, Wendy Ansley, Larry Aranda, Nancy Arnn, Deborah Berg, Sarah Boeh, Jeremy Burton, Ann Butler, Jane Choate, Sarah Clark, Alice Cleveland, Paul Cohen-Meyers, Gretchen Cohenour, Karin Coyne, John Davis, Jane Denman, Nancy Dey, Vaughan Durkee, Margarett Ekberg, Howard Fine, Laura Fisher, Jonathan Friedman, Rosanna Gamson, Zita-Ann Geoffroy, Heidi Gibbs, Jill Graham, Kathleen Granger, Abby Gross, Daniel Hallock, Jean Hannum-Pulos, Barbara Harrison, Janis Harrison, Lyndia Harrison, Shawn Hiers, Alice Horning, Elizabeth Hursa, Marth Isom, Carl Kaelber, Jane Kahan, Thomas Kanthak, Joann Kawamura, Marion Keen, Shari Kenney, Joanne Korner, Lysa Kotin, Steven Langer, Rebecca Leatherman, Susan Leveton, Diana Lim, John MacGregor, Gwynne MacManus, Nikolas Malyshev, Monica Manning, Jean Marshall, Mary Masuda, Mark McConnell, Cunthia Merrion, Melanie Miller, Cecile Miranda, John Munger, Carolyn Nordstrom, Jenise Parris, Marcia Paulsoen, Maureen Perou, Margaret Pierpont, Susannah Purdy, Martha Renick, Mary Romer, Sheri Rosengard, Sueann Ross, Dana Rownseley, Beverly Ryan, Phyllis Sanfilippo, Kathryn Schmitz, Margaret Snow, Mariamna Soudakoff, Michael Sternfeld, Regina Sweeney, Lindsey Sweet, Anita Trujillo, Lisa Weaver, Doreen Weiss, Karen Wolman, Clair Yarmo, Karla Zhe

1977   Leda Bagwell, Kenneth Baker, Yael Barash, William Barron, Donald Borsh, Belinda Bowler, Rebecca Boyd, Laura Brenton, Becki Brinkerhoff, Rachel Brumer, Raul Burton, Farrell Carson, Sarah Colmery, Marbury Coxe, Janice Cusolito, Paula Davis, Madeline Dean, Pricilla Engelin, Nancy Evans, Nancy Fitts, Leslie Flint, Laurel Fullerton, Dian Gibson, Calvin Grogan, Susan Hadley, Gail Harlor, Barbara Harrison, Heather Hering, Sara Hohe, Carol

Kaminski, Sherri Kenney, Nancy Kittredge, Stephen Koester, Jean Leavenworth, Sandy Leeds, Edward Martinez, Lesli Miles, Russell Miller, John Munger, Kathryn Munger, Lisa Naugle, Lani Okimoto, Kathleen Pignataro, Eulalia Ponce, David Prager, Jean Pulos, Susannah Purdy, Mary Reid, Karen Shechter, Margaret Sturges, Clarissa Townsend, Anita Trujillo, Gina Vincent, Tim Walker, Lisa Wallgren, Sharon Washington, Linda Weiss, Susan Wicke

1978   Anne Baldy, Beth Baydarian, Karen Brown, Thomas Burrington, Louise Cackowski, Catherine Calder, Robert Connor, Jennifer Corrie, Madeline Dean, Sharon Dilworth, Nancy Evans, Peggy Gilchrist, Mary Good, Kimberlie Griffis, Matthew Gunzelman, Debra Handley, Sarah Hauser, Janet Hildebrandt, Drew Hoag, Catherine Hondrorp, Eve Keller, Stephan Koplowitz, Judith Kreith, Tracy Leonard, Merle Matsunaga, Olava Menczkowski, Andrea Mezvinsky, Janet Miller, Leland Montgomery, John Munger, Kathryn Munger, Lisa Naugle, Karleen Neil, Stephen Otto, Carole Pfannenstein, Kristan Pritz, Deborah Reshotko, Rosa Rodriguez, Janet Russell, Sue Schnitt, Mark Scott, Demarise Sellens, Cathi Shover, Spencer Snyder, Anita Soloman, Barbara Stentzelberger, Martha Sullivan, Kim Sutton, Ann Swanberg, Ann Swigart, Charlene Tarver, Edit Tor, Candy Travis, Sarah Trissel, Dara Van Laanen, Sharon Washington, Judith Wido, Robin Williams, Patricia Yeager, Georgina Zadravec, Beth Zeeman

1979   Norma Adler, Elizabeth Amos, Ellen Baker, Elizabeth Becker, Tara Borella, Raul Butron, Beth Chamberlain, Leslie Elledge, Margaret Erdle, Joseph Feldman, Amy Formanek, Lynn Foussard, Pascha Gerlinger, Gina Gibney, Dorothy Goodman, Marsha Goren, Becky Haman, William Harren, Laura Harvey, Megen Hlavacek, Anne Hogan, Robert Howe, Teri Jalenak, Bronwyn Judge, Diane Ketelle, Amy Kligerman, Stephan Koplowitz, Cheryl Krown, Karin Levitas, Linda Loftis, Debra Marrs, Cyndy McCrossen, Theresa Mockler, Anne Moulton, Julia O'Sullivan, Diane Rayor, Sandra Rebollo, Alicia Reckford, Kaye Robertson, Della Rodriguez-Moher, Robyn Rosenfeld, Ruth Sander, Dale Schmid, Diane Shull, Spencer Snyder, Diane Spergel, Dewell Springer, Patricia Stewart, Brian Taylor, Jeanne Travers, Dara Van Laanen, Tomiko Viera, Margaret Vincent, Timothy Walker, Sarah Wank

1980   Mary Abate, Stacey Adams, Elizabeth Aggiss, Michael Anderson, Martha Basinger, Bobby Bracewell, Vivien Bridson, Raul Butron, Farrell Carson, Mili Clayton, Dennis Collada, Alyson Colwell, Pamela D'Arc, Mark Degarmo, Cynthis Dunnahoo, Bianca Edmonds, Nancy Fee, Joseph Feldman, Margery Fernald, Judy Fisher, Lynn Garber, Lisa Gibbs-Ciaffone, Linda Goegel, Jan Hanvik,

Ruth Harkin, Dale Hartigan, Ann Hebert, Deborah Heltzer, Mary Hilbert, Elizabeth Hutson, Gail Iida, Therese Jordan, Joan Karff, Suzanne Kavin, Eve Keller, Naomi King, Margaret Kopald, Karen Kramer, Cheryl Krown, Kathaleen Krujawa, Nancy Lehnhardt, Lori Lewis, Jerry Ljung, Emilio Lobato, Linda Loftis, Rebecca Long, Marilyn Lucchi, Scott MacDonald, Kathleen Malloy, Judy Marriott, William McClelland, Faith Merritt, Melissa Mullineaux, Robert Neu, Stephen Otto, Derek Phillips, Susan Prouty, Susan Scigliano, Deborah Segaul, Dewell Springer, Sarah Stanton, Cecelia Tait, Brian Taylor, Elia Thies, Katherine Thompson, Menno Vantoorenburg, Susan Weiner, Mark Wischmeyer

1981 Monica Angle, Bruce Atkinson, Martha Basinger, Virginia Bladen, Lisa Brodeur, Rita Bureika, David Butron, Farrell Carson, Dennis Collaado, Erik Cota-Robles, Susan Cotter, Mark Degarmo, Terri Diaz, Lisa Farlee, Joseph Feldman, Margery Fernald, Lawrence Fortunato, Rebecca Fox, Tari Gallagher, Sarah Gamble, Nancy Gardenhire, Dolly Gardner, Janine Gastineaux, Jan Hanvik, Deborah Heltzer, Jennifer Jones, Laura Jones, Therese Jordan, Sharon Kent, Nancy Lee, Nancy Lehnhardt, Elizabeth Lewis, Cynthia Merrion, Kathleen Moran, James Murphy, Elise Nagel, Kathy Nelson, Robert Neu, Theresa Nockler, Patricia Pardini, Derek Phillips, Deborh Pirri, Melissa Pope, Jean Pulos, Susan Roebuck, Kristin Schleiep, Carol Schober, Laurel Smith, Lisa Snyder, Tracy Sprong, Jon Sterling, Lisa Stewart, Cecelia Tait, Sarah Trissel, Victoria Vadala, Menno Vantoorenburg, Dennis Vasquez, Sherrie Waggener, Lynn Wenning, Mark Wischmeyer, Joseph Youngblood

1982 Earl Balcos, Henry Beer, Robin Bennett, Thomas Cary, Erik Cota-Robles, Reinaldo De Palmer, Barbara Dralle, Carol Dzuro, Barbara Firkins, Michael Flowers, Annette Ghee, Kay Gile, Melora Griffis, Kim Grover, Vicki Hatch, Mary Hilbert, Stephen Ho, Holly Jaycox, Nancy Jimenez, Cynthia Kamoroff, Sharon Kent, Robert Neu, Anne Phelan, Julianne Rice, Diana Sherwood, Susan Sidman, Josephine Smith, Laurel Smith, Spencer Snyder, Christa Sterling, Treva Tegtmeier, Elizabeth Trissel, Mark Vaner, Martina Vermaaten, Mark Wischmeyer

1983 Angela Adamson, Joseph Arcand, Deborah Baker, Alan Beecher, Christopher Caines, Anne Carey, Valda Craig, Dianna Dorgelo, Martha Goss, Arne Hartmann, Deborah Heltzer, Stephen Ho, Holly Humble, Kristin King, Amy Lange, Heather Lee, Jaime Lujan, Sandra Mandelbaum, Dana Montroy, Yukimi Mori, Craig Oldfather, Hideaki Onuki, Amy Orsborn, Jeanine Shields, Kimberly Smith, Sarah Stanley, Cynthia Stevens, Lisa Thurrell, Joseph Youngblood, Brigitte Zuger

Appendix Two
PROGRAMS OF HANYA HOLM
CONCERTS AT COLORADO COLLEGE,
1941-1983

Note: The information supplied is from printed programs provided courtesy of the Hanya Holm Collection, Dance Division, New York Public Library, and a 1973 program courtesy of John Munger. Inconsistencies in spellings have been left as originally printed.

Abbreviations:

ch:	choreographed by
m:	music composed by
d: or ds:	danced by
dir:	directed by
p:	pianist
inst:	instrumentalists
cs:	chorus
con:	conducted by
cos:	costumes designed by

1941, AUGUST 7-9. Hanya Holm and Company in a Dance Concert. Instrumental Prelude, *Soliloquy and Dance,* m: Roy Harris, p: Johana Harris, viola: Robert Becker. All dances ch: Holm. *Dance of Introduction,* m: Henry Cowell, ds: Frances Davies, Robin Gregory, Barbara Hatch, Kipp Kiernan, Louise Kloepper, Gregory McDougall, Elizabeth Nichols, Paul Sweeney, Martha Wilcox, cos: Liz Rytell. *From This Earth,* m: Harris, "Dawn—mother's lullaby," d: Holm; "Childhood—children at play," ds: Gregory, Hatch, Jinx Heffelfinger, Eleanore McDougall, Sweeney; "Love—courtship-marriage-festivities," ds: Kloepper, G. McDougall, Holm, Shirley Brimberg, Gregory, Hatch, Heffelfinger, Kiernan, E. McDougall, Sweeney; "Work—treadmill and exhaustion," ds: Gregory, Kiernan, G. McDougall, Sweeney; "Dusk—restrospection," ds: Holm, Brimberg, Gregory, Hatch, Heffelfinger, Kiernan, Kloepper, G. McDougall, E. McDougall, Sweeney, con: Harris, Aug. 7; Peter Page, Aug. 8, 9. inst: Albert Rahier, Margaret Foote, Charles Foidart, Joseph Wetzels, Vincent De Sciose, Cecil Effinger, Tom Ross, Alfred Prud'homme, William Fristoe, Guillaume Mombaerts, Charles Robinson, cos: Liz Rytell. *Metropolitan Daily,* m: Gregory Tucker, "Financial Section," ds: Davies, Gladys DeBarry, Deborah Froelicher, Gregory, Hatch, Elizabeth Hayes, Vickery Hubbard, Kiernan, Kloepper; "Scandal Sheet," ds: Gregory, Patty Kerr, Kloepper, Sweeney; "Society Page," ds: DeBarry, Hatch, Hayes, G. McDougall; "Want Ads," ds: Holm, Kloepper; "Foreign News," ds: DeBarry, Froelicher, Gregory, Hatch, Hayes, Hubbard, Kerr, Kiernan as Conservative Reporter, Sweeney as Sensational Reporter; "Comics," ds: Davies, DeBarry, Gregory, Kerr, Kiernan, G. McDougall, Elizabeth Nichols, Sweeney; "Sports Page," ds: Davies, DeBerry, Gregory, Hatch, Hayes, Kerr, Kloepper, Nichols, cos: Betty Beebe, p: Freda Miller, Helen Davis.

1942, AUGUST 8, 9. Hanya Holm and Company, Roy Harris, Composer-Conductor, Arch Lauterer, Director-Designer in a Dance Concert. *What So Proudly We Hail,* m: Harris, ch: Holm, staging: Lauterer. "The Girl I Left Behind Me," ds: Holm, Jessica Fleming, Robin Gregory, Jinx Heffelfinger, Rheba Koren, Paul Sweeney; "Western Cowboy," ds: Holm, Fleming, Gregory, Heffelfinger, Koren, Harriet Roeder, Sweeney; "Rock of Ages," ds: Holm, Fleming, Gregory, Heffelfinger, Koren, Roeder; "I'll Be True to My Love," ds: Gregory, Sweeney; "Rhythms of Today," ds: Fleming, Gregory, Heffelfinger, Koren, Roeder, Sweeney, con: Harris, inst: Johana Harris, Robert Gross, Margaret Kelly, Mary Judd, Frances Fletcher, Katherine Shreves, cs: Ella Ann Davies, Barbara Platt, Mary Randall, Marie Watkins, Edalyne Bledsor, Margaret Jones, Lillian McCue, Jean Reed, Larry Clarke, Leslie Goss, Kenneth Moore, Adam Sallee, John St. Edmunds, Clifford Kolsrud, Allen Mathies, Edwin Norton, William Root. *Chaconne,* m: Bach-Busoni, p: J. Harris. *Namesake,* m: Harris, ch: Holm, scenario and design: Lauterer, dir: Holm, Lauterer. The Memories: Martha Childress, Sweeney; Patience Turner: Martha Wilcox; Addie Mason: Koren; Ann Lyndon: Heffelfinger; Polly Doty: Roeder; Hannah Moody: Fleming; Mary Smith: Holm; Milla Gaylord: Gregory; The Unnamed: Shirley Broughton, Marjory Kinney, Mary Lou Lee, p: J. Harris, viola: Gross, voice coaching: John C. Wilcox.

1943, AUGUST 14, 17. Hanya Holm and Company in a Dance Concert. *Parable—with reference to the popular incident of the Wise and Foolish Virgins,* m: Couperin, Narrator: Paul Sweeney, ds: Wise Virgins: Molly Howe, Mildred Kaeser, Rheba Koren; Foolish Virgins: Mary Anthony, Joan Palmer, Holm, p: John Colman, cos: George Blockman. *Orestes and the Furies,* m: Colman, ds: Orestes: Sweeney; Apollo: Anthony; Athena: Koren; Leader of the Furies:

Martha Wilcox; Ghost of Clytemnestra: Frances Davies; Vision of Clytemnestra (first scene) Clytemnestra: Howe; Orestes: J. Vanz Fitzer; The Furies: F. Davies, Norma Davies, Mary Teresa Gushurst, Howe, Ruth Jacobs, Kaeser, Patty Kerr, Koren, Margaret Murphy, Louise Musman, Edna Jane Nesbitt, Palmer, Vera Sieradz, p: Colman, James Sykes. *Suite of Four Dances,* m: Harris, "First Dance—The Girl I Left Behind Me," ds: Anthony, Howe, Palmer, Koren, Holm, Sweeney; "Second Dance—Western Cowboy," ds: Anthony, Howe, Kerr, Palmer, Koren, Holm; "Duo—I'll Be True to My Love," ds: Palmer, Sweeney; "Finale—Rhythms of Today," ds: Anthony, Howe, Kerr, Palmer, Koren, Sweeney, cos: Arch Lauterer, con: Roy Harris, inst: Johana Harris, Robert Gross, Sue Thomas, Mary Judd, Robert Becker, Fredrick Knorr, cs: Gertrud Blanchard, Honora McKay, Barbara Platt, Gwendolyn Weide, Edalyne Bledwoe, Lillian McCue, Velna Miller, Marian Lee, Herbert Beattie, Robert Evett, Harvey Hinshaw, Boris Kremenlief, Peter Page.

1944, AUGUST 19, 22. An Evening of Theater Arts: Hanya Holm, Martha Wilcox and Her Group. "El Cristo," play by Margaret Larkin, dir: Woodson Tyree. *What Dreams May Come,* ch and dir: Holm, m: Alex North, ds: The Dreamer: Holm; Bright Refraction: Frances Davies; Dark Refraction: Wilcox; Shadowy Refraction: Mildred Kaeser; Shapes: Batya Heller, Joan Palmer, Florita Roup, Vera Sieradz; Passers-by: Joan Brodie, Davies, Mary Geppert, Mazie Guzakoff, Marie Hans, Heller, Kaeser, Palmer, Jeanne Roberts, Roup, Sieradz, Alice Taylor, Wilcox; Performers: Dulcy Amter, Patricia Urner, Lillian Covillo, p: Gui Mombaerts, Louise Metz. *Waltz,* m: Richard Strauss, dir: Wilcox, ch: Amter, Kaeser, ds: Palmer, Amter, Kaeser, Patty Kerr, Sieradz, p: Mombaerts, Metz. *For Our World,* m: Robert Evett, dir: Wilcox, ch: Kaeser, Wilcox, ds: Wilcox, Amter, Davies, Kaeser, Kerr, Nancy Martsolf, Sieradz, p: Metz.

1945, AUGUST 18. Hanya Holm Dance Concert. *Walt Whitman Suite,* ch: Holm, m: Roy Harris. "To Thee Old Cause," ds: Louise Carrol, Tilla Hevesi, Joan Kruger, Miriam B. Levinson, Elizabeth L. Mason, Florita Raup, Diana Smith, Lee Thomas; "The Year That Trembled," ds: Carrol, Hevesi, Rheba Koren, Kruger, Levinsohn, Mason; "Drums," ds: Holm, Jerome Andrews, Koren, Levinsohn, Mason, cs: Bernice Jensen, Honora McKay, Jean Osmun, Gwendolyn Weide, Jane Bower, Elisabeth Clark, Ruth Kice, Lillian McCue, Ruth Tyree, Theo Fenlon, Lt. Joseph Gaudio, Irving Sims, Cpl. Russell Danburg, Ernest Kitson, Allen Mathies, Peter Page, Seventh Service Command String Ensemble: Pvt. Albert Pratz, Pfc. Leon Rudin, T/5 Erik Kathison, Pvt. Avram Lavin, Pvt. Max Lanner, con: Harris. *Portrait of a Lady,* ch: Koren, m: Kitta Brown, d: Koren, p: Helen Davis. *What Dreams May Come,* ch: Holm, m: Alex North, ds: The Dreamer: Holm; Bright Refraction: Frances Wessells; Dark Refraction: Martha Wilcox; Shadowy Refraction: Koren; Shapes: Eileen Fezler, Bernice Mendelsohn, Joan Palmer, Raup; Passersby: Lena Belloc, Barbara Bennison, Virginia Harris, Carol Jackson, Kruger, Lois Miller, Palmer,

Raup, Edna Schiff, Thomas, Mary Titus, Marjorie Turner, Londa Verrill, Wessells; Performers: Barbara Bennion, Eileen Fezler, Marjorie Turner; The Male Figure: Andrews, p: Helen Davis, De Wright. *My Love Has Flown the Coop*, ch: Koren, m: Freda Miller, d: Koren, p: Davis. *The Gardens of Eden*, ch: Holm, m: Darius Milhaud, ds: Adam Smith: Joseph Salek; Eve Smith: Wilcox; Adam Jones: Andrews; Eve Jones: Holm; The Intruders: Mason, Turner, inst: Seventh Service Command String Ensemble.

1946, AUGUST 17. Hanya Holm Dance Concert. *Dance For Four*, m: Wallingford Riegger, ch: Holm, ds: Joan Kruger, Maxine Munt, Alfred Brooks, Alwin Nikolais. *Fable of the Donkey*, m: Freda Miller, ch: Nikolais, narration: Lillian de la Torre, set: Christine Elrod, Woodson Tyree, Narrator: Leslie Goss, ds: The Donkey: Glen Tetley; The Father: Harry Bernstein; The Son: Leah Aberson; The Girls: Rosemary Harmier, Paula Levine, Jacquelyn McMahill, Eve Smith, Vivian Watkins; The Acrobats: Norman Chelquist, Oliver Kostock; The Mother and the Children: Chris Neubert, Katherine Mendum, Barbara Quirin, Elaine Sarnoff; The Gossips: Sandy Gibson, Martha Howe, Marion Watson. *Windows*, m: Miller, ch: Holm, set: Tyree, "Prologue: Late Afternoon," ds: Holm, Bernstein, Louise Carroll, Katya Delakova, Gibson, Kruger, Munt, Nikolais, Tetley; "Bedtime Story," ds: Carroll, Eya Rudhyar; "Alone," d: Holm; "Hep Session," ds: Bebe Alpert, Sonia Borenstein, Brooks, Tetley; "Triad," ds: Holm, Delakova, Fred Berk; "The Spirit Moves," ds: Gibson, Munt, Bernstein, Kostock, Nikolais; "Epilogue: Early Morning," ds: as "Prologue." *Walt Whitman Suite*, m: Roy Harris, ch: Holm, ds: Holm, Alpert, Borenstein, Carroll, Gibson, Nancy Gregson, Patty Kerr, Kruger, Munt, Libby Nichols, Diana Smith, Bernstein, Brooks, Kostock, Nikolais, Tetley, cs: Mary Bennett, Dana Butler, Joan Downing, Paulina Fink, Elaine Hansen, Bernice Jensen, Lilian McCue, Honora McKay, Virginia Paris, Carol Welty, Warren Boudinot, James Erb, Harold Frantz, Frank Gilles, Allen Mathies, Charles Potter, Frederick Tooley, inst: Johana Harris, Burrill Phillips, Josef Gingold, Robert Gross, Ferenc Molnar, Carl Stern, con: Harris.

1947, AUGUST 15. Hanya Holm Dance-Drama Production and Demonstration. *Demonstration of Modern Dance Technique*, ds: Joan Kruger, Sherry Traver, Gertrude Green, Freidann Parker, Elizabeth Brooks, Glen Tetley, Oliver Kostock, Gregory MacDougall, John Castello. *Student Compositions:* "Richard Cory," poem: E. A. Robinson, reader: Jack Moore, ch and d: Tetley; "Americana," m. arrangement: Percy Grainger, ch: William Murphy, ds: Antoinette Beck, Jane Denham, Marion Edmonds, Sybil Gramlich, Castello, Murphy. *"And So Ad Infinitum,"* Script: Karel and Josef Capek, dir: Holm assisted by Nikolais and in collaboration with Reginald Lawrence, "Prologue: In the Woods," Tramp: Eldor Mainville, Lepidopterist: Murphy; "Act I: The Butterflies," Felix: Tetley, Iris: Kruger, Clytie: Gramlich, Otto: MacDougall, Victor: Castello, Flappers: Green, Denham, Mary Miller, Dorothy Gotterer;

"Act II: Creepers and Crawlers," Chrysalis: Traver, Mr. Beetle: Melville Larned, Mrs. Beetle: Marianne Winz, Another Beetle: Charles Loubier, Ichneumon Fly: Bruce Balbirnie, His Daughter: Ann Alsup, Mrs. Cricket: Beck, A Parasite: Castello; "Act III: The Ants," Chrysalis: Traver, Blind Timekeeper: Evelyn Freed, Chief Engineer: George Boudinot, Second Engineer: Kostock, Inventor: Murphy, Signal Officer: Moore, Philanthropist: Ann Neprud, Commander in Chief of the Yellows: Tetley, Messengers: Loubier, Castello; Workers and Soldiers: Beck, Brooks, Penny Corya, Esther Craft, Marion Edmonds, Miriam Jerebek, Patty Kratz, Jacqueline MacMahill, Patti Musson, Edna Nahon, Neprud, Mary O'Connell, Freidann Parker, Barbara Voichick, Green, Miller, Denham; "Epilogue: Death and Life," Chrysalis: Traver, Moths: Green, Denham, Gotterer, Miller.

1948, August 13. Dance Demonstration and Concert under the direction of Hanya Holm assisted by Alwin Nikolais. *Demonstration of Technique,* speaker: Holm, ds: Penny Corya, Mildred Kaeser, Mary Miller, Della Parker, Jean Riley, Marc Breaux, Leo Duggan, Oliver Kostock, Jack Moore, Glen Tetley, m: Marilyn Knorr. *Dance Etudes:* 1. "Studies in straight paths," Group Etude, m: Armas Jarnefelt, ch: Holm, ds: Corya, Miller, Parker, Kaeser, Riley, Breaux, Duggan, Kostock, Tetley. Solo Etude, m: Ted Coons, ch and d: Miller. Solo Etude, m: percussion, ch and d: Breaux. 2. "Study in Curved Path," m: Knorr, ch: Holm, ds: Sara Aman, Corya, Kaeser, Miller, Riley. 3. "Study in nonrepeat movement," m: percussion, ch and d: Riley. 4. "Etude for Men Dancers," m: Knorr, ch: Holm, ds: Breaux, Duggan, Kostock, Tetley. 5. "Primitive Study," m: percussion, ch and d: Kaeser. 6. "Trio Etude in Unrelated Movement," unaccompanied, ch: Holm, ds: Riley, Breaux, Tetley. 7. "Dramatic Etude," m: Marshall Bialosky, ch: Nikolais, ds: Aman, Patricia Barrett, Antoinette Beck, Cornelia Cerf, Barbara Dwyer, Patti Musson, Ann Neprud, Nancy Robb, Holly Robinson, Shirley Spackmann, Sonja Svig, Marjorie Turner, Carol Walgenbach. *Xochipili,* ch: Holm, scenes and cos: Ricardo Martinez, ds: Scene I "Men of Earth," Duggan, Breaux, Kostock, Tetley with Aman, Barrett, Spackmann, Turner, Walgenbach; Scene II "The Temple Builders," Holm, Riley, Kaeser, Carl Jones, Moore; Scene III "The Recurring Pulse," as Scene I.

1949, August 18, 19. Concert of Modern Dance under the direction of Hanya Holm assisted by Alwin Nikolais and with music conducted by Nicolas Slonimsky. *Extrados,* ch: Nikolais, m: Alfred Pew, ds: Misses Bailen, Cooper, Choate, Lundbeck, Robb; Messrs. Fillin, Fuchs, Griffin, Holt, Wood, p: Lucille Delaney, Carol Welty, flutist: Doris von Holst, cs dir: James Erb, cs: Misses Choate, Horsch, Jones, Leitzinger, Muensinger; Messrs. Crabb, Gitlin, Moman, Redfield, Savig. Nicolas Slonimsky's *Little Suite for Wood-wind, Percussion and Portable Typewriter,* inst: Harvey Boatright, Catherine Emig, Richard Joiner, Carl Paarman, Edward Lenichek, John Lunn, Walter Light, Gilda Carmel. Igor Stravinsky's *History of a Soldier,* dir and ch: Holm, inst: Frank

Costanzo, Stuart Sankey, Richard Joiner, Carl Parrman, Lenichek, Lunn, Light; Narrator: Calvin Holt, Soldier: Melvin Fillin, Devil: David Wood or John Reese, Princess: Deborah Choate or Mildred Kaeser. Edgard Varese's *Ionization,* m: Edgard Varese, ch: Holm, ds: Misses Adam, Bailin, Bassett, Castator, Choate, Cook, Cooper, Crosby, Dixon, Goldberg, Howe, Jones, Kaeser, Landi, Lischner, Lundbeck, Mahoney, Miller, O'Neill, Ongley, Reynolds, Rice, Richards, Robb, Senter, Spitznagel, Toman, Werrill, Williams; Messrs. Amerman, Fillin, Fuchs, Gitlin, Griffin, Holt, Moman, Redlich, Reese, Wood.

1950, AUGUST 5. An informal Dance Recital directed by Hanya Holm. *Opening Dance,* m: Erik Satie, ds: Barbara Byrne, Judith Callaway, Judith Haskell, Mary Miller, Melvin Fillin, John Reese, p: Lucille Delaney. *Dances of Youth,* m: Claude Debussy, Bela Bartok, d: Ray Harrison, p: Delaney. *Impetus,* m: Shirley Genther, ch: Robin Gregory, ds: Katherine Cockey, Martha Cornick, Sara Fitzpatrick, Phyllis Hamilton, Patricia Harley, Lenore Landau, Catherine Planche, Dorothy Robinson, Gregory, p: Delaney, Jeff Duncan. *Concert Royal,* m: François Couperin, ds: Byrne, Callaway, Haskell, Miller, Fillin, Harrison, Oliver Kostock, Reese, inst: Don Hopkins, Janet Stewart, p: Delaney. *Irish Jig,* m: Traditional. *Memphis Blues,* m: W. C. Handy, ch and d: Harrison, p: Delaney. *Jeune Filles aux Jardin,* m: F. Mompou, ch: Kostock, ds: Byrne, Callaway, Haskell, Landau, Miller, Patricia Sullivan, p: Delaney. *Five Old French Dances,* m: Marin Marias, ds: Holm, Harrison, viola: Ferenc Molnar, p: Max Lanner.

1951, AUGUST 13. An Evening of Dance and Drama directed by Hanya Holm and Woodson Tyree. *A Phoenix Too Frequent,* Comedy by Christopher Fry staged and dir: Tyree. *Prelude,* m: Arman Jarnefelt, ch: Holm, p: Delaney, Julia Sutton, ds: Sonja Easterly, Patti Musson, Melvin Fillin, Jeff Duncan. *Jeunes Filles aux Jardin,* m: F. Mompou, ch: Oliver Kostock, p: Delaney, ds: Donna Gillett, Katherine Haak, Natalie Jaffe, Shirley Nelson, Karla Olsen, Jean Zahorsky. *Trifles:* 1. "No Movement," words: Gertrude Stein, ch and d: Molly Lynn; 2. "Opus ½," words: Stein, ch and d: Paul Arthur; 3. "Bent Woman and Queens," words: Stein, ch: Lynn, ds: Lynn, Marilyn Wood; 4. "Scarcely," m: George Gershwin, piano arr.: Delaney, ch: Lynn, p: Delaney, Sutton, Caller: Fillin, ds: Haak, Jaffe, Rogermae Johnson, Judd Sperry, Paul Chambers, Clifford Kirwin, Jim Ray, Al Schulman. *Quiet City,* m: Aaron Copland, ch: Holm, inst: Colorado College String Orchestra and Walter Lindskoog, Konstantine Epp, con: Edgar Schenkman, ds: The Woman of the Street: Johnson, The Evil One: Arthur, The Stranger: Kostock, The Lovers: Lynn, Fillin, The Innocent: Easterly, The Fugitive: Schulman, People in the Street: Rebecca Ball, Charlotte Cole, Haak, Ann Ingram, Jaffe, Musson, Grace Rapaport, Wood, Zahorsky, Chambers, Jack Copland, Duncan, Kirwan, James Metcalf, Ray.

1952, JULY 26. An Evening of Dance and Drama directed by Hanya Holm and Woodson Tyree. *The Lady's Not For Burning* by Christopher Fry, dir: Tyree.

Little Rondo, m: Paul Hindemith, ch: Molly Lynn, ds: Caroline Loring, Barbara Turley, Paul Chambers, Clifford Kirwan, Jim Ray. *Vignettes:* 1. "Old Mother Hubbard," m: traditional, ch and d: Fannie Aronson; 2. "Etiquette," text: Emily Post, ch: Lynn, ds: Aronson, Karen Kanner, Lois Tomlinson, Ray, Grace Butler; 3. "Etudes," A, ch and ds: Sonja Easterly, Jane Hauser, Marilyn Wood, accomp.: Robert Wood; B, ch and accomp.: Wood, ds: Jeniel Reeves, Joyce Rutherford, Tomlinson; C, m: Dimitri Kabalevsky, p: Lucille Delaney, ch and ds: Easterly, Penny Simmons, Ray, Don Redlich. *Waltz,* m: Eric Satie, ch: Oliver Kostock, p: Delaney, ds: Faith Gulick, Hauser, Waltraud Herrmann, Kirwan, Ray, Redlich. *Kindertotenlieder,* Songs no. 4 and no. 1, m: Gustav Mahler, ch: Holm, ds: Jennifer Allen, Kaliope Candianides, Marti Culbert, Joanne Finkelor, Naome Goldberg, Vera Goldsmith, Julie Hamilton, Katherine Hutchison, Loretta Li, Virginia Liese, Janice Rabinowitz, Ann Ritterbush, Joy Sallick, Simmons, Beverly Webster, Caroly Wilcox. *Concertino da Camera,* m: Jacques Ibert, ch: Holm, ds: Lynn, Ray Harrison, Jeri Crowther, Easterly, Rutherford, Jere Stevens, Wood, Chambers, Kirwan, Redlich.

1953, AUGUST 3. An Evening of Dance and Drama directed by Hanya Holm and Woodson Tyree. *God's Trombones,* Five Negro Folk-Sermons by James Weldon Johnson, dir: Tyree. *Preface,* m: John La Montaine, ch: Oliver Kostock, p: Lucille Delaney, ds: Pat Ablett, Dolores Hammond, Elaine Hess, Ellen Moore, Ruth Schubach, Helen Thaxton, Paul Chambers, Clifford Kirwan, A. A. Leath. *Ritual,* m: Bela Bartok, ch: Holm, p: Delaney, ds: Mildred Kaeser, Jere Stevens, Fannie Aronson, Barbara Bench, Kay Brown, Peggy Barclay, Norma Carter, Ann Choate, Lois Christianson, Diane Diener, Betty Alice Godwin, Helen Harris, Virginia Harris, Doris Hysler, Mary Josepheson, Marilyn Maycock, Peggy Merle-Smith, Barbara Mills, Betty Sawyers, Janie Vaughn. *Temperaments and Behavior,* ch: Holm, m: Bela Bartok, inst: James Badger, Margaret Smith, Tosca Kramer, Julia Zaustinsky: 1. "Adolescent," ds: Mildred Barnhart, Kaliope Candianides, Diener, Marquel Pettit; 2. "Romantic," ds: Stevens, Jim Ray; 3. "Fearful," d: Don Redlich; 4. "Womanly," d: Kaeser; 5. "Restless," d: Stevens, m: Igor Stravinsky, inst: Don Caldwell, Albert Desiderio, John Rabe-Steele, Thomas Ward; 6. "Mischevous," ds: Chambers, Kirwan, Ray; 7. "Neurotic," d: Lynn; 8. "Somnambulant," d: Redlich. *Dance Mania,* m: Bartok, ch: Lynn, ds: Jeri Crowther, Ray, Barnhart, Candianides, Choate, Ivy Lee Cole, Royce Colon, Geulah Greenblatt, Rita Parr, Pettit, Dora Sanders, Don Sobieske, Jo Zaccaro.

1954, AUGUST 6. An Evening of Dance and Drama directed by Hanya Holm and Woodson Tyree. "A Reading From the Life of Socrates" from Maxwell Anderson's *Barefoot in Athens,* dir: Tyree. *Prelude I,* m: Herbert Elwell, ch: Holm, p: Carlton Gamer, ds: Julie Hamilton, Linn Howard, Rita Parr, Dora Sanders, Ruth Schubach. *Prelude II,* m: Elwell, ch: Holm, p: Gamer, ds: Norman Cornick, Bruce King, Ray Harrison. *Pastoral,* m: Darius Milhaud, ch: Holm, ds: Susan Cary, Mel Fillin, Jerry Bywaters, Ellen McQuaid. *Presage,* m: Elwell, ch: Holm, p: Gamer, ds: Dorothy Jarnac, Molly Lynn, Peggy Barclay, Nancy Berquist, Bywaters, Elece Cox, Margaret Fox, Joanna Gewertz, Teres Hancock, Howard, Doris Hysler, Joyce Jensen, Marilynn Jones, Delores Koster, Joan Levinson, Gayle Madsen, McQuaid, Valda Mock, Sylvia Mocroft, Bernadine Muller, Shirley Nelson, Barbara Nims, Rita Poehlin, Mary Reardon, Dora Sanders, Sophie Sieniewicz, Wylma White, Martha Williams, Jane Woodbridge, Howard Girvin, Ray Kingston, James Staheff. *Cakewalk,* m: Robert Russell Bennett, ch: Lynn, ds: Anne Bogart, Cornick, Pat Ablett, Yvonne Crittendon, Janie Harnack, Jeanne Hurley, Dee Maxwell, Martha Spann, Girvin, Kingston. *As I See It:* 1. "Abstract Painting," ch and d: Jarnac, narrator: James Sanders; 2. "Bound," ch and d: Jarnac; 3. "Fatigue Fandango," m: Lloyd Glenn, ch and ds: Jarnac, Cornick; 4. "Graduation Speech," ch and d: Jarnac, narrator: Sanders; 5. "Scarf Dance," m: Ponchielli, ch and d: Jarnac, p: Gamer. *Frevo,* m: Peres Prado, ch: Cornick, ds: Susan Cary, Hamilton, Florence Howard, Parr, Joan Penman, Schubach, Cornick, King.

1955. No printed program. For description see text and see Oliver Kostock, "Hanya Holm's Fifteenth Summer at Colorado College," *Dance Observer,* November 1955, p. 131.

1956, AUGUST 3. An Evening of Dance directed by Hanya Holm. Guest artists, Katherine Litz and Ray Harrison. *Partita No. 3,* m: Johann Sebastian Bach, violin: Raymond Gniewek: 1. "Preludio," ch: Holm, ds: Marilyn Muegge, Consuela Sandoval, Susan Watson, Mary Ann Young, Jim Ray, Don Redlich; 2. "Loure," ch: Holm, ds: Litz, Margaretta Bobo, Pola Nirenska, Rita Parr, Cheryl Richardson; 3. "Menuet," ch: Oliver Kostock, ds: Jo Fields, Sally Hanson, Norma Spieth, Olga Zampos, Raleigh Fleming, Lath Sanford; 4. "Bourrée," ch and d: Harrison; 5. "Gigue," ch: Harrison, ds: Harrison, Carol Kluss, Ann Robertson, Spieth, Ralph Lee, Sanford. *Story of Love From Fear to Flight,* m: Antonio Vivaldi, ch and d: Litz. *Toward Assent,* m: Paul Hindemith, ch: Mary Young, p: John Colman, Jo Garner, ds: Ann Hersey, Kluss, Richardson, Robertson, Jane Yosepian. *Summer Idyll,* m: Maurice Ravel, ch and ds: Litz, Harrison, p: Colman. *Exhortation,* m: percussion, ch: Redlich, Leader: Parr, Attendants: Gerry Culp, Muegge, Sandoval, cs: Kay Brown, Julia Carver, Yvonne Crittenden, Lynn Gerstenfeld, Helen Keith, Marilyn Leibovitz, Sally Nash, Janice Tenney. *Intrigue,* m: Claude Debussy, ch and ds: Litz, Harrison, p: Colman. *The Introvert,* m: Bela Bartok, ch and d: Redlich. *Twilight of a Flower,* m: Ravel, ch and d: Litz. *Eighth Avenue Character,* m: traditional, ch and d: Harrison. *Lapidopterists,* m: Roger Sessions, ch: Bobo, ds: Brown, Sanford. *Nymph and Shepherd,* m: Bartok, ch and ds: Redlich, Young. *Archy and Mehitabel,* m: Colman, ch and ds: Litz, Harrison.

1957, AUGUST 7. An Evening of Dance Workshop directed by Hanya Holm. *English Suite No. 4,* m: Johann Sebastian Bach, p: John Colman, 1. "Prelude," p: Colman; 2. "Allemande," ch: Paul Chambers, Clifford Kirwan, ds: Barbara Davidson, Nona Paulsen, Sally Snead, Lee Wagner, Chambers, Lawrence Hayward, Kirwan, Thomas Ruh; 3. "Courante," ch: Cynthia Jones, ds: Ann Amter, Barbara Bierner, Betty Bryant, Alida Dureau; 4. "Sarabande," ch: Thais Roberson, ds: Karen Hobbs, Christine Nicoloff, Roberson, Nola Ruspini, Joan Schwartz, Evelyn Woerheide; 5. "Menuet 1 and 2," ch: Loabelle Black, ds: Emily Gamboa, Margaret Hyden, Hetty Mitchell, Joan Rundell, Susan Salam, Amanda Taylor, Jim Drowns, Michael Matchie, Lathan Sanford; 6. "Gigue," ch: Marjorie Stuart, ds: Terry Dolson, Carol Fried, Normandie Karr, Harriet Slaughter, Judith Willis. *Woodland Impressions,* m: Claude Debussy, ch and d: Laurie Archer. *Syrinx,* m: Debussy, ch and d: Don Redlich. *Chanson Triste,* m: Guillaume Dufay, ch: Holm, ds: Archer, Gamboa, Slaughter, Taylor, Willis. *You Can't Go Home Again,* m: Paul Hindemith, ch: Holm, The Returned: Michael Maule, The Gambler: Redlich, The Beloved: Archer, The Husband: Hayward, Children: Fried, Gamboa, Karr, Gamblers: Chambers, Kirwan, Matchie. *Marche Militaire No. 3, Opus 51,* m: Franz Schubert, p: Jo Garner, Colman. *El Vito,* m: Infante, ch and d: Maule. *Tangents in Jazz,* m: Jimmy Giuffre, ch: Redlich, ds: Black, Schwartz, Redlich. *The Hunter,* m: Hindemith, ch and d: Archer. *Three Satires,* m: Bela Bartok, ch: Redlich: 1. "Nymph and Shepherd," ds: Karr, Redlich; 2. "Giva and Shiva," ds: Archer, Redlich; 3. "Electra and Orestes," ds: Schwartz, Redlich. *Suffragettes on Recruit,* m: Jaques Ibert, ch and ds: Roberson, Schwartz, Slaughter, Taylor. *Field Day,* m: Traditional Marches, p: Colman, ch: Oliver Kostock, ds: Bryant, Dureau, Cynthia Jones, Christine Nicoloff, Paulsen, Roberson. *Ozark Suite,* m: Elie Siegmeister, ch: Holm, ds: Amter, Black, Karr, Schwartz, Chambers, Kirwan, Redlich, Sanford.

1958, August 6, 7. An Evening of Dance: Workshop directed by Hanya Holm. *Etudes*: 1. "Salutation," m: John Colman, ch: Holm, ds: Paul Chambers, Clifford Kirwan, Don Redlich; 2. "Flight," m: percussion, ch: Redlich, ds: Ann Amter, Dorothy Masursky, Janetta McNamara, Jefferson Miller, Teressa Oliver, Nancy Thysell, Judy Willis; 3. "Dissension," m: Bartok, ch and ds: Bernadine Madole, Jane Poor; 4. "Curve," ch: Oliver, ds: Miller, Oliver, Thysell, Helen Weser, Willis; 5. "March," m: Schubert, ch: Oliver Kostock, ds: Terry Brown, Larry Brugoon, Chambers, Dick Foose, Kirwan. *Two Sketches,* m: Copland, ch and d: Elizabeth Harris. *Three Figures of Delusion,* m: Bartok, ch and d: Redlich. *Journey,* m: Bartok, ch and d: Harris. *Strange Idyll,* m: Britten, ch: Molly Lynn, The Young Girl: Carol Fried, The Boy: Hal O'Neal, Children: Jeannine Kocher, Miller, Oliver, Willis, Women: Sarah Ford, Karen Larsen, Masursky, Betsy Rasumny, Weser, Men: Brown, Foose, Michael Matchie, Don Walker. *Allegro,* m: Colman, p: Colman. *Mark of Cain,* m: Stravinsky, ch and d: Redlich. *The Warrior's Courtesan,* m: percussion, ch and d: Harris. *Syrinx,* m: Debussy, ch and d: Redlich. *Ozark Suite,* m: Siegmeister, ch: Holm, ds: Amter, Harris, Lynn, Madole, Poor, Chambers, Kirwan, O'Neal, Redlich.

1959, August 3-5. The Young Choreographers' Workshop Under the Supervision of Hanya Holm. (August 3 and 5) *Field Day,* m: Vittorio Rieti, ch: Molly Lynn, ds: Shirley Appleman, Joan Cooper, Barbara Dilley, Elizabeth Harris, Rosalind Schmutz, Andrew Bailey, Ray Broussard, Don Steel. *Theatre Piece,* m: Arnold Schoenberg, ch: Joyce Trisler, ds: Don Redlich, Laurie Archer, Lucinda Childs, Dilley, Jefferson Miller, Larry Burgoon. *Allegro Buffo,* m: John Colman, p: Colman. *The Procession,* m: Carlos Surinach, ch: Archer, Saints: Trisler, Sandra Faxon, Beverlee Patton, Rose Rochman, People: Molly Lynn, Childs, Robyn Baker, Bessie Caldwell, Norma Carter, Joan Cooper, Barbara Davidson, Diana Dunagan, Sally Hatfield, Carol McCue, Jane Morrow, Marya Randall, Sandra York. *Passin' Through,* m: Traditional, ch and d: Redlich. *The Hunter,* m: Paul Hindemith, ch and d: Archer. *A Tangled Tale,* m: Wallingford Riegger, The Verse of Lewis Carol and Edward Lear recorded by Cyril Ritchard, ch: Harris, The Man in the Bowler Hat: Burgoon, The Barrister: Barbara Davidson, The Young Crowd: Marcia Barratt, Alice Hankins, Judith Hogan, Julia Maguire, Schmutz, Geraldean Smith, Andrew Bailey, Broussard, Steele. (August 4) *Eventide,* m: Norman Della Joio, ch: Redlich, ds: Redlich, Archer. *Journey,* m: Charles Ives, ch and d: Trisler. *Covenant,* m: Bela Bartok, ch and d: Harris. *The Gypsy's Dream,* m: Traditional, ch and d: Archer. *Mark of Cain,* m: Igor Stravinsky, ch and d: Redlich. *The Warriors Courtesan,* m: Michael Colgrass, ch and d: Harris. *Variegations,* m: John Wilson, ch: James Truitte, d: Trisler.

1960, August 10, 11. The Young Choreographers' Workshop Under the Supervision of Hanya Holm. *Pieces for A Capella Chorus,* m: G. Palestrina, H. Schuetz, S. Barr, con: John Colman, cs: T. Boggs, B. Clayton, E. Foote, C. Hutchinson, B. Ritchie, J. Semotan, D. Waters, L. Wray, B. Braman, K. Ashcroft, J. Axelson, S. Booth, J. Boatright, M. La Bach, S. O'Rourke, J. Maguire, L. Burgoon, A. Bruce, J. Stannard, B. Toews, R. Windsor, H. Boatright, J. Fetler, G. Finney, H. Gitelman, O. Kostock, P. Kutsche, A. Reid. *Roundelay,* m: medieval chansons and French folk music, ch: Claudia Gitelman, ds: Gitelman, Albert Reid, Kay Ashcroft, Julie Axelson. *Primavera,* m: Vittorio Rieti, ch and d: Elizabeth Harris. *The Duel,* m: Pierre Boulez, Henry Brant, ch: Harris, The Man: Robert Windsor, The Woman: Laurie Archer, The Catalyst: Larry Burgoon. *Instumental Pieces:* a. "Square Dance Set," arr.: Colman, viola: Paul Doktor, p: Colman; b. "Quodlibet on American Folk Tunes," m: Ingolf Dahl, 2 pianos, 8 hands: J. Boatright, P. Carpenter, C. Hutchison, Colman. *Country Dance,* m: Paul Creston, ch: Oliver Kostock, ds: Sue Bisgeier, Seece Boyce, Diana Dunagan, Suzi Farmer, Nancy Gilbert, Billy Hutchings, Kari Larsen, Patti McConnell. *Species Hominis Urbanis,* sound accompaniment, ch: Molly Lynn, Moles: Boyce, Dunagan, Pat Grover, Mary Kerns, Mary Kohlhaas, Cynthia Molkenbur, Sharon Rushing, Iris Seligman, Richard Bruce, Cranes: Betsy Braman, Sarah Burnham, Larsen, Beetles: as Moles. *Daydreams of Betty Mitty,* m: Kurt Weil, Bernie Green, Luening-Ussachevsky, Quarterlodeons, ch: Archer, Street Cleaner: Kostock,

Betty Mitty: Archer, Lion Tamer: Julia Maguire, Committeemen: Bruce, Bryan Toews, Robert Windsor, Woman on the Moon: Gitelman, Moon People: Jeannine Bramwell, Lynn, Toby Wiley, Bruce, Toews, Windsor, Silent Screen Star: Harris, Lover: Burgoon. *Phases,* m: Lou Harrison, ch: Lynn, ds: Tobey Hiller, Maguire, Katherine Posin, Wiley, Burgoon, Reid, Toews, Windsor.

1961, AUGUST 8. Hanya Holm Dance Concert: An Evening of Dance, Music, and Poetry at Broadmoor International Theatre starring Vera Zorina, Janet Collins, featuring Elizabeth Harris, Don Redlich, choreography by Hanya Holm, music and chorus directed by John Colman. *String Quartet No. 21,* m: Virgil Tompson, "Allegro Moderate" and "Tempo Valzer," d: Collins; "Adagio Sostenuto," ds: Harris, Redlich; "Allegretto," ds: Collins, Harris, Phyllis Haskell, Jan Ihrie, Lou Collier, Deveda Erikson, Redlich, inst: Giorgio Ciompi, Sue Fulghum, Paul Doktor, George Bekefi. *Pieces for Mixed Chorus,* m: Clemens non Papa, Orlando di Lasso, Ludwig Senfl, Stephen Barr. *Six Psalms,* m: Heinrich Schutz, solo d: Collins, dance cs: Virginia Adams, Ina Begerow, Susan Brehm, Collier, Erikson, Joan Ernst, Haskell, Heidi Hauser, Roberta Herbison, Sandra Horton, Billie Hutchings, Ihrie, Kathryn Karipides, Julia Maguire, Pat McConnell, Jane Robbins, Emily Roberts, Barbara Rutherford, Sharlyn Smoot, Nancy Topf, cs: Jenny Burgie, Diane Davidson, Josephine Estil, Esther Foote, Sue Fulghum, Evelyn Grubb, Rachel Hatton, Barbara Karl, Mary King, Jennis Phillips, Olive West, Julie Chatham, Mary Chatham, Ann Fiedler, Nellie Kavelin, Marcia Mize, Ruth Moon, Ann Slater, Lexine Weeks, William Beatty, George Garrigue, Mark Goodbody, Bill Moon, Horace Work, Jack Abel, Edward Gates, Charles Griffin, Oliver Kostock, Tom Ross, Robert Twitchell, Pete Tyree, Richard Watkins, The Quartet: Josephine Estill, Ruth Moon, George Garrigue, Stuart Creighton. *Facade,* m: William Walton, poems: Edith Sitwell, spoken by Vera Zorina, con: Colman, inst: Harvey Boatright, Earl Juhas, Richard Hubbard, Clayton Brant, William Ferguson, George Bekefi. *Music for an Imaginary Ballet,* m: Henry Brant, ch: Holm, ds: Harris, Redlich, Erikson, Horton, Karipides, inst: Boatright, Bekefi, Colman, lighting: Klaus Holm, technical dir: David Hand, cos: for *Psalms,* Julia Maguire.

1962, AUGUST 9. Summer Dance Demonstration, Hanya Holm, director, Oliver Kostock, assistant, John Colman, director of music, Allan Miles, Labanotation. *Dance Demonstration. Labanotation,* Presentation of Notation Symbols, Two Dance Etudes, ch: Holm, notated Miles, m: Colman and William Fischer. *Eurythmics,* dir: Colman. *Dance Studies (solutions to problems assigned in Dance Composition):* "Counterpoint," ch: Wilson Barrilleaux, drum Robert Fletcher, ds: Beverly Brown, Vicki Dils, Judith Shelby; "Triode," m: Edgar Varese, ch: Heidi Hauser, ds: Julian Burwell, Trudi Galloway, Marilyn Lowen; "March of the Marionettes," m: Charles Gounod, ch: Brown, ds: Barrilleaux, Dils, Lowen, Shelby, Spencer Snyder; "Conformity," ch: Christine Clark, drum, Fletcher, ds: Brown, Al Wiltz, Barbara Zakarian; "Circus

Pieces," m: Carlos Surinach, "Carnival," ch: Wiltz, ds: Burwell, Lowen, Jean Pinkerton, Robert Roth, Karen Stronach, Betty Shuford, Toni Urso, Joan Wohlstetter; "Circus Dancers," ch: Zakarian, ds: Brown, Susan Dunn, Martha Hixon, Rosalie Jones, Pricilla Miller, Zakarian; "Sentimental Duet," ch and ds: Barrilleaux, Shelby; "Clowns," ch: Donna Kearness, ds: Hauser, Snyder, Mills Tandy; "Acrobats," ch: Dils, ds: Clark, Fletcher, Galloway, Mary Quinn, Jennifer Way. Other participating dancers: Seece Boyce, Elissa DeWitt, Susan Dunn, Henry Everett, Nancy McDonald, Terry Navioux.

1963, August 8. **Summer Dance Demonstration**, Hanya Holm director, Oliver Kostock, Molly Lynn, assistants, Leonard Taffs, director of music, Allan Miles, Labanotation. *Dance Demonstration. Labanotation,* Presentation of Notation Symbols, Three Dance Etudes, ch: Holm, notated Miles, m: Taffs. *Dance Studies (solutions to problems assigned in Dance Composition)* "Gum," ch and ds: Gretchen Schneider, Regina Wray; "Bubble Up," ch and ds: Merrily Vincent, Roger Seward; "Time Machine," ch and ds: Mary Sue Woodcox, Gail Turner; "The Web," ch and ds: Linda Osborne, Margaret Kurz, Jinx Bryant; "Shapes," ch and ds: Wray, Vincent, Woodcox; "Duet in 5/4 Time," m: Bela Bartok, ch and ds: Woodcox, Seward; "A Day at the Races," ch and d: K. Dunkley. *Undertones and Comments,* ch: Lynn, "Chant," m: Alan Hovhanness, ds: Seece Boyce, Osborn, Terry Reeves, Barbara Zakarian; "Argument," m: Ronald Lo Presti, ds: Clifford Kirwan, Paul Chambers; "Soliloquy," m: Theodore Strongin, ds: Carol Sahlstrand and group; "Old Refrain," m: Popular, ds: Alice Olds, Christine Clarke, Wilson Barrillcaux; "Cacaphonia," ds: Barrilleaux and group. *Figure of Predestination,* m: Wallingford Riegger, ch: Holm, ds: Dunkley, Kirwan, Chambers. *Transfiguration, a Rite,* improvised accompaniment: Taffs, ch and d: Elizabeth Harris. *Toward the Unknown Region,* poem: Walt Whitman, m: Taffs, cs: Gini Andrews, Dorothy Brown, William Buckley, Florence Darby, Trent Ellis, Sue Fulghum, Margaret Godfrey, Lanny Green, Rachel Hatton, Clifford Horton, Ruth Horton, Arlene Kushnir, Ruth Laughren, Cecilia Lomo, Beth Mayse, Charlene Miller, Terry Naviaux, Eleanor Otto, Pat Redman, Barbara Thomas, Sheila Volkman, p: Ben Gahart, soprano solo: Volkman, ch: Holm, ds: Harris, Lynn, Dunkley and group. Other participating dancers: Carolyn Byrum, Mary Emanuel, Henry Everett, George Freelove, Patricia Kallien, Betty Malezi, Judy Morton, Betsy Sacks, Margot Starr, Barbara Waddill, Diane Walker.

1964, August 5. **Summer Dance Demonstration.** Hanya Holm, director, Oliver Kostock, associate, Leonard Taffs, director of music, Allan Miles, Labanotation. *Dance Demonstration. Dances of Children (solutions to problems assigned in Dance Composition Class I)* m: Carl Orff, "Entrance," ds: group; "Sextette," ch and ds: Donna Busby, Nancy Green, Don Heinselman, Carol Ramstad, Alta Townes, Sam Tapia; "Quartette," ch and ds: Judith Annia, Bev Cook, Sheila Donaghe, Diane Sandys; "Choo-Choo Train and Waltz," ch and ds: Nina Bellak, Happy Holstrom, Lothian Langhorst; "March," ch and ds: Bellak, Chardelle Cooper, Sheila Corbitt; "Trio," ch and ds: Cooper, Corbitt, Tapia; "Horses," ch: Bev Cook, ds: Busby, Holstrom, Langhorst, group. *Music for Dance Class,* dir: Taffs, "Bodily Experience of Musical Rhythm." *Labanotation Class. Dance Studies (solutions to problems assigned in Dance Composition Class II)* m: first 5 studies, Bela Bartok, last 3 studies, Igor Stravinsky, "Youth," ch and ds: Jacquie Davis, Sharon Jones, Patricia Kallien; "The Woman," ch and d: Nina Pauff; "The Disturbed," ch and d: Henry Everett; "The Romantic," ch and ds: K. Dunkley, Mary Sue Woodcox; "The Restless," ch and d: Lauren Persechetti; "The Enmeshed," ch and d: Gretchen Schneider; "The Troubled," ch: Dunkley, ds: Dunkley, Everett, William Hansen, Don Heinzelman, Sam Tapia; "The Dreamer," ch and d: Persichetti. *Trolls,* m: Al Hirt, ch: Kostock, ds: Cooper, Langhorst, Persichetti, Sandys. *Theatrics,* m: Henry Brant, staged by: Holm, ds: Bellak, Cook, Cooper, Dunkley, Hansen, Holstrom, Jones, Persichetti, Tapia. Other participating dancers: Mary Gallagher, Lucy Huddell, Diana Johnson, Charlene McDonald, Diane Rose.

1965, AUGUST 2-4. A Dance Festival Honoring Hanya Holm. Chs: Valerie Bettis, Elizabeth Harris, Nancy McKnight Hauser, Murray Louis, Alwin Nikolais, Don Redlich. Dancers from Colorado College Summer Session: Alma Martinez, Beverly Cook, Wilson Barrilleaux and Janis Ansley, Joan Brown, Kay Dunkley, Greta Flodquist, Mary Freese, Lauren Persichetti, Grechen Schneider, Diana McKelvey, Gail Turner, Catherine Vandertuin, Penny York, Emily Wadhams, Gale Ormiston, Tom Hustvet, Carleton Chard, Sam Tapia.

1966, AUGUST 4. Summer Student Workshop in Dance under the direction of Hanya Holm, assisted by Molly Lynn, Oliver Kostock, Allan Miles, musical director, Leonard Taffs. *Studies in Group Directions,* music improvisations by Taffs; "Straight Path": 1. Jean Milani, Chris Brant, Nadine Emerald, Kathleen Seymour, Josephine Sutlive, Kathleen Morris; 2. Arlene Zuefle, Linda Ruzich, Penny Fray, Lucy Brooks, Judith Novak; "Curved Path": 1. ch: Mary Bird, ds: Jane Abramson, Suzie Haynes, Jim Julian, Judith Sonnek, Kathy Stelly, Catherine Vandertuin; 2. ch: Pamela Pleasant, ds: Regina Wray, Pat Rogers, Marsha Hale, Gilda Grant, Pat Wehner, Enid Obee. *Solos With Vocal Sounds:* 1. Sandra Harris, 2. Fray. *Duets:* 1. Sutlive, Harris; 2. Fray, Lucy Brooks; 3. Pleasant, Sonnek; *Trios:* 1. Alice Reyes, Obee, Brant; 2. Sutlive, DiAnne Damro, Harris; 3. Brooks, Fray, Seymour; 4. "Work Theme," ch: Sonnek, ds: Bird, Reyes, Sonnek; 5. "And They Watched," ch: Hale, ds: Arlene Zuefle, Wray, Haynes. *Group Theme and Variations,* music improv.: Taffs, ch and ds: Wray, Hale, Pleasant, Rogers, Haynes, Reyes. *Group Dance,* m: Corelli, ch: Lynn, ds: Reyes, Jim Julian, Marsha Hale, Wray, Bird, Zuefle, Haynes, Rogers. *Labanotation Class,* dir: Miles. Dances learned from notation scores: "Lilac Fairy Variation" from *The Sleeping Beauty,* ch: Petipa, m:

Tchaikovsky, d: Bird; "Tarentella," ch: Sergievsky, m: Rossini, ds: Bird, Haynes, Obee, Hale. *Philippine Folk Dances,* staged by Alice Reyes, member, Bayanihan Philippine Folk Dance Group, "Ifugao," ds: Alice Frost, Sonnek, Reyes, Vandertuin, Gary Masters, Christ Brant, Julian; "Polkabal," ds: Wray, Fray, Gant, Abramson; "Kandingan," ds: Lynn, Kostock; "Singkil," d: Reyes, clappers: Bird, Masters, Gant, Pleasant, Sonnek, Fray; "Pandango sa Ilaw," ds: Pleasant, Sonnek, Reyes, Masters, Julian, Brant; "Itik-Itik," ds: Wray, Gant, Fray, Abramson; "Binasuan," d: Reyes; "Tinikling," ds: Pleasant, Masters.

1967, AUGUST 2. Summer Students Workshop in Dance under the direction of Hanya Holm and Oliver Kostock, musical director, Leonard Taffs. *Salutation,* m: G. F. Handel, ch: Esther Geoffrey, ds: Saundra Dugan, Toby Hankin, Natalie Richman, Terry Stoner, Sara Wiener, Marie Winckler, Regina Wray. *Theme and Variations I,* prepared piano: Taffs, ch and ds: Cathryn Cornelius, Suzanne Hellmuth, Jane Quentin, Kathleen West, Mary Anderson. *Symmetry-Asymmetry Studies,* unaccompanied, ch and ds: Helmuth, Holly Hajjar; Corine Windus, West; Cornelius, Quetin. *Duet,* percussion: Alice Reyes, ch and ds: Dugan, Wray. *Echoes,* m: Bela Bartok, ch: Winckler, ds: Dugan, Wiener, Wray. *Theme and Variations II,* accomp.: Taffs, Karen Steele, ch: Steele, ds: Hajjar, Denise Lapaglia, Gerald Pearson, Steele, Windus. *Set of Five Dances,* m: Charles Ives, ch: Don Redlich, restaged by Linda Osborne, ds: Osborne, Heidi Hauser, Stoner with Wray, Dugan, Wiener, Winckler, Daphne Mantis, Richman, Steele, Pearson. *Valses "Nobles et Sentimentales,"* m: Maurice Ravel, p: Taffs. *Pastorale,* m: Igor Stravinsky, ch: Kostock, ds: Dugan, Lapaglia, Hauser, Reyes, Wray. *Upon Enchanted Ground,* m: Alan Hovhaness, ch and d: Osborne. *Untitled,* m: Dello Joio, ch: Reyes, ds: Reyes, Stoner with Osborne, Dugan, Richman, Steele, Winckler, Wray. *Three Fragments,* unaccompanied, A. "Teasing," ch and ds: Hankin, Richman; B. "Study in Tension," m: the dancers, ch and ds: Hajjar, Lapaglia; C. "Contrasts," m: the dancers, ch: Lapaglia, ds: Suzanne Pierre, Quetin. *Birds,* m: Jerry Goldsmith, ch: Hajjar, ds: Hajjar, Lapaglia, Pierre. *Spooks,* m: F. Poulenc, ch: Holm, ds: Dugan, Geoffrey, Hajjar, Sheila Laughlin, Eddy Martinez, Dee McCandless, Pearson.

1968, AUGUST 7. Summer Students Workshop in Dance under the direction of Hanya Holm and Oliver Kostock. Guest artist, Molly Lynn, musical director, Leonard Taffs, Labanotation, Allan Miles, lighting and scenery, Klaus Holm. *Dance Demonstration,* musical improvisation: Taffs. *Studies—Composition Class I,* "Symmetry-Asymmetry," "Metronome," "Study With Prop," and "Studies With Spoken Word." *Laban Dance Notation,* dances re-created from notation: "Pavane," ch: Thoinot Arbeau; "Branle," ch: traditional; "Galliard," ch: traditional; "Schottische," ch: traditional. *Dances for Children— Composition Class I,* m: Carl Orff, "Shoes," ch: Treva Folkers; "Play With Me," ch: Margo Bassity; "Choo-Choo Train," ch: Charlotte Barker; "Waltz," ch: Gretchen Phillips, Bob Rose; "Drums," ch: Gayle Wult; "Bells," ch: Susan

Krohn; "Horses," ch: Eve Dearborn. *Solo Dance for Children,* m: Ernst Toch, ch
and d: Mary Cerny. *Games,* ch: Kostock. *Seven Pieces—Composition Class II,* m:
Bela Bartok, Igor Stravinsky, "The Romantic," ch and ds: Cerny, Eilif
Jesperson; "The Disturbed," ch and d: William Marsh; "The Serene," ch
and d: Natalie Richman; "The Driven," ch and ds: Denise Lapaglia, Frances
LaBarre; "The Enmeshed," ch and d: Joanne Saltsman; "The Troubled," ch:
Diana Cole; "The Dreamer," ch and d: Cole. *Three Dances,* ch: Lynn,
"Unravel-Ravel," m: John Coltrane; "Anti-Moves," m: Gunther Schuller; "Re-
lays," m: Paul Fetler. *Not By Love Alone,* m: Shchedrin, ch and d: Gail Turner.
Nimblewit, m: J. S. Bach, ch and d: Richman. *Theatrics,* m: Carlos Surinach, ch
and d: [*sic*] Holm. Other participating dancers: Paggy Anderson, Alexa
Brill, Sandy Dexheimer, Penny Fray, Gayle Graff, Jorja Jahrig, William Marsh,
Ed Martinez, Janet Monninger, Joan Muckenhirn, Dolores O'Connor, Tess
Roberts, Mary Safire, May Steele, Earlaine Young, Jane Huffman, Elaine
Ivaldy.

1969, AUGUST 6. Summer Students Workshop in Dance under the direction of Hanya Holm and Oliver Kostock. Guest artist, Molly Lynn, musical
director, Leonard Taffs, lighting and scenery, Klaus Holm. *Entrances,* m:
Carl Orff, ch: Holm. *Studies From Composition Classes:* "Symmetry and Asym-
metry: Duets"; "Theme and Variation #1," ch: Nancy Davis, improvised m:
Taffs; "Duet," ch and ds: Gretchen Phillips, Jessie Sayre; "Theme and Varia-
tion #2," ch: Alita Robnak, improvised m: Taffs; "He and She," ch and ds:
Elaine McHugh, Charlotte Hildebrand; "Theme and Variation #3," ch:
McHugh, improvised m: Taffs; "Male and Female," ch and ds: Marcia Schram,
Fred Sherwood; "Rundadinella," ch: Sayre. *Dance With Props,* m: Orff, ch:
Lynn. *Celestial Mechanics,* m: Teo Macero, ch: Lynn. *Celebration,* m: Orff, ch:
Gretchen Phillips. *March and Couple Dance,* m: Orff, ch: Kostock. *Solo Dance,*
m: Orff, ch and d: Pat Hodges. *Studies With Words and Sounds,* ch and ds: Joan
Friedman, Debbie Loewen. *The Grey Bench,* m: excerpts from Quicksilver
Messenger Service, "Happy Trails," ch: Holm. *Ballad of Mr. Latour,* m: Orff,
ch: Lynn. *Exits,* m: Orff, ch: Holm. Other participating dancers: Christo-
pher Burnside, Diana Cole, Eileen Cook, Linda De Lissovoy, Beth Finke,
Carolyn Foyse, Ned Halloway, Connie Hammer, Susan Hellmuth, Ann
Howbert, Paul Jarocki, Jean Jennings, Robin Johnson, Sharon Kelly, Susan
Lane, Carie Lo Castro, Sarah Mangelsdaof, Eddie Martinez, John McVay,
Creighton Miller, Kathy Norris, Gwen Pollack, Joseph Rocha, Glayds Ro-
man, Susan Sandler, Susan Smith, Varya Soudakoff, Cinde Switzer, J. Sydow.

1970, AUGUST 6. Summer Workshop in Dance under the direction of Hanya
Holm and Oliver Kostock. Guest choreographer, Molly Lynn. "The De-
scent of Rhythm and Harmony," a Renaissance Intermedio reconstructed
by Dr. Julia Sutton, visiting professor of music and dance. *Dance to Ariel,* ch:
Gretchen Phillips, m: Haufrecht. *Studies From Composition Class:* "Dances for
Children," m: Orff, ch: Charlotte Barker, Mary Horner, Claudia Edwards,

Teru Osato, Kathy Morris, Joe Rocha, J. Sydow, Marianne Livant; "Sound,
Sense, and Nonsense," ch and ds: Penny Burr and Elizabeth Garren,
Gabrielle Lawrence and Rika Burnham, Debby Quinn and Ken Fischer,
Phillips; "Themes and Variations," ch: Lawrence, Elizabeth Garren; "Style
Piece No. 1," ch: Lynn, m: Stravinsky; "Characters," ch and d: Judith Ragir,
Osato and Hornor, Phillips; "Style Piece No. 2," ch: Lynn, m: Xenakis. Other
participating dancers: Kathryn Biesanz, Lisa Brinton, Rosanne Drillich, Cathy
Einhorn, Carolyn Foyse, Nancy Frost, Amy Grossman, Jacqueline Hand,
Marya Huseby, Sheri Ille, Elaine Ivaldy, Nancy Lee, Kristin Lindley, Eddie
Martinez, Dolores O'Connor, Sally Oosterhous, Deborah Pleskow, Sylvia
Poole, Lauren Schubart, Nancy Stern, Anna Taffs, Barbara Thornburgh,
Deborah Vacha, Larry Wilson. *The Descent of Rhythm and Harmony*, producer,
staging, editing: Holm, dance reconstruction, musical, poetic ed.: Sutton,
chorus dir and con: Taffs, scenery and lighting, Klaus Holm; characters,
Apollo: Charles Garth, Harmony: Lynn, Rhythm: Sydow, Bacchus: Rocha,
Three Muses: Foyse, Morris, Phillips, Messenger: Frank Hoffmeister, inst:
Patrick Lindley, Margaret Smith, Grace Bragonier, Muriel Baay, Elizabeth
Aldrich, Gunther Paetsch, Mildred Lacour, cs: Kat Bradley, Ellen Frerichs,
Quinn, Missye Bonds, Livant, Nancy Theeman, Jo Brewer, Burr, Paula
Cheever, Margie Clark, Bonnie Moulton, Pleskow, Powell, Janet Sprouse,
Marilyn Turner, Fischer, Hoffmeister, Martinez, Pat Perry, John Daane,
Richard Hilt, Paul Ricker, Dirk Baay, Robert Feldsien, Jesse Hill, Kostock,
Richard Neidhardt.

1971, AUGUST 4. Hanya Holm Workshop in Dance under the direction of
Hanya Holm and Oliver Kostock, musical director, Leonard Taffs, scenery
and lighting, Klaus Holm. *The Glorianna*, m: Benjamin Britten, ch: Marcia
Schramm, ds: Anita Feldman, Jonette Lancos, Schramm, Anna-Kate Taffs,
Art Bridgeman, Timothy Crafts, Carey Erickson, Lee Gurga, Larry Wilson.
Quartet, ch: Kostock, percussion: Taffs, played by Taffs, Schramm, Lancos,
Joe Smith. *Asymmetry Etude*, ch and ds: Bridgeman, Eugenie Doyle. *Etudes
With Sounds*, ch and ds: Diana Drake and Wendie Abend, Bridgeman and
Elinor White, Amy Grossman and Leslie Cunningham. *Theme and Variation
Etudes*, m: Partch, ch: Pat Lillis, m: George Harrison, sung by Leon Russell,
ch: Crafts. *Duet*, ch and ds: Jennifer Donohue, Richard Haisma. *Inguernica*,
m: K. Gaburo, reading: Joan Baez, ch and d: Gretchen Phillips. *Still*, m:
Britten, ch: Lynn, ds: Susan Crate, Gerald Pearson. *Forces*, m: Varèse, ch:
Holm, set: K. Holm. *Ritual*, ch: Haisma. *Dance With Props*, m: Charles Ives,
ch: Lynn. *Dance for Dreamers*, m: Ken Gaburo, ch: Phillips. *Group—J. Thurber's
Last Flower*, ch: Ken Yoder. *Birds*, ch and ds: Wendy Freed, Yoder. *I'll Be in Your
Dreams if You'll Be in Mine*, ch and d: Phillips. *Pardners*, m: Leo Kottke, ch and
ds: Ann Arends, Gabrielle Lawrence. *Magnetic Rag*, m: Scott Joplin, ch and
ds: Sara and Gerald Pearson. Other participating dancers: Nancy Allyn,
Barbara Bennett, Paula Bluebaugh, Eileen Cooley, Leslie Cunningham,
Dallas Dexter, Carol Friedman, Jane Friedman, Ferris Frost, Nancy Frost,

Martha Harpstrite, Sandra Hendrick, Sheri Ille, Sara Keith, Hilary Leibsohr, Patricia Lillis, Leslie Litin, Ann Little, Gary Lund, Eddie Martinez, Lucy Marx, Constance McKeon, Lyn Miller, Dena Mullen, Eileen Nemeth, Colleen Nepstad, Craig Neustaedter, Christina Nichols, Lea Peterson, Constance Pfitsch, Margaret Pierpont, Debra Powell, Ellen Rafel, Jeanette Robertson, Patricia Rockwood, Howard Sabatt, Mary Sames, Pamela Samuel, Holly Schiffer, Elizabeth Schlosser, Gretchen Schneider, Sallie Shepardson, Deborah Vacha, Patricia Ward, Lawrence Wilson.

1972, AUGUST 9, 10. Hanya Holm Dance Concert under the direction of Hanya Holm, Oliver Kostock, and Gretchen Phillips, musical director and pianist, Leonard Taffs, scenery and lighting designer, Klaus Holm. With the American Brass Quintet: Gerald Schwarz, Louis Ranger, Douglas Edelman, Robert Biddlecome, Edward Birdwell. *Etudes (selected from dance composition class)* A. "Three Children's Pieces," m: Bela Bartok, p: Taffs, ch: Dena Brown, Lowell Britson, Wendy Kennan, Ethel Coe, Cyndie Bellen, Becky Hansen, Beth Johnson, Laurie Dill; B. "Little Studies," ch: Carol Ginsberg, John Munger, Tamar Kotoske, Ginsberg, Dennis Breeze, Sue Hawkins. *Court Dance,* m: Henry Purcell, harpsichord: Patrick Lindley, ch: Kostock. *Ritual,* m: Carl Orff, Igor Stravinsky, ch: Kostock. *Corroboration Rag,* m: Scott Joplin, p: Taffs, ch: Phillips. *Contrapunctus,* m: J. S. Bach, inst: American Brass Quintet, ch: Holm. *Flags,* ch: Holm, trumpets: Schwartz, Ranger. *Waltzes,* m: Maurice Ravel, p: Taffs, ch: David Rotholz, Maria Cheng, Beverly Ryan, Amy Targan, Gloria Goodale, Penny Burr, Gordon Shepard. *Clowns,* m: Francis Poulenc, inst: American Brass Quintet, ch: Phillips. Other participating dancers: Heidi Alford, Diane Bearman, Betsy Binder, Joyce Cadle, Nancy Coburn, Holly Conway, Timothy Crafts, Janice Cronin, Lucinda Durham, Janis Dybdahl, Carter Ellison, Patricia Ethridge, Kay Evans, Pamela Francis, Barbara French, Lane Gifford, Sandie Gookin, Alan Hadley, Libby Hager, Ann Hammack, Eric Haskell, Joseph Holloway, Susan Hostetler, Pam Kariotis, Steven Keith, Vickie King, Carolyn Klismith, Gary Lund, Pamela Magrill, Eddie Martinez, Theresa McGuire, Robin McNelly, Clair Nagel, Laurie Near, Kathy Norris, Sherry Ogg, Perry Paterson, Barbara Peterson, Daren Petrie, Margy Pierpont, Cheryl Pleskow, Alli Price, John Rankin, Patty Rockwood, Mitchell Rose, Cathy Rusoff, Ginger Sarber, Sallie Shepardson, Dinah Smith, Michael Smith, Carol Soleau, Nancy Stern, Anna Taffs, Paula Traktman, Cathy Turocy, Donald Van Horn, Judy Van Wyk, Jessica Woody.

1973, AUGUST 8, 9. Hanya Holm Dance Concert under the direction of Hanya Holm, Oliver Kostock, and Gretchen Phillips, musical director and pianist, Leonard Taffs, scenery and lighting designer, Klaus Holm, with Melvin Kaplan, oboe, and John Solum, flute. *Entrances and Exits,* m: Carl Orff. *Etudes (selected from Dance Composition classes)* A. "Directions" (August 8) ch and d: Andrea Lovato, drums: Richard Lillehei (August 9) ch and d:

Janice Cronin, p: Taffs; B. "Parallel Studies" (August 8) ch and ds: Phyllis Pollack and Connie Swisher, Fern Bartner and Kathy Guy, Jeremy Burton and Varya Soudakoff (August 9) ch and ds: Judy Fischer, Lee Ann Eldridge, Haila Strass and Marlene Pitkow, Dawn Beattie and Nancy Stavn, p: Adrienne Stamatos; C. "Asymmetry" (August 8) ch and ds: Katie Higgins and Pris Doernbach, Jane Kahan and Jane Roeder (August 9) Marcia Breit and Jane Jacobson; D. "Symmetry" (August 8) ch and ds: Kristin Olson and Nancy Madden, Char Hummel and Betsy Heffelfinger (August 9) Nina Egert and Doernbach, p: Egert, Jim Kelley and Betsy Davidson; E. "Voices and Props" (August 8) ch and ds: Doug De Witt, Olson and Hummel, Carol Ginsberg, Missy Hoagland (August 9) Heffelfinger and Geraldine Smith, Cronin; F. "Theme and Variations" (August 8) ch and d: Hummel, sound: Gus Mundt (August 9) Heffelfinger; G. "Compositions to Music" (August 8) m: Carl Orff, ch and ds: Heffelfinger, Irma Fyfe, Smith, Davidson, m: Erik Satie, ch and d: Cronin (August 9) m: Octavio Pinto, ch and ds: Linn Walker, Pam Budner, Sylvie Blaustein, Ceil Walsky, m: Francis Poulenc, ch and d: Hoagland (August 8 and 9) m: Arnold Schoenberg, ch and d: Carol Ginsberg, m: Dmitri Kabalevsky, ch and ds: Guy, Strauss, Clasina Vanderwert, John Munger. *Moon-Bone Cycle,* ch: Phillips. *Allemande-Courrente,* m: J. S. Bach, ch: Kostock. *Three Stories From "The Me Nobody Knows,"* m: Wallingford Riegger, ch: Mimi Kagan Kim, 1. The early bird catches the worm, but not always; 2. The hopeless tree; 3. When I go to sleep, I get drowsy and I see things like little fireworks; inst: Kaplan, Solum. *"That's the Show,"* text: Samuel Beckett, ch and reading: Kim. *Metamorphoses After Ovid,* m: Benjamin Britten, ch: Holm, 1. Pan-Munger, 2. Niobe-Kim, 3. Arethusa-Bartner, Beattie, Margy Pierpont, Tamar Smith, Devon Wall, oboe: Kaplan. *Density 21.5,* m: Edgar Varèse, ch: Holm, ds: Kelly, Eddie Martinez, Munger, flute: Solum. *Three Pieces,* m: Alberto Ginastera, ch: Holm, ds: Cronin, De Witt, Guy, Heffelfinger, Francis Leftwich, Munger, Marlene Pitkow, G. Smith, David Struthers, inst: Kaplan, Solum. Other participating dancers: Linda Cohen, Catrina Cramer, Kris Darnell, Joyce Davidoff, Cindy Dean, Patricia De Lee, Robbie Diamond, Barbara French, Libby Hager, Sherry Hilding, Jan Isaacs, Michelle Javornik, Lisa Judge, Dana Keeler, Wendy Kennan, Don Ladig, Jacqueline Lang, Phoebe Lawrence, Jacqueline Low, Valerie Luiz, Nancy Merkel, Kate Michaels, Cece Miranda, Audrey Montano, Carol Nicol, Gwen Noel, Sherry Ogg, Sally Pennington, Witney Ray, Jara Reed, Renee Rockoff, Beverly Ryan, Betty Schneider, Sandra Smith, Mary Stroud, Holly Summer, Constance Swisher, Cynthia Vollmer, Linn Walker, Devon Wall, Debra Weiss, Sally White, Karin Wood, Thom Yarnal.

1974, AUGUST 7, 8. Hanya Holm Dance Concert under the direction of Hanya Holm, Oliver Kostock, and Gretchen Phillips, musical director and pianist, Leonard Taffs, scenery and lighting designer, Klaus Holm, with the Festival Winds: Melvin Kaplan, Allen Blustine, Arthur Weisberg. *Entrances and Exits,* m: arr. Taffs. *Little Studies for Technique,* ch: Mimi Kim, guest choreographer, m: Taffs. *Etudes (selected from Dance Composition classes)* A. "Symmetry, Asymmetry, and Parallel" (August 7) m: Dick Hyman, J. Kelly, D. Ladig, ch: Doug DeWitt and others (August 8) m: as Wed., ch: DeWitt and others; B. "Quartets," ch: Wendy Ansley, m: Claude Debussy; ch: Matia Karrell, Kristen Eliasberg, m: Tom Kathak, Carol Corbus. C. "Theme and Variation," ch: Leslie Cox, Karrell, Kathy Schweizer, Cynthia Merrill, Karla Hackstaff, Schweizer, m: Bo Hanson, the Beach Boys, Cynthia Merrill, Antonio Vivaldi; D. "Counterpoint," ch: the dancers, m: Taj Mahal, J. S. Bach; E. "ABA Form," ch: the dancers, m: Kelly, French, Ryan, Taj Mahal; F. "Props, Masks, and Caricatures," ch: Betsy Rowland, Suellen McAndrews, Judy Shapiro, Barbara French, others. *Honolulu Punch,* ch: Gretchen Phillips, m: Ernest Toch, con: Taffs. *Composition for Clarinet and Tape,* m: Charles Whittenberg, inst: Blustine, ch: Holm, solo ds: Phillips, Jim Kelly. *Two Pieces,* m: G. F. Handel, inst: Festival Winds, ch: Kostock. *Eight Pieces,* m: Darius Milhaud, inst: Festival Winds, ch: June Panagakos, Alli Price, Beverly Ryan, Merrill, Didi Day, Matia Karrell, Schweizer, Dana Block, Rowland, Kelley Amerson, Brett Larson, Richard Abbott. *Composition in Three Movements,* m: Igor Stravinsky, inst: Blustine, ch: Phillips, ds: Leanne Eldridge, Eddie Martinez. *Tackymetric Auricle,* m: Georges Auric, inst: Festival Winds, ch: Phillips. Other participating dancers: Judy Anderson, Larry Aranda, Teri Bain, Dawn Beattie, Joann Boyle, Jeremy Burton, Mary Burton, Patty Campbell, Ellen Carey, Yvette Cornelius, Allison Davis, Pamela Elder, Elaine Evans, Janet Fattore, Maggie Gibbe, Deborah Gibson, Steve Gray, Paula Harrington, Heather Harris, Elizabeth Heffelfinger, Janel Hopper, Elizabeth Huebner, David Hughes, Susan Kennedy, Mona Ketchersid, Betty Kolner, Don Ladig, Lola Lee, Vicki LeFevre, Terry Lehman, Gail Lewis, Bobbie Lippman, Diane Malik, Linelle McCune, Ellen McLarty, Cindy Meyer, Tom Michel, Cece Miranda, Ed Myers, Emily Odza, Perry Patterson, Yancey Perkinson, Jan Perry, Jim Pogue, Linda Priest, Patricia Ratcliffe, Whitney Ray, Susan Roebuck, Marta Schaefer, Lin Shook, Julia Sides, Lisa Spiegel, Danny Spinuzzi, Michelle Stevens, Sandy Strahan, David Struthers, Lee Sweetland, Anna Taffs, Anne Tantillo, Andrea Torrice, Maria White, Eula Yancey, Lillian Zamora.

1975, August 6, 7. Hanya Holm Dance Concert under the direction of Hanya Holm, Oliver Kostock, and Claudia Gitelman, musical director, Marilyn Rosenberger, with the New York Saxophone Quartet: Raymond Beckenstein, David Tofani, Albert Regni, Walter Kane. *Entrances and Exits,* m: Traditional. *Etudes (selected from Dance Composition classes)* A. "Parallel, Symmetry and Asymmetry," B. "Duets." *Dances to Music,* A. "Dances for Children," m: Carl Orff, ch: Victoria Marks, Judith Silverman, Steven Gray, Nancy Frost; B. "Five Little Pieces," m: Elliott Carter, inst: New York Saxophone Quartet, ch: Wendy Ansley, Jim Kelly, Dale Thompson, John Munger, Tom Kanthak, Joyce Mills; C. "Rondo," m: Michael Oldfield, ch: the dancers; D. "Hoedown," m: Aaron Copland, ch: Caren Paul. *Canon and Fugue,* m: J. S. Bach, inst: New York Saxophone Quartet (and all following) ch: Kostock, ds: Ansley, Anne Bryan, Kanthak, Brett Larson, Marks, Munger. *Blues,* m: Eugene DiNovi, ch: Gitelman, ds: Ansley, Susan Blankensop, Gitelman, Gray, Jan Gundelfinger, Kanthak, Larson, Donna Pelle, Dianna Rawnsley, Carl Watley. *Quartet for Saxophones,* m: George Handy, ch: Holm, ds: Blankensop, Gray, Kelly, June Panagakos. *4 + 14,* m: Milan Kaderavek, ch: Gitelman, ds: Bryan, Jeremy Burton, Gail Casson, Don Ladig, Mills, Munger, Jill Novascone, Deborah Olin, Silverman, Chris Small, Anne Tantillo, Thompson, John Towbin, Julie Williams. *Bach Menagerie,* m: Henry Brandt, ch: Holm, ds: Ansley, Dawn Beattie, Gray, Kanthak, Kelly, Amy Klein, Ladig, Larson, Eddie Martinez, Merle Matsunaga, Jim Pogue, Carol Scoville, Small, Charles Gross, Heidi Gundlack, Brenda Hassenbein, Marjorie Huebner, Margaret Morris, Panagakos, Pelle, Tantillo. Other participating dancers: Mary Bennison, Barbara Bolt, Kathy Brann, Marcia Breit, Alice Cleveland, Ursula Dennis, Rick Flippin, Charles Gross, Linda Harkavy, Brenda Hassenbein, Marjorie Huebner, Deborah Jelin, Carol Kuyper, Lola Lee, Gail Lewis, Betilyn Mahaffy, Charon Marco, Meg McGough, Jill Novascone, Deborah Olin, Linda Peacock, Patricia Peterson, Carol Scoville, Kay Tani, Julie Williams, Chase Winton, Karen Wolman, Emilie Zonsius.

1976, August 4, 5. Hanya Holm Dance Concert under the direction of Hanya Holm, Oliver Kostock, and Claudia Gitelman, scenery and lighting designer, Klaus Holm, with Jeanne Piland, mezzo-soprano. *Entrances and Exits,* m: Leonard Taffs. *Etudes (from Dance Composition Classes)* A. "Symmetry, Parallel, Asymmetry," B. "Studies initiated by parts of the body," C. "Studies on a Theme," D. "Etudes with variable sound accompaniments," E. "Dances to Music," F. "Eight Pieces," m: Paul Bowles, ch: Marcia Paulsen, Phyllis Sanfillippo, Jon Friedman, Paul Cohen-Myers, Gretchen Cohenour, Sheri Kenney, Sarah Boeh, John Munger, Tim Davis, Jane Kahan, Rosanna Gamson, Beverly Ryan. *Rite,* m: Reginald-Smith Brindle, dir: Kostock, ds: Ann Butler, Sarah Clark, Davis, Friedman, Lysa Kotin, Munger, Paulsen, Margy Pierpont, Jean Pulos, Dianna Rawnsley, Mary Romer, Ryan. *Homage to Mahler,* m: Gustav Mahler, sung by Piland, p: Taffs, ch: Holm, ds: Gitelman, Terry Kaelber with Howard Fine, Kenney, Diana Lim, John MacGregor, Eddie Martinez, Mary Ann Masuda, Cecile Miranda. *Partita,* m: G. P. Telemann, ch: Gitelman, ds: Ansley, Cohen-Myers, Friedman, Kaelber, Kanthak, Joanne Korner, Jenise Parris, Karla Zhe. Other participating dancers: Julia Allen, Larry Aranda, Deborah Berg, Ann Butler, Alice Cleveland, Karin Coyne, Jane Denman, Ursula Dennis, Nancy Dey, Peggy Ekberg, Laura Fischer, Zita Geoffroy, Jill Graham, Abby Gross, Shawn Hiers, Suzanne Horning, Elizabeth Hursa, Martha Isom, Joann Kawamura, Alyssa Keen, Rebecca Leatherman, Susan Leveton, Monica Manning, Jean Marshall, Carolyn Nordstrom, Maureen Perou, Sukey Purdy, Martha Renick, Sheri Rosengard, Suzy Ross, Katy Schmitz, Margaret Snow, Michael Sternfeld, Lindsey Sweet, Doreen Weiss, Claire Yarmo.

1977, Aᴜɢᴜsᴛ 3, 4. Hanya Holm Dance Concert under the direction of Hanya Holm, Oliver Kostock, and Claudia Gitelman, musical director and pianist, John Colman, scenery and lighting designer, Klaus Holm. *Demonstration,* m: Colman. *Studies Based on Symmetry, Asymmetry, and Parallel,* ch: Madeline Dean and Susan Hadley, Dian Gibson and Jean Levenworth, Don Borsh and Lisa Naugle, Yael Barash and Rachel Brumer, Jean Pulos and Sukey Purdy, Katy and John Munger. *Independent Projects:* 1. "Lullaby," m: Traditional Israeli, ch: Barash, Brumer, Chris Evans, ds: Brumer, Evans, cs: Barash, Evans, Leslie Flint, Purdy, inst: Belinda Bowler, David Prager III; 2. "Jazz-Inspired," ch and ds: Cal Grogan, Hadley, Russell Miller, Mary Reid, voice and percussion: Raúl Butrón, Paul Davis, Eddie Martinez; 3. "Dream," m: Pulos-Xenakis, ch: Pulos, ds: Barash, Belinda Bowler, Dian Gibson, Hadley, Jean Leavenworth; 4. "Solo With Prop," m: Atteignant, ch: Dean and Clarissa Townsend, d: Dean; 5. "Las Alazanas," m: Traditional Mexican, dir: Butrón, ds: Barash, Molly Coxe, Janice Cusolito, Evans, Kathleen Pignataro, Reid, Gina Vincent. *Dances for Children* (August 3) m: Orff, ch: J. Munger, ds: Barash and Naugle, ch: Butrón, ds: Janice Cusolito, Leslie Flint, Martinez, Reid, Vincent, ch: Susan Wicke, ds: Hadley, Kenney, Sandy Leeds, Lisa Wallgren, ch: Bill Barron, ds: Don Borsh, Bowler, Molly Coxe, Dean, ch: Evans, Purdy, ds: Brumer, Kathleen Pignataro, Grogan, Stephen Koester, Miller, Prager; *Games* (August 4) m: Bizet, ch: Jean Leavenworth, ds: Barash, Bowler, Laura Brenton, Dian Gibson, Carol Kaminski, Levenworth, Pignataro, ch: Coxe, ds: K. and J. Munger, Reid, Townsend, Wicke, ch: Prager, ds: Butrón, Heather Hering, Sara Hohe, Prager, Anita Trujillo, Vincent, ch: Koester, ds: Brumer, Leslie Flint, Grogan, Hadley, Koester, Lani Okimoto, Pulos, Lisa Wallgren. *Space Design: Dances Created for a Given Dramatic Space Design:* 1. "Exploring Depth," m: Bartók, ch: Hadley, ds: Bowler, Dean, Levenworth, Pignataro, Vincent; 2. "Columns," m: Bartók, ch: Barash, ds: Kenney, Naugle; 3. "The Web," ch: Borsh: ds: Coxe, Paula Davis, Reid, Wallgren, Wicke; 4. "Single Focus," m: Bartók, ch and d: Brumer; 5. "Cave," m: Stravinsky, ch Evans, ds: Grogan, Purdy, Miller; 6. "Pool of Light," m: Stravinsky, ch: J. Munger, ds: Butrón, Martinez, K. and J. Munger; 7. "The Ramp," m: Stravinsky, ch: Koester, ds: Brenton, Cusolito, Flint, Gibson, Hering, Kaminski, Leeds, Okimoto, Pulos, Townsend, Trujillo. *Parsley, Sage, Rosemary, and Thyme,* m: Simon and Garfunkle, ch: Kostock, ds: K. and J. Munger. *A Suite for Players,* m: Stravinsky, ch: Gitelman, ds: Barron, Borsh, Kenney, Koester, Leeds, Miller, Naugle, Prager, Purdy, Wicke, masks: Lisa, Hillary and Alix Gitelman. Other participating dancers: Ursula Dennis, Laurie Fullerton, Karen Holm, Margaret Munro, Karen Shechter.

1978, Aᴜɢᴜsᴛ 9, 10. Hanya Holm Dance Ensemble Concert including choreography by Hanya Holm, Nancy Hauser, Oliver Kostock, John Colman, musical director. *Exits and Entrances,* m: Colman. *Symmetry, Asymmetry, and Parallel,* ch: John and Katy Munger, Rosa Rodriguez and Barbara Stetzelberger, Madeline Dean and Robert Connor, Drew Hoag and Stephen

Koplowitz. *Shapes,* ch: Ann Swanberg, ds: Karen Brown, Stephen Otto, Rodriguez, Spencer Synder. *Contrasts,* m: Subotnik, ch and ds: Dean, Nancy Evans, William Harren, J. Munger. *Props,* m: Gunther Schuller, ch: Lisa Naugle, ds: Tom Burrington, Robert Connor, Dean, K. Munger, Naugle; m: Eliot Carter, ch: Merle Matsunaga, ds: Evans, Matthew Gunzelman, Sarah Hauser, Catherine Hondorp, Koplowitz. *Humor:* 1. "Just the Three of Us," m: Captain and Tenille, ch and ds: Mary Good, Hoag, Gunzelman; 2. "A Kind of September," m: Sigmund Romberg, ch: J. Munger, ds: Tom Burrington, Robert Connor, J. and K. Munger; 3. "Orestes and the Bermuda Triangle," ch and ds: Matsunaga, Snyder, Dara Van Laanen. *ABA Form,* m: Basque Folk, ch: Rodriguez, ds: Janet Russell, Van Laanen, Rodriguez. *Three Independent Solo Projects,* ch: Stetzelberger, J. Munger, Matsunaga. *Everness,* m: F. Chopin, Villa Lobos, ch: Hauser, ds: Heidi Jasmin, Dean, Good, Evans, Naugle. *Allemande,* m: J. S. Bach, ch: Kostock, ds: Burrington, Eddie Martinez, J. and K. Munger, Naugle, Anita Solomon, Stetzelberger. *Two Dances,* m: Cole Porter, ch: Holm, ds: Evans, Gunzelman, Harren, Otto, Matsunaga, Van Laanen.

1979, August 5, 7, 8. The Thirty-Ninth Annual Hanya Holm Dance Concert under the direction of Hanya Holm, Nancy Hauser, and Oliver Kostock, John Colman, musical director, Klaus Holm, scenery and lighting design. Part I: Compositions by faculty and students. *Parallel and Symmetry,* m: Stephan Koplowitz, ch and ds: Dorothy Goodman and Linda Loftis, Beth Chamberlain and Browyn Judge, Joe Feldman and Debra Marrs, Raúl Butron and William Harren. *Sound and Dynamics,* ch and ds: Goodman, Dara Van Laanen, Koplowitz. *Heavy and Light,* ch and ds: Judge, Maggie Vincent, Tim Walker. *Prop Piece,* m: Tarrega, inst: Tom Stringer, ch: Alicia Reckford, ds: Judge, Marrs, Dale Schmid. *Solos, Duets, Trio:* 1. "An Invitation to Summer," m: Claude Debussy, ch and d: Brian Taylor; 2. "Echo," m: Victor Speigal, ch and ds: Chamberlain, Tomiko Viera; 3. "Dual Rockers," m: Todd Rundgren, ch and ds: Amy Formanek, Terry Mockler; 4. "Candlelight," m: R. Towner and C. Walcott, ch and ds: Chamberlain, Viera; 5. "It's Gonna Rain," ch: Ruth Sander, ds: Tara Borella, Loftis, Marrs; 6. "Feet for Two," m: Coleman Hawkins, ch and ds: Chamberlain, Koplowitz. *Pulse Studies,* m: Vangelis, ch and ds: Norma Adler, Elizabeth Becker, Feldman, Formanek, Gina Gibney, Loftis, Marrs, Sander, Dewell Springer. *Choric Study,* m: Albinoni, ch: Hauser, ds: Borella, Butron, Chamberlain, Feldman, Formanek, Lynn Faossard, Gibney, Goodman, Anne Hogan, Jeff Howe, Diane Ketelle, Koplowitz, Karin Levitas, Loftis, Cyndy McCrossen, Schmid, Spencer Snyder, Jeanne Travers, Van Laanen, Viera, Walker. Part II: *The Insect Comedy,* a play by Josef and Karel Capek, text adapted and arranged by Lilian McCue, dir and ch: Holm, cos: Betty Ross. Tramp: Bill Smith, Lepidopterist: Douglas McKay, Butterflies: Harren, Judge, Elizabeth Becker, Springer, Taylor, Flappers: McCrossen, Gibney, Viera, Voice of Chrysalis: Joanna Burtón, Mr. Beetle: Kenneth Burtón, Mrs. Beetle: Margaret Garrison, Strange Beetle: Butron, Ichneumon Fly:

Feldman, Larva: Van Laanen, Mr. Cricket: Travers, Parasite: Snyder, Blind Ant: Koplowitz, Chief Engineer: Larry Richardson, Second Engineer: Harvey Rabbin, Signal Officer: Springer, Yellow Ant: Taylor, First Messenger: Feldman, Second Messenger: Schmid, Ants: Borella, Butron, Chamberlain, Formanek, Gibney, Goodman, Jeff Howe, Loftis, Marrs, McCrossen, Mockler, Sander, Schmid, Van Laanen, Walker, Chrysalis: Harren, Moths: Judge, Travers, Viera.

1980, AUGUST 6, 7. Grand Finale I and Grand Finale II of Hanya Holm 40th Anniversary Festival. The Holm Technique: Compositions by Hanya Holm's Advanced Composition Students under the direction of Hanya Holm, Nancy Hauser, and Oliver Kostock, musical director, David Gregory. *Parallel and Symmetrical Studies,* ch and ds (August 6) Linda Loftis and Mark Wischmeyer, Dennis Collado and Ruth Harkin, Stephen Otto and Dewell Springer (August 7) Mili Clayton and Brian Taylor, Michael Anderson and Raúl Butrón. *Study in Directions,* ch and ds (August 6) Bobby Bracewell, Vivien Bridson, Linda Goebel, Elizabeth Hutson (August 7) Butrón, Collado, Alyson Colwell, Nancy Fee, Eddie Martinez. *Studies in Dimensions,* ch and ds (August 6) Fee, Lynn Garber, Lisa Gibbs, Loftis, Suzanne Kavin, Butrón, Collado, Otto (August 7) Thérèse Gabriel, Ann Hébert, Robert Neu, Joe Feldman, Goebel, Malcolm MacDonald, Elizabeth Aggiss, Vivien Bridson, Menno Vantoorenburg. *Studies in Contrast,* ch and ds (August 6) Michael Anderson, Collado, Loftis, Otto, Mark DeGarmo, Goebel, Derek Phillips (August 7) Ruth Harkin, Suzanne Kavin, Springer, Margery Fernald, Garber, Rex Kujawa, Bianca Edmonds, Feldman, Hébert, Elizabeth Hutson. *Study in Characterization, the Celebrant,* m: anonymous, ch and d: Brian Taylor. *Studies With Vocalization,* ch and ds: Wischmeyer, Bridson, Clayton, Vantoorenburg. *Independent Student Works:* 1. "Street-Wise," m: Igor Stravinsky, ch: Taylor, ds: Michael Anderson, Butrón, Loftis; 2. "Genesis," m: M. Mussorgsky, ch and d: Collado; 3. "Two Studies—Angular and Circular," m: percussion, ch and d: DeGarmo; 4. "Mirror Dyslexia," m: Brian Eno, ch: Vantoorenburg, ds: Butrón, Clayton, Vantoorenburg; 5. "Saltare," m: Bach, Mozart, ch: Otto, ds: Alyson Colwell, DeGarmo, Garber, Taylor. *Rota,* ch: Holm (1975) m: George Crumb, cos: Sally Ann Parsons, ds: Don Redlich Dance Company, Kathryn Appleby, Jim Clinton, Robyn Cutler, Joan Finkelstein, Redlich. *Four Nocturnes,* ch: Holm, m: Crumb, inst: Sergia Luca, Anne Epperson, ds: Advanced Composition students, Mary Abate, Aggiss, Stacia Adams, Bridson, Butrón, Clayton, DeGarmo, Feldman, Goebel, Jan Havik, Hébert, Loftis, MacDonald, Martinez, Phillips, Springer, Taylor, Vantoorenburg. *Sonata for Piano and Violin,* "Blues," and "Continuum," ch: Holm, m: Maurice Ravel, ds: Don Redlich Dance Company, inst: Luca, Epperson, cos: Parsons.

1981, JULY 31, AUGUST 1. **Bartok** *Cantata Profana,* choreographed by Hanya Holm for the Don Redlich Dance Company and Chorus with additional works by the Redlich Company. Student ds: Dennis Collado, Mark DeGarmo, Lawrence Fortunato, James Murphy, Menno Vantoorenburg, Mark Wischmeyer, Joseph Youngblood, Tari Gallagher, Melissa Pope, Jean Pulos, Susan Roebuck, Cea Tait, Sherrie Waggener, understudies: Jan Hanvik, Eileen Bendersky.

1981, AUGUST 5. This Is My Work, Dance Recital of original works choreographed and performed by members of the Hanya Holm School of Dance. *Symmetry, Asymmetry, and Parallel Design,* ch and ds: Joe Feldman and Nancy Gardenhire, Margery Fernald and Mark Wischmeyer, Joseph Youngblood and Dennis Collado, Lawrence Fortunato, Menno Vantoorenburg and James Murphy. *Vocal Accompaniment,* ch and ds: Vantoorenburg and Eileen Bendersky, Sarah Gamble and Dreke Phillips, Feldman and Wischmeyer, Gardenhire, Gallagher and Therese Gabriel, Fortunato, Laura Jones, Susan Roebuck, Murphy. *Curve or Straight Path Studies:* 1. "Courante," ch and ds: Sherrie Waggener, Victoria Vadala, Jean Pulos, m: J. S. Bach; 2. "March," ch and ds: Fortunate, Lynn Wenning, Deborah Pirri, Gardenhire, m: J. P. Sousa. *Studies With Props:* 1. "Chair," ch and d: Dennis Collado, harmonica: Wischmeyer; 2. "Wood Easel," ch and ds: Kathy Moran, Phillips, Kristin Schliep; 3. "Rope," ch and ds: Feldman, Melissa Pope; 4. "Bone Mask," ch and ds: Laura Jones, Robert Neu, m: Herbie Handcock; 5. "Shopping Cart," ch and ds: Fortunato, Gallagher, Dennis Vasquez; 6. "Concrete Cylinders," ch and ds: Murphy, Elizabeth Lewis, Vantoorenburg; 7. "Sonata for Sweat Socks," ch: Fortunato, ds: Fortunato, Phillips, Vasquez, m: Louis Armstrong. *Friends of Long Ago,* ch: Waggener, m: Art of Japanese Bamboo Flute, ds: Mark deGarmo, Gallagher, Jan Hanvik, Pulos, Vadala. *Each Apart,* ch: Vantoorenburg, m: Brian Eno, Harold Budd, ds: Fortunato, Martha Basinger, Eileen Bendersky, Murphy, Gallagher, Margery Fernald, Hanvik, Gardenhire, Youngblood, Vantoorenburg. *Equinox,* ch: Sarah Gamble, m: Jean Jarre, ds: Gamble, Collado, Hanvik, Murphy, Vantoorenburg, Wischmeyer, Youngblood.

1982, AUGUST 4. Hanya Holm Workshop in Dance under the direction of Hanya Holm and Oliver Kostock with guest instructors Nancy Hauser and Don Redlich, musical director, William Elliott, production designer, Klaus Holm. *Directional, Symmetrical, and Parallel,* "Duet," m: Brian Eno, ch and ds: Carol Dzuro, Mark Wischmeyer; "Trio," m: Eddie Martinez, ch and ds: Martina Vermaaten, Laurie Smith, Josie Smith; "Duet," m: Eno, ch and ds: Earl Balcos, Wischmeyer. *Rhythmic,* "Duet," m: Leo Kottke, ch and ds: Vickie Hatch, Susan Sidman; "Duet," m: Elliott, ch and ds: J. Smith, Reinaldo De Palmer; "Duet," m: Kottke, ch and ds: L. Smith, Mark Vanek; "Duet," m: Lipps Inc, ch and ds: Henry Beer, De Palmer; "Trio," m: Electric Light Orchestra, ch and ds: Julianne Rice, Vermaaten, Wischmeyer. *Vocal and Percussive Accompaniment,* "Solo," ch and d: Stephen Ho; "Duet," ch and ds: Holly Jaycox, Ann Phelan; "Duet," ch and ds: Kay Gile, Melora Griffis; "Duet," ch and ds: Balcos, Rice; "Duet," ch and ds: Vanek, Wischmeyer; "Trio," ch and ds: Lynn Firkins, Diana Sherwood, Barbara Dralle. *Studies With Props,* "Duet," ch and ds: Holly Jaycix, Phelan; "Duet," m: Ultra Vox, ch and ds: L. Smith, Vermaaten; "Solo," m: Traditional, ch and d: Ho; "Trio," ch and ds: De Palmer, Spencer Snyder, Vanek. *Quest,* m: Chick Corea, ch: Kim Grover, ds: J. Smith, Barbara Dralle, Jaycox, Phelan, Vicki Hatch, Diana Sherwood. *Dependencies,* m: percussion and Phil Aaron, ch: Snyder, ds: Balcos, Beer, Vanek, Wischmeyer, Vermaaten, Gile, Dzuro, Sherwood, Snyder. *Monotonie,* m: Vangelis, "Variations," ch and ds: Gile, Balcos, Rice, Vanek; Ho, Treva Tegtmeier, Kim Grover; Lynn Firkins, L. Smith, J. Smith; Beer, Dralle, Hatch, Griffis; Gile, Vanek; Dzuro, Sidman, Snyder, Vermaaten; Michael Flowers, Jaycox, Phelan; Wischmeyer; Sterling, Sherwood, De Palmer, Wischmeyer.

1983, August 10. Hanya Holm Dance Concert under the direction of Hanya Holm, Oliver Kostock, and Nancy Hauser, musical director, William Elliott, scenery and lighting design, Klaus Holm. *Solos*—Independent Studies, ch: Dana Nontroy, Jeanine Shields, Christopher Caines, Cynthia Stevens, Hideaki Onuki, Holly Humble, Amy Orsborn. *Symmetry, Assymetry, Parallel,* ch: Jaime Lujan and Lisa Thurrell, Martha Gross and Anne Carey, Deborah Heltzer and Stephen Ho, Brigitte Zuger and Joseph Youngblood. *Vocalization,* ch: Cynthia Stevens and Shields, Caines and Orsborn, Arne Hartmann and Kimberly Smith, Joseph Arcand and Craig Oldfather. *Spaces*—Problems in space were given to students, and floor plans and a model were provided for visual orientation. "Vertical Division," m: Bela Bartok, ch: Caines, ds: Angela Adamson, Deborah Baker, Martha Goss, Sandra Mandelbaum, Smith; "Pools of Light," m: Bartok, ch and ds: Ho, Onuki; "Three Columns," m: Bartok, ch: Orsborn, ds: Kristin King, Stevens, Thurrell, Zuger; "Center Focus," m: Bartok, ch and d: Shields; "Horizontal Division," m: Igor Stravinsky, ch: Heather Lee, ds: Anne Carey, Dianna Dorgelo, Deborah Heltzer, Humble, Lujan, Sarah Stanley; "Levels," m: Stravinsky, ch: Arcand, ds: Hartmann, Montroy, Oldfather, Youngblood, Dennis Vasquez. *Props,* poem: Margaret Atwood, ch and ds: Caines, Baker, Adamson; m: Traditional Chinese, ch and d: Ho; m: Pachelbel, John Williams, ch and ds: Onuki, Lujan; m: Cosma, ch and ds: Arcand, Youngblood; m: tape collage, ch and ds: Humble, Carey, Arcand. *Marches,* ch and ds: Hartmann, Onuki; m: Fats Waller, ch and ds: Caines, Ho, Orsborn.

*N*OTES

Chapter 1: Forty-three Summers

1. Sali Ann Kriegsman wrote eloquently of the great Bennington Summer School of the Dance in *Modern Dance in America: The Bennington Years* (Boston: G. K. Hall, 1981). Jack Anderson provided a season-by-season description of performances at the equally important American Dance Festival in *The American Dance Festival* (Durham, NC: Duke University Press, 1987). Lucille Bogue composed a charming account of the Perry-Mansfield School in Steamboat Springs, Colorado, in *Dancers on Horseback: The Perry-Mansfield Story* (San Francisco: Strawberry Hill, 1984).
2. For a history of Colorado Springs, see Marshall Sprague, *Newport in the Rockies: The Life and Good Times of Colorado Springs* (Denver: Sage, 1961).
3. Bessie Schönberg, interview, Bronxville, NY, February 8, 1996. Quotation to follow is from this interview.
4. J. B., *Dance Observer,* February 1943, pp. 20, 21.
5. Walter Sorell's biography, *Hanya Holm: The Biography of an Artist* (Middletown, CT: Wesleyan University Press, 1969), is flawed by sentimentality.

Chapter 2: Frontier Crossings

1. Margaret Lloyd, *Christian Science Monitor,* August 16, 1938, expressed the opinion that modern dance would not fulfill its possibilities as art unless it appealed to the layperson without pretense and cult. Critics who discussed the issues in *Theater Arts* 24, no. 9 (September 1940) are

quoted in Sali Ann Kriegsman, *Modern Dance in America: The Bennington Years* (Boston: G. K. Hall, 1981), pp. 97, 98. Walter Terry deplored cultism in modern dance in the *New York Herald Tribune,* September 15, 1940. In his December 15, 1940, column Terry quoted Martha Graham on the alienation of audiences because of "grimness of theme and a non-theatrical approach."

2. *Dance Observer,* November 1941, p. 125.

3. Martha Hill, speaking at the Hanya Holm one-hundredth birthday celebration, St. Marks Church, New York City, March 3, 1993. Hanya Holm Memorial Birthday Tribute, 1993 [videorecording], Dance Division, New York Public Library for the Performing Arts [hereafter NYPL].

4. Juan J. Reid, *Colorado College: The First Century, 1874–1974* (Colorado Springs: Colorado College, 1979), p. 138.

5. KOA radio script, Hanya Holm Collection, NYPL.

6. KLZ radio script, Hanya Holm Collection, NYPL.

7. Martha Hill, telephone interview, September 3, 1993.

8. John Colman, interview, New York City, March 15, 1994; telephone interviews, 1994–1995.

9. Speakers are quoted in an unsigned article in the *Colorado Springs Gazette,* July 27, 1941, and by Elizabeth Hylbom in the same newspaper, July 29.

10. Hanya Holm Collection, NYPL; Walter Sorell quotes the declaration in *Hanya Holm: The Biography of an Artist* (Middletown, CT: Wesleyan University Press, 1969), p. 45.

11. Thurston Davies, quoted in "From This Earth," *American Dancer,* April 1942, pp. 17, 39.

12. Bessie Schönberg, interview, Bronxville, NY, February 8, 1996.

13. Hanya Holm Collection, NYPL.

14. Virginia Stewart and Merle Armitage (eds.), *The Modern Dance* (New York: E. Weyhe, 1935), p. 82.

15. Elizabeth Hylbom, *Colorado Springs Gazette,* July 27, 1941.

16. Told to Doris Hering. Hering, telephone interview, September 5, 1996.

17. Elizabeth Hayes, telephone interview, August 13, 1996.

18. Frances Wessells, telephone interviews, June 26, 1996, and December 23, 1997.

19. Susan Manning, in *Ecstasy and the Demon: Feminism and Nationalism in the Dances of Mary Wigman* (Berkeley: University of California Press, 1993), sets up a theory of utopian reconciliation between authority and autonomy (p. 86) and goes on to describe the working method at the Wigman School in Dresden (pp. 89–96).

20. Dean E. D. Hale, *Colorado Springs Gazette,* August 15, 1941.

21. John C. Wilcox, quoted in Marya McAuliff, "Dance Mosaic," *Music News,* October 2, 1941, p. 7.

22. Martin, *New York Times,* February 1, 1942.

Chapter 3: The Dance and the War

1. Dorothy Madden, interview, New York City, June 14, 1994.
2. Janet Mansfield Soares, *Louis Horst, Musician in a Dancer's World* (Durham, NC: Duke University Press, 1992), p. 174.
3. Mimi Kim, interview, Oakland, CA, June 12, 1996.
4. Thurston Davies, quoted in "From This Earth," *American Dancer,* April 1942, pp. 17, 39.
5. Arch Lauterer, "Form in Action," unpublished ms. Tobin Collection of the McNay Art Museum, San Antonio, TX.
6. Elizabeth Hylbom, *Colorado Springs Gazette,* August 9, 1942.
7. C. T., "Hanya Holm–Roy Harris–Arch Lauterer at Colorado College, 1942," *Dance Observer,* August-September 1942, p. 89.
8. J. B., "Hanya Holm Group," *Dance Observer,* February 1943, pp. 20, 21.
9. G.W.B., "Hanya Holm and Company," *Dance Observer,* May 1943, pp. 54, 55.
10. John Colman, interview, New York City, March 15, 1994, and telephone conversations, 1994–1995. Quotations to follow are from these interviews.
11. Mary Anthony, interview, New York City, June 30, 1993. Quotations to follow are from this interview.
12. John C. Wilcox, "Colorado Springs Holds Fine Arts Conference," *Music News,* September 9, 1943, pp. 18–19.
13. Elizabeth Hylbom, *Colorado Springs Sunday Gazette,* August 15, 1943.
14. John Martin, *New York Times,* September 19, 1943.
15. Edwin Denby, *New York Herald Tribune,* January 30, 1944.
16. Frances Wessells, telephone interviews, June 26, 1996, and December 23, 1997.
17. George W. Beiswanger, *The Colorado College Tiger,* August 25, 1944, p. 1; "Hanya Holm Presents New Work at Colorado Springs," *Dance Observer,* October 1944, p. 100.
18. Hortense Loeb, telephone interview, July 18, 1996.
19. Margery Turner, telephone interview, May 21, 1995, and subsequent correspondence.
20. Bernice Mendelsohn Bronson, telephone interview, April 23, 1995.
21. Edna Jane Nesbitt Dexter, telephone interview, July 9, 1994.
22. Elizabeth Hylbom, quoted in Jan Gay, "Hanya Holm at Colorado College," *Dance Observer,* October 1945, p. 96.

Chapter 4: Connecting to the American Dream

1. *Colorado Springs Gazette-Telegraph,* August 16, 1949.
2. *Colorado Springs Gazette-Telegraph,* August 11, 1946; *Rocky Mountain News,* August 11, 1946.
3. Harry Bernstein, telephone interview, January 16, 1994.
4. Alfred Brooks, telephone interview, June 28, 1996.
5. Dane Rudhyar, *Colorado Springs Gazette-Telegraph,* August 18, 1946.

6. Doris Baker, "Hanya Holm's Summer Productions," *Dance Observer,* November 1946, p. 113.
7. Sybil Shearer, "My Hanya Holm," *Ballet Review* 21, no. 4 (winter 1993), pp. 4–7.
8. *Colorado Springs Gazette-Telegraph,* August 16, 1949.
9. *Colorado Springs Gazette-Telegraph,* July 29, 1947.
10. Dorothy Adlow, "Hanya Holm in Colorado," *Dance Observer,* October 1947, pp. 88, 89.
11. Sharry Traver Underwood, interview, New York City, June 7, 1996. Quotation to follow is from this interview.
12. Sharry Traver Underwood, "Ballet Ballads," *Dance Chronicle* 9, no. 3 (1986), pp. 279–327.
13. Several Broadway dancers discussed the subject in a colloquium moderated by Marcia B. Siegel and published in "Hanya Holm: Life and Legacy," *Journal for Stage Directors and Choreographers* 7, no. 1 (spring-summer 1993), pp. 41–49.
14. Dorothy Adlow, "Hanya Holm and Her Dancers at Colorado College," *Dance Observer,* August-September 1948, p. 87.
15. *Colorado Springs Gazette-Telegraph,* August 1, 1948.
16. Walter Terry, *New York Herald Tribune,* January 9, 1949.
17. John Martin, *New York Times,* January 30, 1949.
18. "Salute to Hanya Holm" (Capezio advertisement), *Dance Magazine,* January 1949, p. 46.
19. Martin, *New York Times,* January 30, 1949.
20. Murray Louis, interviews, New York City, 1996. Quotations to follow are from these interviews.
21. Dorothy Adlow, *Colorado Springs Gazette-Telegraph,* August 19, 1949.
22. Joan Woodbury, telephone interview, August 2, 1994.
23. Adlow, *Colorado Springs Gazette-Telegraph,* August 19, 1949.

Chapter 5: A Company of Irregulars

1. Molly Lynn, interview, Minneapolis, MN, October 29, 1995. Quotations to follow are from this interview.
2. *Colorado Springs Gazette-Telegraph,* July 27, 1952.
3. Oliver Kostock, interviews, Cayucos, CA, June 11–13, 1993. Quotations to follow are from these interviews.
4. I discuss these issues in "Finding a Place for Hanya Holm," *Dance Chronicle* 23, no. 1 (2000), pp. 49–71.
5. Donald Redlich and I were colleagues at Mason Gross School of the Arts, Rutgers University, 1985–1994. This and following quotations are from interviews during this period.
6. Mary Wigman, "Composition in Pure Movement," *Modern Music* 8, no. 2 (January-February 1931), pp. 20–22.
7. Allen Young, *Denver Post,* August 11, 1950.

8. Andrea Di Sessa, *Colorado Springs Gazette-Telegraph,* August 17, 1951.
9. Ibid., July 27, 1952.
10. John Fetler, *Colorado Springs Gazette-Telegraph,* August 4, 1953.
11. Hannelore Yager, *Free Press,* September 6, 1953.
12. Ellen Moore, telephone interview, July 23, 1996.
13. Geulah Greenblatt Abrahams, telephone interview, July 6, 1995.
14. Jerry Bywaters Cochran, telephone interview, August 27, 1995.
15. Joanna Harris, e-mail to author, August 7, 1995.
16. Norman Cornick, telephone interview, June 9, 1995.
17. *Free Press* and *Colorado Springs Gazette-Telegraph,* August 8, 1955.
18. Oliver Kostock, "Hanya Holm's Fifteenth Summer at Colorado College," *Dance Observer,* November 1955, p. 131.
19. Theodore Fisher, *Free Press,* August 5, 1956.
20. John Fetler, *Colorado Springs Gazette-Telegraph,* August 7, 1956.

Chapter 6: A Partnership Reaffirmed

1. Ellen O'Connor, *Denver Post,* July 7, 1957.
2. Theodore Fisher, *Free Press,* August 9, 1957.
3. Laurie Archer, telephone interview, August 19, 1996; interview, Santa Fe, NM, December 28, 1997.
4. Fisher, *Free Press,* August 9, 1957.
5. Holm, quoted in *Colorado Springs Gazette-Telegraph,* July 27, 1958.
6. Scripts, letters to Holm, and copies of her letters are in the Hanya Holm Collection, Dance Division, New York Public Library for the Performing Arts (hereafter NYPL).
7. Besides Redlich, Harris, Archer, and Trisler, Lucinda Childs, Barbara Dilley, and Kathryn Posin attended, as did educators Annelise Mertz, Paul Chambers, and Clifford Kirwin. See Appendix One for a full list of registered students.
8. Nancy Topf, interview, New York City, August 21, 1996. Quotations to follow are from this interview.
9. *Colorado Springs Gazette-Telegraph,* August 8, 1960.
10. Some of Kostock's notebooks are in the Hanya Holm Collection, NYPL. Direct quotation: Oliver Kostock, interviews, Cayucos, CA, June 11–13, 1993.
11. John Cage, quoted in Martin Duberman, *Black Mountain: An Exploration in Community* (New York: E. P. Dutton, 1972), p. 228.
12. John Wallen, quoted in ibid., p. 236.
13. Ibid., p. 63.
14. Donald Redlich, conversations, Mason Gross School of the Arts, Rutgers University, 1985–1994. Quotations to follow are from these conversations.
15. John Fetler, *Colorado Springs Gazette-Telegraph,* August 11, 1961.
16. *Rocky Mountain News,* August 9, 1961.

17. Reports of Fred Sonderman, director of Summer Session. Special Collections, Tutt Library, Colorado College.
18. Fred Bruning, *Free Press,* August 2, 1964.
19. Allan Miles, telephone interview, September 8, 1996.
20. Nik Krevitsky, "Dance Festival Honors Hanya Holm," *Dance Magazine,* September 1965, p. 98.
21. Donald Janson, *New York Times,* August 4, 1965.
22. Mary Ann Lee, *Free Press,* August 4, 1965.
23. Krevitsky, "Dance Festival Honors Hanya Holm."
24. Phyllis Lamhut, interview, New York City, September 5, 1996.
25. Jack Anderson, "Hanya Holm Asks and Answers," *Dance Magazine,* August 1965, pp. 32–33.
26. K. Wright Dunkley, "Dance Art," edited transcript of Holm's classes at Colorado College during the summer of 1964, pp. 8, 20, 21, Hanya Holm Collection, NYPL.

Chapter 7: Dancing into the Boom

1. John Fetler, telephone interview, June 24, 1995.
2. Lloyd E. Worner (Colorado College president), "The Ford Challenge Met," *Colorado College Magazine,* fall 1965, pp. 2, 3, 33–41.
3. Gilbert Johns, telephone interviews, July 1993. Quotations to follow are from these interviews.
4. Oliver Kostock, interviews, Cayucos, CA, June 11–13, 1993. Quotations to follow are from these interviews.
5. Molly Lynn, interview, Minneapolis, MN, October 29, 1995. Quotations to follow are from this interview.
6. Tom Kanthak, interview, Garden City, NY, August 18, 1996.
7. Choreographer Yvonne Rainer issued a one-paragraph statement in 1965 that has become known as the "NO Manifesto." See Sally Banes, *Terpsichore in Sneakers* (Middletown, CT: Wesleyan University Press, 1987), p. 43.
8. Jessica Sayre, telephone interview, September 7, 1996. Quotations to follow are from this interview.
9. Chris Burnside, telephone interview, October 23, 1996.
10. Julia Sutton, telephone interview, September 22, 1996.
11. Hanya Holm Collection, Dance Division, New York Public Library for the Performing Arts (hereafter NYPL).
12. Mimi Kim, interview, Oakland, CA, June 12, 1996.
13. Tom Kanthak, "Dancing with Hanya: A Memory," *Minnesota Dance,* Newsletter of the Minnesota Dance Alliance (winter 1992), pp. 8–9.
14. Ibid.
15. Lindsay Fischer, telephone interview, September 28, 1996.
16. Karen Trautlein, interview, Wilkes-Barre, PA, June 30, 1996.
17. Hanya Holm Collection, NYPL.

Chapter 8: Escalation and Reflection

1. Judith Finley, interview, Colorado Springs, October 29, 1996.
2. Gilbert Johns, telephone interviews, July 1993.
3. A 1997 reconstruction of Holm's *Homage to Mahler* is described at http://dance.rutgers.edu/hanyaholm.
4. Rose Anne Thom, "Past, Present, Future," *Dance Magazine,* May 1997, p. 116; Murray Louis, "From the Inside: On Curtain Time," *Dance Magazine,* April 1977, pp. 102–103; reprinted in *Inside Dance* (New York: St. Martin's, 1980), pp. 91–92.
5. Don McDonagh, *New York Times,* April 12, 1977.
6. Diary entries given to the author.
7. James Kelly, interview, New York City, September 22, 1997.
8. Glen Tetley spoke about this at the one-hundredth birthday celebration memorializing Holm on March 3, 1993. Hanya Holm Memorial Birthday Tribute, 1993 [videorecording], Dance Division, New York Public Library for the Performing Arts.
9. Edward Martinez, interview, Colorado Springs, CO, October 22, 1996. Quotations to follow are from this interview.

Chapter 9: Holm on the Range and Other Amusements

1. This and other letters from Johns are in the Hanya Holm Collection, Dance Division, New York Public Library for the Performing Arts (hereafter NYPL).
2. Elena Jarvis, *Colorado Springs Gazette-Telegraph,* June 9, 1979.
3. Gilbert Johns, telephone interviews, July 1993. Quotations to follow are from these interviews.
4. Tobi Tobias, "Hanya Holm: A Young Octogenarian," *Dance News,* March 1979, pp. 1, 10.
5. Terri Tangney, *Colorado Springs Sun,* August 3, 1979.
6. Stephan Koplowitz, interview, New York City, March 19, 1997.
7. Hanya Holm Collection, NYPL.
8. Program booklet in Hanya Holm Collection, NYPL, and Special Collections, Tutt Library, Colorado College.
9. Tim Fuller, dean of Colorado College, interview, Colorado Springs, CO, October 30, 1996.
10. Margaret Nicoll, *Colorado Springs Gazette-Telegraph,* August 17, 1980.
11. Glenn Giffin, *Denver Post,* June 17, 1980.
12. Ibid., August 7, 1980.
13. William Hockmann, Colorado College Summer School dean, interview, Colorado Springs, CO, October 25, 1996. Hockmann lamented that he was obliged to do all his summer planning with a spreadsheet in front of him, whereas Gilbert Johns had not been so restrained.
14. Irene Clurman, *Rocky Mountain News,* August 1, 1981.
15. Giffin, *Denver Post,* August 3, 1981.

16. Edward Martinez, interview, Pueblo, CO, October 23, 1996. Quotations to follow are from this interview.

Chapter 10: Curtain

1. Judith Finley, interview, Colorado Springs, CO, October 29, 1996.
2. Bessie Schönberg, interview, Bronxville, NY, February 8, 1996.
3. Hanya Holm Collection, Dance Division, New York Public Library for the Performing Arts (hereafter NYPL).
4. Edward Martinez, interview, Pueblo, CO, October 22, 1996.
5. James Malcolm, telephone interview, October 21, 1996.
6. Norman Cornick, telephone interview, June 9, 1995.
7. "Hanya: Portrait of a Pioneer," Dance Horizon Video coproduced by Marilyn Cristofori and Nancy Mason Hauser, 1985.
8. Outtakes from the video documentary "Hanya: Portrait of a Pioneer" are in J. Henry Meyer Library, Stanford University, Palo Alto, CA.
9. Elmer Peterson, interview, Colorado Springs, CO, October 22, 1996.
10. Donald Redlich, interviews, Mason Gross School of the Arts, Rutgers University, 1985–1994.
11. Luc Peton, interview, Basel, Switzerland, August 3, 1993.
12. Valda Craig, "The Hanya Holm Summer School of the Dance at Colorado College: 1941–1983" (master's thesis, George Washington University, Washington, DC, 1985).
13. Jean Pulos, quoted by Linda DuVal, *Colorado Springs Gazette-Telegraph,* September 17, 1983.
14. Gilbert R. Johns, *Colorado Springs Gazette-Telegraph,* September 30, 1983.
15. Glenn Giffin, *Denver Post,* October 9, 1983.
16. This article with Giffin's note, as well as letters quoted later, was sent to Holm. Hanya Holm Collection, NYPL.

Chapter 11: Aftermath

1. Hanya Holm Collection, Dance Division, New York Public Library for the Performing Arts (hereafter NYPL).
2. Ursula Gray, interview, Colorado Springs, CO, October 25, 1996.
3. Stephanie Reinhart, personal communication, January 27, 1997.
4. Jennifer Dunning, *New York Times,* November 4, 1992. The *Village Voice* published a tribute written by Deborah Jowitt on November 24, 1992, p. 97.
5. *Colorado Springs Gazette-Telegraph,* November 5, 1992.
6. Hanya Holm Memorial Birthday Tribute, 1993 [videorecording], NYPL.

ADDITIONAL SOURCES

Anderson, Jack. *Art Without Boundaries.* Iowa City: University of Iowa Press, 1997.

Colorado College: Memories and Reflections. Collected by Maxwell F. Taylor. Colorado Springs: Colorado College, 1999.

Connor, Lynn. *Spreading the Gospel of Modern Dance: Newspaper Dance Criticism in the United States, 1850–1934.* Pittsburgh: University of Pittsburgh Press, 1997.

Cristofori, Marilyn, ed. "Hanya Holm: A Pioneer in American Dance." *Choreography and Dance* 2:2 (July 1991).

Finley, Judith. *Time Capsule 1900: Colorado Springs a Century Ago.* Colorado Springs: Pastwords, 1998.

Gitelman, Claudia. "Hanya Holm." *Dance Theatre Journal* 10:2 (winter 1992–1993), p. 15.

———, ed. *"Liebe Hanya": Mary Wigman's Letters to Hanya Holm,* forthcoming.

Graff, Ellen. *Stepping Left: Dance and Politics in New York City, 1928–1942.* Durham, NC: Duke University Press, 1997.

Hershey, Charlie Brown. *Colorado College: 1874–1949.* Colorado Springs: Colorado College, 1952.

Holm, Hanya. "The Dance Is Drama Set to Music." Unpublished lecture given at Colorado College, 1942. Dance Division, New York Public Library.

———. "Mary Wigman." *Dance Observer* 2:8 (November 1935), pp. 85, 91–92.

———. "The Mary Wigman I Know," in *The Dance Has Many Faces,* ed. Walter Sorell, pp. 182–191. New York: Columbia University Press, 1966.

Lloyd, Margaret. *The Borzoi Book of Modern Dance.* Princeton: Princeton Book Co., 1949; Dance Horizons, reprint, 1987.

Loevy, Robert D. *Colorado College: A Place of Learning, 1874–1999.* Colorado Springs: Colorado College, 1999.

Martin, John. *America Dancing.* New York: Dance Horizons, 1968 [1936].

———. *Introduction to the Dance.* New York: Dance Horizons, 1965 [1939].

———. *The Modern Dance.* New York: A. S. Barnes, 1933.

Maynard, Olga. *American Modern Dancers.* Boston: Little, Brown, 1965.

Mazo, Joseph H. *Prime Movers: The Makers of Modern Dance in America.* New York: William Morrow, 1977.

McDonagh, Don. *The Complete Guide to Modern Dance.* Garden City, NY: Doubleday, 1967.

New Grove Dictionary of Music and Musicians, ed. Stanley Sadie. London: Macmillan, 1980.

Partsch-Bergson, Isa. *Modern Dance in Germany and the United States.* Chur, Switz.: Harwood Academic, 1994.

Rosenberg, Bernard, and Ernest Harburg. *The Broadway Musical: Collaboration in Commerce and Art.* New York: New York University Press, 1993.

Schlundt, Christena. *Dance in the Musical Theatre: Jerome Robbins and His Peers, 1934–1963.* New York: Garland, 1987.

Siegel, Marcia B. *At the Vanishing Point: A Critic Looks at Dance.* New York: Saturday Review Press, 1968.

———. "Hanya Holm." *Ballet Review* 9:1 (spring 1981), pp. 5–30.

Sorell, Walter. *Looking Back in Wonder: Diary of a Dance Critic.* New York: Columbia University Press, 1986.

Stehman, Dan. *Roy Harris: An American Musical Pioneer.* Boston: Twayne, 1984.

Watts, Billie Jean. "Arch Lauterer: Theorist in the Theatre." Ph.D. diss., University of Oregon, 1970.

"Yesterday Shapes Today: Tracing the Roots." Television interview, Celia Ipiotis, *Eye on Dance,* PBS-TV, 1985.

INDEX